D1395534

The Security Dilemmas of Southeast Asia

The Security Dilemmas of Southeast Asia

Alan Collins
Lecturer in Politics
University of Wales
Swansea

 in association with
INSTITUTE OF SOUTHEAST ASIAN STUDIES,
SINGAPORE

Published by PALGRAVE MACMILLAN
Houndmills, Basingstoke, Hampshire RG21 6XS and
175 Fifth Avenue, New York, N. Y. 10010
Companies and representatives throughout the world

PALGRAVE MACMILLAN is the global academic imprint of the Palgrave
Macmillan division of St. Martin's Press, LLC and of Palgrave Macmillan Ltd.
Macmillan® is a registered trademark in the United States, United Kingdom
and other countries. Palgrave is a registered trademark in the European
Union and other countries.

Outside North America
ISBN 0-333-91890-9

In North America
ISBN 0-312-23525-9

This book is printed on paper suitable for recycling and
made from fully managed and sustained forest sources.

A catalogue record for this book is available from the British Library.

Library of Congress Catalog Card Number: 00-031120

Transferred to digital printing 2002

Contents

List of Tables

List of Abbreviations

AFP	Armed Forces of the Philippines
AFPFL	Anti-Fascist People's Freedom League
AFTA	ASEAN Free Trade Area
APEC	Asia-Pacific Economic Cooperation
ARF	ASEAN Regional Forum
ASA	Association of South-East Asia
ASEAN	Association of South-East Asian Nations
ASEM	Asia-Europe Meeting
BCP	Burma Communist Party
BN	*Barisan Nasional*
CBMs	Confidence Building Measures
CCP	Chinese Communist Party
CMC	Central Military Commission
CPM	Communist Party of Malaya
CPT	Communist Party of Thailand
DAP	Democratic Action Party
EEZ	Exclusive Economic Zone
FALSG	Foreign Affairs Leading Small Group
FDI	Foreign Direct Investment
FPDA	Five Power Defence Arrangements
GATT	General Agreement on Tariffs and Trade
GRIT	Graduated Reciprocation in Tension-Reduction
ISG	Inter-Sessional Support Group
ISM	Inter-Sessional Meetings
MCA	Malaysian Chinese Association
MIC	Malaysian Indian Congress
MILF	Moro Islamic Liberation Front
MNLF	Moro National Liberation Front
NEP	New Economic Policy
NLD	National League for Democracy
NOD	Non-Offensive Defence
PAP	People's Action Party
PAS	Parti Islam Se-Malaysia
PKI	Indonesian Communist Party
PLA	People's Liberation Army
PLAAF	People's Liberation Army Air Force

PLAN	People's Liberation Army Navy
PLANAF	People's Liberation Army Navy Air Force
PMC	Post-Ministerial Conference
SAF	Singapore Armed Forces
SEANWFZ	Southeast Asian Nuclear Weapons Free Zone
SEATO	South-East Asian Treaty Organisation
SLORC	State Law and Order Restoration Council
SPDC	State Peace and Development Council
TAC	Treaty of Amity and Cooperation
UMNO	United Malays National Organisation
UNCLOS	United Nations Convention on the Law of the Sea
UNRCA	United Nations Register of Conventional Arms
VFA	Visiting Forces Agreement
WTO	World Trade Organisation
ZOPFAN	Zone of Peace, Freedom and Neutrality

Preface

In the early months of 1995 as I was putting the finishing touches to my PhD I submitted an application to the British Academy to study the applicability of the security dilemma to Southeast Asia. In the aftermath of the Cold War the region was one of the few in which the acquisition of military weapons was on the rise and concerns were being raised that an arms race was underway. With the procurement of power projection weapons and the existence of an institution – the Association of South-East Asian Nations (ASEAN) – the region seemed ideal to study the relevance of the security dilemma and the mitigation effects, if any, of the regional security regime. The first meeting the year before of the ASEAN Regional Forum also raised the question of whether the norms of behaviour that operated within the ASEAN security regime could be transferred to the wider Asia-Pacific region, and in particular constrain the activities of China.

In the summer I was awarded a three-year British Academy Postdoctoral Fellowship, little was I to know what dramatic changes would occur in the region during these three years. In the late months of 1998 as I began to revise some overly optimistic conclusions about ASEAN's mitigating effects, and time-bounding other findings, I began to appreciate what it must have felt like to be writing on NATO strategy in the late 1980s. The chill winds of an economic crisis has brought about events that could not have been foreseen in 1995, the most tangible being the fall of the Suharto regime in Indonesia and the prospect of independence for East Timor. While the events of the latter 1990s have been a cause of frustration as yet another development forces a rewrite, I remain immensely thankful that I chose Southeast Asia. Not only because it has given me an opportunity to write in interesting times, but it has been tremendously rewarding coming to terms with the mix of cooperation and conflict that exists among the ASEAN membership.

It is not only Southeast Asia that has changed since 1995, but the security dilemma itself has been revisited and applied to new referent objects of security. The 1990s has witnessed the security dilemma, hitherto the preserve of the international system, applied to ethnic tensions in Eastern Europe and the former Soviet Union. Thus, in addition to determining the dilemma's applicability to the international security issues in the region I have also examined its usefulness in understanding the ethnic tensions that exist within the region. The book therefore uses the security dilemma, where it is applicable, to reveal the security dynamics at work in the region's ethnic tensions, intra-ASEAN rivalries and finally the evolving relationship between the ASEAN members and China.

As with other writings this book could not have been completed without the assistance of various institutions and individuals who have provided both financial, intellectual and emotional support along the way. I am particularly grateful to the British Academy for the award of the Post-doctoral Fellowship without which this project would not have been embarked upon, and in particular, to Ken Emond for his assistance and general encouragement. My thanks for the support, both intellectual and financial, from the Department of International Politics at the University of Wales, Aberystwyth, where I held the Fellowship; particular thanks goes to Nicholas Wheeler for his comments on earlier drafts of Chapter 1. Thanks also to Paul Roe for our conversations in which we were able to clarify each other's thoughts on the security dilemma, especially over malign/benign intent and real/illusory incompatibilities. The British Academy also provided the bulk of the finances needed to support the fieldwork I conducted in 1998, and my thanks to the Department of International Relations in the School of Pacific and Asian Studies at the Australian National University and the Institute of Southeast Asian Studies in Singapore for providing a stimulating environment within which to conduct my research. The assistance provided during this trip by Stuart Harris, and in particular Greg Austin, was immense and Chapter 5 on China and ASEAN is much the richer for our discussions. I am also grateful to John Funston for his comments on ethnic tensions in Malaysia and Chapter 3 benefited greatly from his thoughts. Discussions with Derek da Cunha, Hari Singh and Narayanan Ganesan helped to clarify my thinking more than they probably realised, and I am immensely grateful to Professor Zakaria Ahmad for his invitation to attend the Security and Interdependence in Pacific Asia conference held in Kuala Lumpur in April 1998, and also to Rajayah for shuttling me between conference centre, hotel and railway station. It was so very much appreciated. Special thanks must go to Tim Huxley and Gerald Segal for their views on the implications for the region of the economic crisis and enlargement of ASEAN. It is in this regard that I am particular grateful to Allen Whiting for reading over draft chapters and being especially supportive during the last couple of months, when I began to fear that the changes were undermining the analysis. Finally, thanks are due to the staff at the Department of International Relations at Keele University, and the Department of Political Theory and Government at The University of Wales Swansea.

The road to completing a book is not made possible just by the assistance of scholars, but also by friends and family that help to keep spirits high when set-backs arise and doubts creep in. To all these people I offer my thanks, but in particular to my wife, Sue, whose continual support was critical, especially towards the end.

All these people have had a role in making this book possible and I am grateful for their time and patience.

ALAN COLLINS

1
Introduction: Evolution of the Security Dilemma

The 1990s has proven to be a decade of great change for the members of the Association of South-East Asian Nations (ASEAN). The beginning of the 1990s brought fears that ASEAN would be unable to adjust to the new post-Cold War era. In 1989 the then Foreign Minister of Singapore, Wong Kan Seng warned, 'the continued relevance of the organisation, post-Cambodia, cannot be taken for granted', and that ASEAN would need 'new rallying points or risk drifting apart to the detriment of regional cooperation and bilateral relationships'.[1] The combination of weapons procurements by the ASEAN members; the thawing of territorial disputes frozen during the Cold War; the emergence of China as a regional hegemon; and the prevalence of ethnic tensions throughout the region, all indicated that Southeast Asia was entering a period of uncertainty at best and rising tension at worst. Yet prior to the economic crisis of the late 1990s ASEAN was touted as a success story. The association had not only managed to avoid drifting apart, but with the accession of Vietnam in 1995, Burma and Laos in 1997 and Cambodia in 1999 its membership increased to include all the states of Southeast Asia – the goal of an ASEAN-Ten has been achieved. ASEAN also took centre-stage in the creation and operation of the ASEAN Regional Forum (ARF), while the member states were courted by the major powers. Confidence was high with outspoken leaders, such as Malaysia's Prime Minister Mahathir Mohamad and Singapore's Senior Minister Lee Kuan Yew, preaching the virtues of 'Asian Values'. The end of the decade though has brought fears of an ASEAN drifting apart back to the fore. The social and political consequences of the regional economic crisis, coupled with the difficulties of admitting new members has raised doubts about ASEAN's continued viability. In 1999, echoing the thoughts of Wong Kan Seng,

1

an Asian diplomat based in Rangoon said, 'Asean is no longer the same ... It has lost its edge, its sense of direction'.[2] At the turn of the century Southeast Asia, bereft of prosperity, once again faces uncertainty at best, and rising tension at worst.

This study is concerned with examining three distinct, though not mutually exclusive, security concerns for ASEAN members through the prism of the security dilemma. In so doing the aim is not only to explain the dynamics at work in Southeast Asian security, but also to expound upon the concept of the security dilemma itself. The study will reveal the difficulties in applying the security dilemma to new referent objects of security, and the reasons why despite propitious conditions, the dilemma's operation is largely ameliorated in the region. The study is divided into three sections, reflecting the security concerns of the region and also the application of the security dilemma. The first concentrates on ethnic tensions within the region and provides an opportunity to examine the most recent utilisation of the security dilemma. The second is concerned with inter-state tension within ASEAN, and provides an examination of the 'ASEAN Way' and the current challenges to its principles and processes. The final section focuses on China as a rising hegemon, and uses the security dilemma in a different guise to suggest how the members of ASEAN might influence this evolving relationship. The study therefore seeks to provide two outcomes. First, a better understanding of the security dilemma and its application, and second, an account of the security issues facing the members of ASEAN and how they might be overcome.

The security dilemma has been referred to as the quintessential dilemma of international relations and it derives from the realist tradition of international relations theory.[3] The study of Southeast Asia's international relations had by the beginning of the 1990s been dominated by the realist tradition. The emphasis lay with states as the international actors and concerns with security were dominant. In his coverage of the study of Southeast Asia, Tim Huxley explains that the 'dominance within the study of Southeast Asia's international relations of security-related questions, defined until the 1990s almost exclusively in realist terms, was hardly surprising in view of the nature of Western interest in the region between the 1940s and 1980s'.[4] The dominance of Western writers on Southeast Asian security has changed with the establishment of various think-tanks and academic institutes in the region, and the literature now boasts an increasing number of regionally based scholars. While the 1990s has witnessed an increasing interest in economic factors and multilateral regional cooperation

(Asia-Pacific Economic Cooperation and the ARF), realist assumptions have, however, remained the key underlying themes. The regionalism of Southeast Asia is designed to strengthen, not weaken the state structure. The creation of supra-national organisations, such as an equivalent to the European Union, has never been an ambition for the region's state leaders. Hence Muthiah Alagappa, writing in 1998, noted that '[u]nlike in Europe, there is little cause to argue that the state is in decline in Asia'.[5] Thus, Huxley concludes, 'the ASEAN states continue to rely on realist means of ensuring their security in the more multipolar and less predictable regional strategic environment of the 1990s'.[6] The degree to which the security dilemma operates in this strategic environment receives coverage in chapters four and five.

Although the security dilemma originated out of realist thinking, it is by no means wedded to realism. Indeed it has found favour in the critical security studies literature where it has been used as a tool for expanding the parameters of security studies.[7] The first section of this study will examine one of the areas in which the security dilemma has increasingly been used in the 1990s – explaining the dynamics at work in ethnic tension/conflict. Before this, it is necessary to explain what the security dilemma is, and how its meaning has evolved. This chapter will therefore provide an analysis of the security dilemma's history, sketching new meanings that have been added and providing the conceptual grounding for the dilemma's application to Southeast Asia in each of the subsequent chapters.

A. The history of the security dilemma

A number of contemporary writers have noted the historians Xenophon and Thucydides describing circumstances between political units which have since been labelled the security dilemma.[8] The term security dilemma is relatively new though and John Herz can be credited with its first use in *Political Realism and Political Idealism*, written in 1951.[9] However, while it is Herz who is accredited with coining the term, the 'grandfather' of the security dilemma is the British historian Herbert Butterfield. Published in the same year as Herz's monograph, Butterfield's *History and Human Relations* highlights the key to understanding the security dilemma; it's a tragedy.[10] The security dilemma describes a situation in which war can occur between two or more participants where none of those involved desired such an outcome. Thus war can occur without the participation of a revisionist or revolutionary state seeking to alter the status quo. Hence Butterfield's claim that, '[t]he greatest war in history could be produced without the intervention of any great criminals who might be out to do deliberate harm in the world. It could be produced between two Powers both of which were desperately anxious to avoid a conflict of any sort'.[11] In explaining how such a tragedy could occur Butterfield highlights a key element to understanding the security dilemma: uncertainty. He notes the uncertainty that statesmen have determining others' intentions and focuses upon the fear and suspicion such uncertainty causes. In his now famous passage Butterfield writes:

> It is the peculiar characteristic of the situation that I am describing ... that you yourself may vividly feel the terrible fear that you have of the other party, but you cannot enter into the other man's counter-fear, or even understand why he should be particularly nervous. For you know that you yourself mean him no harm, and that you want nothing from him save guarantees for your own safety; and it is never possible for you to realise or remember properly that since he cannot see the inside of your mind, he can never have the same assurance of your intentions that you have.[12]

He refers to this fear as Hobbesian fear thus suggesting the statesmen's uncertainty is a direct consequence of the international system's anarchic nature (Hobbes' state of nature). However, Butterfield focuses on the individual rather than the international system and claims that 'man's universal sin', since it is inherent to all humans, ensures there is no escape from this Hobbesian fear. Hence his assertion that, 'this condition of absolute predicament or irreducible dilemma lies in the very geometry of human conflict ... So far as the historian is concerned, here is the basic pattern for all narratives of human conflict'.[13] In essence, therefore, the uncertainty that statesmen have of each other's intentions leads to fear and suspicion that others may intend harm and thus a war can occur despite neither desiring such an outcome. The very character of the security dilemma is one of tragedy since all participants have benign intent.

While Herbert Butterfield was noting the importance of uncertainty in generating a war, on the other side of the Atlantic, John Herz was labelling Butterfield's predicament the security dilemma. For Herz the predicament Butterfield notes occurs because humans are capable of killing one another but they are also reliant upon one another for their well-being. Therefore, humans cannot solve the threat that each human poses by seeking to eliminate others because humans are dependent upon each other for providing the necessities of life. Thus, humans must have social interaction and it is because this is dangerous that Herz states, '[i]t is his uncertainty and anxiety as to his neighbours' intentions that places man in this basic dilemma, and makes the "homo homini lupus" (man's inhumanity to man) a primary fact of the social life of man'.[14] Like Butterfield, Herz highlights the importance of uncertainty. He refers to the predicament as a dilemma since humans appear incapable of solving this cause of their insecurity. Herz concludes that since this threat cannot be resolved, humans remain in a constant search for means of perpetuating their safety. In other words, the 'security dilemma leads directly to social competition for the means of security'.[15] Since this competition is insoluble and operates within different sized communities (whether it be ethnic groups, nations or between states) Herz refers to it as all-pervasive.[16] Despite this fatalist approach to the security dilemma Herz concludes that escape is possible in a 'person whose sympathy … reaches out to and includes all groups and all human beings, and who makes no distinction between his own narrow group and any other part of humanity [and] … is ready to answer the demands arising from the power dilemma with a clear and unambiguous No!'.[17] It is clear though that Herz considers such individuals rare and unlikely to gain a position of power. Butterfield concurs that such individuals are rare – his example being St Francis of Assisi.

Thus at the very outset the security dilemma is seen to have two characteristics: uncertainty; and, because it is a tragedy, benign intent. Both authors focus on individuals, though Herz is clear that the security dilemma is a social problem, not an anthropological or biological one. Finally both are fatalistic in their judgement considering the security dilemma to be inescapable.

Both authors return to the security dilemma in the 1960s, with Herz acknowledging the work of Butterfield in *International Politics in the Atomic Age*. While Herz agrees with much of Butterfield's analysis, he regards Butterfield's assertion that the dilemma lies at the heart of all conflicts an exaggeration. Focusing on Nazi Germany, Herz refutes Butterfield by claiming the Second World War was 'provoked by Hitler's policy of world domination. It can hardly be maintained that it was a German security dilemma which lay at the heart of that conflict, but rather one man's, or one regime's, ambition to master the world'.[18] Thus, despite considering the security dilemma all-pervasive, for Herz the malign intent inherent in Germany's political ambition refutes the existence of the security dilemma. In Butterfield's own words, Hitler was a great criminal who was deliberately seeking to do harm.

Butterfield continues to focus on Hobbesian fear and as a consequence finds suspicion and fear in all narratives of conflict.[19] Herz meanwhile produces his most lucid work on the subject. He suggests that during the seventeenth and eighteenth centuries European states could 'satisfy minimum requirements of security without creating insecurity in their neighbours'.[20] It was only in the nineteenth century when European states found they were competing with one another as their empires expanded that they faced the security dilemma. An action by one was now seen to impose upon the interests, and this invariably included security interests, of another. Herz concludes that during the Cold War, 'bipolarity [gave] the security dilemma its utmost poignancy'.[21] He reiterates the role of uncertainty and tragedy in the security dilemma and produces one of the most famous references in the literature: 'it is one of the tragic implications of the security dilemma that mutual fear of what initially may never have existed may subsequently bring about exactly that which is feared most'.[22] Here, not only does Herz capture the tragedy of the security dilemma, but he also implies what other writers later reveal as the third characteristic of the security dilemma, paradoxical policies.

In the 1970s and 1980s the security dilemma underwent a detailed examination by the American political scientist, Robert Jervis. Jervis' work is regarded by many as the most thorough on the security dilemma. His first substantial contribution can be found in his highly regarded monograph, *Perception and Misperception in International Politics*. It is here that Jervis highlights the value of perceptions in explaining why the security dilemma can be difficult for statesmen to recognise and ultimately why their prudent policies are paradoxical. He accomplishes this by using a deterrence and spiral model of international relations.

The difference between the deterrence and spiral model centres on the adversaries' intentions. In the deterrence model the adversaries' intentions are malign and it is only by deterring the adversary that decision-makers can protect their state. This model therefore is marked by the perception that resolve on all matters, regardless of their intrinsic value, is necessary in dealing with the adversary since any sign of weakness will be exploited. In contrast the spiral model emphasises the setting in which statesmen conduct state relations. In this model the anarchic nature of international relations compels statesmen to provide for their own security. In so doing a problem arises:

> When states seek the ability to defend themselves, they get too much and too little – too much because they gain the ability to

carry out aggression; too little because others, being menaced, will increase their own arms and so reduce the first state's security.[23]

This fear that the other intends harm can lead both states to acquire more and more arms which in turn creates an arms race. The spiral model is clearly relevant to the security dilemma. Uncertain of others' intent statesmen pursue the prudent option of acquiring security via unilateral means. The others witnessing this acquisition respond in order to safeguard their security. None of the actors intend harm to each other – their intent is benign – yet they have begun to view each other with suspicion and fear. Thus, while in the deterrence model competitive policies indicate resolve and deter the aggressor, in the spiral model they compound the problem by reinforcing the image of the other as an aggressor. Echoing Butterfield's famous line concerning the inability of statesmen to enter into the other's counter-fear, Jervis claims, 'statesmen ... rarely ... consider seriously the possibility that such a policy will increase the danger of war instead of lessening it'.[24] Therefore, although no harm is intended the statesmen's uncertainty leads them to pursue prudent policies, but since these are the cause of the rising tension and suspicion they are also paradoxical policies.

Jervis explains why statesmen come to view benign powers as aggressive neighbours in a series of examples that highlight the importance of perceptions. In particular he notes that because the statesmen know that they do not intend harm they find it difficult to appreciate that their own actions are partly the cause of their insecurity. They come to the conclusion that since they do not intend harm, and assume that others know this, others' arms acquisitions can only be explained in terms of aggressive intent. Hence Jervis' use of John Foster Dulles' exclamation that, 'Khrushchev does not need to be convinced of our good intentions. He knows we are not aggressors and do not threaten the security of the Soviet Union'.[25] The belief that a Soviet response would indicate aggressive intent can be witnessed in the exchange between the US Secretary of State, Dean Acheson, and the Senate Foreign Relations Committee chairman, Tom Connally, when the North Atlantic Treaty was discussed. Asked whether any state need fear this treaty Acheson's reply led Connally to assert that only those intending harm need be afraid. The analogy Connally used was that only a burglar, in other words those with malign intent, had anything to fear from a new criminal law. The implication being that should the USSR respond aggressively to the Treaty this was an indication of its malign intent. Once this image of the other as malign has entered the statesmen's consciousness they are likely to interpret all actions from this perspective. Writing at the end of the Cold War Charles Glaser quotes Caspar Weinberger, the US Secretary of Defense in 1983, revealing how this image of the Soviet Union had become ingrained in US decision making:

> The other reason they have no need to worry is that they know perfectly well that we will never launch a first strike on the Soviet Union. And all their attacks, and all their military preparations – I should say, and all of their acquisitions in the military field in the last few years have been offensive in character.[26]

Once this image of the other has become ingrained, reversing a deteriorating relationship becomes extremely difficult. Convinced that the other is intent on doing harm statesmen fail to appreciate that the very policies they perceive as necessary for their defence are actually undermining their security. Their inability to appreciate that their policies are undesirable reveals why states continue to pursue what appear to a third party as clearly self-defeating or paradoxical policies. Jervis captures this in the comments made by the US President, Theodore Roosevelt, in 1904 concerning Britain and Germany. Roosevelt noted that the Kaiser

> sincerely believes that the English are planning to attack him and smash his fleet, and perhaps join with France in a war to the death against him. As a matter of fact, the English harbour no such intentions, but are themselves in a condition of panic terror lest the Kaiser secretly intends to form an alliance against them with France or Russia, or both, to destroy their fleet and blot out the British Empire from the map! It is as funny a case as I have ever seen of mutual distrust and fear bringing two peoples to the verge of war.[27]

The uncertainty, therefore, that statesmen have of one another, which is itself a product of the anarchical nature of the society in which they conduct business, leads them to take measures that while they perceive as achieving security actually fuel their own insecurity. It is this belief that the other does harbour malign intent that makes unwinding the spiralling tension so very difficult. However, even if statesmen were sensitive to the security dilemma this in itself is not sufficient to help mitigate its deteriorating effects. After all the other may indeed harbour malign intent.

Recognising that a security dilemma is in operation is particularly difficult because a similar action-reaction of events can also be witnessed in the deterrence model. However, Jervis is right to note that while this may resemble the operation of the spiral model the malign intent of one of the participants ensures that paradoxical policies are not being pursued and thus it is not a security dilemma. He writes:

> The aggressor, of course, is hostile because its expansion is blocked, but this does not develop the unfounded fear that the status quo power is menacing its existence. It may increase its arms because it sees that its foreign policy aims have outrun its military strength, and the increase of arms and tensions can continue for several cycles as each side matches the other's belligerence. But this process resembles that explained by the spiral model only superficially. It is completely rational. Each side is willing to pay a high price to gain its objectives and, having failed in its initial attempt to win a cheap victory, is merely acting on its unchanged beliefs about the value of the issue at stake. The heightening of the conflict does not represent, as it does in the spiral theory, the creation of illusory incompatibility, but only the real incompatibility that was there from the beginning. Thus the spiral explanation of the process is not correct, and an attempt to apply spiral prescriptions would not have the intended effects.[28]

Spiral prescriptions, such as confidence building measures, are means of lessening statesmen's uncertainty by aiding accurate threat assessment. The implication is that with reduced uncertainty the security dilemma can be mitigated or even escaped as statesmen become more confident about the others' benign intentions. Since such prescriptions are inappropriate in the deterrence model, Jervis is concurring with Herz's analysis of Nazi Germany; the security dilemma is not at the heart of all conflicts. Indeed, Jervis is explicit in noting that too much emphasis on the security dilemma can lead to the false conclusion that 'security, rather than expansion, is the prime goal of most states'.[29] Therefore even if a statesman was sensitive to the security dilemma the heightening of tension in a state's relations with others, manifest by an arms race, for example, does not mean that a security dilemma is the cause. Indeed to initiate spiral prescriptions would be extremely dangerous since such actions would undermine the state's security if its adversary harboured malign intent. Thus, even statesmen who are sensitive to the security dilemma, a rarity in itself, may find they cannot avoid the heightening of tensions and a deterioration of relations. This helps to explain the following claim by Barry Posen:

> Often statesmen do not recognise that [the security dilemma] exists: they do not empathize with their neighbours; they are unaware that their own actions can seem threatening. Often it does not matter if they know of this problem. The nature of their situation compels them to take the steps they do.[30]

The suggestion that statesmen are compelled to act maybe too deterministic but the implication that even statesmen who are sensitive to the security dilemma may be unable to avoid it is probably correct.

By the early 1980s the security dilemma had altered very little. It was still a tragedy in which status quo powers that had not intended each other harm could, because of their uncertainty of each other, pursue paradoxical policies that would bring about exactly that which they had hoped to avoid. The security dilemma was found to contain three characteristics: benign intent, uncertainty, and paradoxical policies. However, the 1980s was to witness an apparent challenge to the first of these characteristics. Writing in the 1990s Nicholas Wheeler and Ken Booth were to label this the deliberate or state-induced security dilemma, which is the next focus of attention.[31]

B. The security dilemma and hegemonic powers

In 1985 Jack Snyder wrote that, '[i]n a security dilemma the adversary's malign intentions' and in so doing appeared to be challenging the orthodox view of the security dilemma.[32] Indeed, he defines the security dilemma as 'a situation in which each state believed that its security *required* the insecurity of others' (emphasis added).[33] The requirement that others be insecure and the existence of malign intent seem at odds with Butterfield and Herz's conception of security dilemma as a tragedy. He introduces to the literature the structural, perceptual and imperialist security dilemmas; it is the latter which is problematic.

In his imperialist dilemma Snyder introduces a revisionist state that from the outset seeks a goal that would require the target state to forfeit a valuable asset (territory, sovereignty). Snyder asserts that the imperialist state would become fearful of the status quo power and explains this using a similar scenario to that noted earlier by Jervis. Snyder writes:

> In order to achieve its expansive ... goals, the aspiring imperialist state develops offensive military forces for the purpose of conquest

or intimidation. When resistance is met, a testing of will and capabilities ensues. An arms race occurs as the imperialist and its opponent both try to prove that they have the capability to achieve their ... aims. Crises are staged as the states test each other's willingness to risk war rather than retreat.[34]

Snyder suggests that if either state believes that it might be taken advantage of during a period of temporary weakness (a window of opportunity) it may initiate a preventive or pre-emptive war. That is, the revisionist state does believe the status quo power intends to do it harm and therefore it arms not only to acquire its original goal, but also to protect itself.

In this scenario, since both are prepared to wage a preventive or pre-emptive war both harbour malign intent. According to Snyder the revisionist's malign intent remains because it mitigates a compromise that is mutually beneficial – 'mutual security guarantees [are] difficult to devise because they may rule out the kinds of capabilities that the imperialist needs for its campaign of limited expansion' – while it appears as though the target state also sees aggression as the only means of achieving security.[35] The incompatibility between the states is real since they both intend the other harm. However, the existence of incompatibility is not enough for the situation to be regarded as a security dilemma; the incompatibility must be illusory. If one state, or both, actually intend to harm the other and they are being foiled by the other state's policies, then those policies are not paradoxical. Jervis' claim noted earlier – that while this type of arms race may resemble a spiral model it is actually the workings of the deterrence model – is right. The states in Snyder's imperialist dilemma may be uncertain of each other's intent but their subsequent fear and suspicion of each other is well founded. However, if Snyder's imperialist dilemma does not appear to be an accurate expansion of the security dilemma's application, the same cannot be said for his definition. Requiring the insecurity of others creates a more complex version of the security dilemma, one that has particular significance for the question of mitigating or escaping the dilemma.

In their synthesis of the literature Wheeler and Booth identify Snyder's version of the security dilemma and distinguish it from the traditional version by labelling the former deliberate, and the latter inadvertent. Their deliberate version, also known as state-induced, consists of two examples. The second involves a revisionist state and suffers the same problems as Snyder's imperialist version.[36] However, it is the first example that provides an exciting expansion for the security dilemma's applicability.

In the first example the security dilemma arises when a status quo power pursues a deliberately aggressive policy vis-à-vis its neighbours in order to intimidate them. The aim is not to overthrow the existing status quo, but rather to consolidate it by making others too frightened to challenge it. This aggressive policy is not a precursor to war, instead it is designed to provide the state with security by requiring others to feel insecure. The state is seeking a position of hegemony and the security dilemma can arise in this situation because the other states are unlikely to be able to distinguish this approach from a revisionist state that harbours malign intent. Indeed given how aggressive the hegemon appears, they are much more likely to interpret its actions as hostile. If they respond to the hegemon's attempt to achieve dominance by enhancing their own power, then the increase in absolute power that the hegemon acquires will not translate into an increase in relative power. The other states' actions are likely to be interpreted as aggressive since the hegemon knows it does not intend them harm but their actions suggest that they are not satisfied with the current status quo. That is, the hegemon and its neighbours are unable to enter into each other's counter-fear and are pursuing paradoxical policies which are leading each to assume the worst. They have fallen victim to a state-induced security dilemma which differs from the traditional, system-induced variant, because in the latter none of the states seek security at each others' expense; they just perceive it this way.

For Snyder the key point concerning one state requiring others to be insecure is the effect this has on the means of mitigating or escaping the security dilemma. In the system-induced security dilemma the states involved can mitigate the dilemma by reassuring each other about their benign intent. In the state-induced security dilemma where one state requires others to be insecure it is unlikely that the other states, even if they assumed the state had benign intent, would accept such vulnerability. It is this problem that led Snyder to assert that, '[i]f threats could not resolve the security dilemma, neither could concessions', because, '[a]ppeasing the security fears of one's neighbour would have entailed accepting one's own insecurity'.[37] Mitigating or escaping this security dilemma would require the other states to change the circumstances or the hegemon's understanding of the circumstances. This creates a more complex approach to mitigation or escape than is required in the system-induced security dilemma, which we now turn to.

By the mid-1980s Snyder has therefore added a subtle but important addition to the security dilemma literature. The emphasis on one state requiring others to be insecure has expanded the security dilemma's applicability to hegemonic powers. Whether this is applicable to the evolving post-Cold War relationship between China and the members of ASEAN will be the focus of Chapter 5.

C. Mitigating and escaping the security dilemma

The question of escaping or mitigating the security dilemma is contentious. Not only do different authors have different opinions but the same author can provide contradictory answers over whether the security dilemma can be escaped. The controversy arises because for some writers the security dilemma is an inherent feature of the anarchical international system. Hence Bradley Klein's comment that 'the international security dilemma is poised by international anarchy',[38] and Barry Buzan's statement that

> [u]nder anarchy, states have to look after themselves to ensure both their welfare and the continued survival of their political and societal values...This structural imperative lies at the core of the power-security dilemma, which is itself the key statement of the security problematique under anarchy.[39]

While Herz considers the security dilemma to be all-pervasive, operating between individuals as well as states, he considers that in the international system, because there is no sovereign, 'the vicious circle of the power and security dilemma works here with more drastic force than in any other field'.[40] It is the belief that this anarchy is a permanent feature of international relations that explains why according to Jervis, '[t]he security dilemma cannot be abolished, it can only be ameliorated'.[41] However, identifying anarchy and the self-help world it creates as the raison d'être of the security dilemma has also led writers on the subject to suggest means of lessening its effects (mitigation) and even nullifying it (escape).[42]

In the early 1980s Buzan introduced the concept of a mature anarchy. He suggested that it was possible to consider a spectrum along which anarchy matures, or becomes more tamed, the more orderly it becomes. He wrote that a mature anarchy would 'be a highly ordered and stable system in which states would enjoy a great deal of security deriving both from their own inner strength and maturity, and from the strength of the institutionalised norms regulating relations among them'.[43] At the mature end of the spectrum, such norms would include the avoidance of force in the settlement of disputes thus equating a mature anarchy with Karl Deutsch's security community. This is important for the security dilemma since in a security community, the defining feature of which is that force is not considered an option for the settlement of disputes, the security dilemma can no longer operate. Also writing in the early 1980s Jervis uses regime theory to claim that if states were able to abide by norms constraining their behaviour – to become part of a security regime – these norms would make statesmen less uncertain of each others' intentions. Such a security regime would lie towards the mature end of Buzan's spectrum, though not at the extreme, and would indicate the security dilemma's detrimental effects were mitigated. In other words, mitigation and escape are possible by reducing uncertainty which in turn reveals to statesmen the others' benign intent thereby enabling their self-defeating or paradoxical policies to be halted. Escape is therefore dependent upon anarchy being subject to change.

In what has become a valuable addition to the literature, Alexander Wendt has argued that states can construct the society in which they exist. His argument is that '[s]elf-help and power politics are institutions, not essential features of anarchy. *Anarchy is what states make of it*' (emphasis in original).[44] He considers self-help to be a process within international relations as opposed to its structure. If statesmen, through a process of learning from interactions with others, are capable of realising that the other is not a threat then, in Butterfield's terms, they will be able to enter into each other's counter-fear and reassure one another about their intentions. Wendt agrees with Herz that the security dilemma is a social or cognitive rather than a behavioural or anthropological effect. Using the example of Mikhail Gorbachev's 'New Thinking' policy, Wendt claims that the USSR was able to alter its own image, its image of the West and, while he was in the process of writing, was altering the West's image of the USSR. What is particularly intriguing with Wendt's assertion is that the process can go beyond mitigating the statesmen's fear to actually escaping it. Thus, while he recognises that via cooperation statesmen can create norms of behaviour and as a result grow more confident in predicting others' intentions and actions, he suggests this process can go further. He argues that in the process of cooperating by not defecting on these norms, statesmen are creating new and communal interests and commitments. These collective interests will be resistant to change, not because there is a penalty for the state that defects, but because all the actors gain from its continued observance. What statesmen perceive as necessary for their state's security has changed. They have acquired mutual or common interests. Similar thinking can be found in the literature on common or mutual security. Here, the emphasis lies on the threat of nuclear devastation creating a shared interest in survival. Whether noted explicitly or implicitly, the claim is made that states can build upon this shared interest in survival to pursue common rather than unilateral goals.[45]

Wendt's suggestion that statesmen through interaction and cooperation can mitigate and ultimately escape the security dilemma is not new. Writing in the 1960s both Charles Osgood and Amitai Etzioni wrote about how statesmen could reduce tension by taking unilateral initiatives which could induce reciprocation from the other state.[46] Both emphasised how by gradually raising the stakes it was possible for the states to cooperate on the issues that caused their greatest concerns regarding one another. This form of cooperation, known as GRIT (Graduated Reciprocation in Tension-Reduction), was centred on the establishment of norms of behaviour thus creating a security regime on the issue at stake. While such a regime lessens the suspicion the statesmen have of one another and thus mitigates the security dilemma, escape can only occur once the statesmen become confident that the other harbours no malign intent and will not resort to the use of force to settle any disputes between them. Wendt suggests that such a shared commitment can arise. If it does then this will be concomitant with a security community in which the security dilemma is escaped. The evolution of norms of behaviour and how they relate to common security, security regimes and the ASEAN experience, in particular the 'ASEAN way', is the focus of attention in Chapter 4.

The idea of statesmen acquiring new and shared interests becomes even more significant when applied to the state-induced security dilemma mentioned above. Since the hegemonic state requires others to be insecure this would, assuming the others are not prepared to accept such insecurity, prevent them solving the security dilemma through the pursuit of GRIT. The hegemon's goal is simply not compatible with those of the other states and thus unilateral action is unlikely to be reciprocated. Hence Snyder's claim that '[a]lthough the security dilemma [is] in some sense a spiral process, it [is] not a spiral that could be unwound by the concessionary policies that spiral theorists usually advocate'.[47] According to Snyder, the hegemon's 'intentions can be made more benign by another state only by changing those circumstances – or the adversary's assessment of them – and not by the use of threats or concessions'.[48] Wendt's focus on states' changing the anarchy in which they conduct relations by acquiring common interests takes on added significance because altering the hegemon's assessment of what is required for security becomes essential. Over a period of time cooperation with the hegemon could alter how the hegemon identifies its relationship with the other states and therefore escape the security dilemma. An example of state interests changing can be found in Europe where, despite its raison d'être disappearing, NATO remains. The alliance retains it value because its members' assessment of European security has altered, or in Wendt's words, 'the European states of 1990 might no longer be the states of 1950'.[49] Whether, by engaging China in a network of security dialogue and cooperation, the ASEAN members have been able to alter China's assessment of its relationship with the states of Southeast Asia receives examination in Chapter 5.

The key to mitigating and ultimately escaping the security dilemma lies in reducing the uncertainty statesmen have about their neighbour's intentions. This can be achieved by a steady improvement in state relations – the maturing of anarchy – via the establishment of recognised codes of behaviour. It is not though the only means by which the security dilemma can be escaped. Writing in the late 1970s, Jervis introduced the offence/defence debate to the security dilemma in his seminal piece, 'Cooperation under the Security Dilemma'.[50] Since then a number of authors, most notably Charles Glaser, have given this aspect of the security dilemma a prominent position in the literature.[51] While escape might be possible via cooperation, achieving such cooperation amongst egoists is fraught with difficulties. This does not make such an approach impossible but it does make an approach that could escape the security dilemma without the need for cooperation very intriguing. It is precisely this prospect that Jervis raises when he writes, '[i]t would ... be possible for states to escape from the security dilemma without developing the sorts of cooperative understandings that help ameliorate political conflicts across a broad range of issues'.[52]

For Jervis the key lies in the types of military forces statesmen procure and the prevailing belief of how to wage war. He claims that 'when offensive and defensive postures are different, much of the uncertainty about the other's intentions that contribute to the security dilemma is removed'.[53] In essence his argument is that where there exists offensive force postures, and offensive actions are perceived to hold the advantage in war, the security dilemma will operate at its highest pitch. Conversely where defence is perceived to be the stronger form of warfare and forces are deployed in defensive formations the security dilemma is mitigated, possibly even escaped. In this latter scenario an increase in defensive weapon acquisitions will not be seen as threatening since they will provide only a limited capability for conducting an invasion. Since status quo powers will not require offensive weapons the procurement of such weapons will indicate an aggressive actor. Thus, rather than seeking cooperation with a perceived foe, Jervis claims that where defence is stronger and distinguishable from offence, '[t]he differentiation between offensive and defensive systems permits a way out of the security dilemma ... There is no reason for a status quo power to be tempted to procure offensive forces, and aggressors give notice of their intentions by the posture they adopt.'[54]

There are problems associated with this approach not least of which is the difficulty in distinguishing offensive and defensive weapons and postures. Snyder has also suggested that since 'offence is virtually never easier than defence ... one of the alleged engines of the structural security dilemma runs in reverse'.[55] It is also unlikely that when defence is perceived to hold the advantage status quo powers will only procure defensive weapons. Despite these problems the ability to escape the security dilemma by altering force postures remains an important part of the equation. It is because non-offensive defence (NOD) plans place limitations on the offensiveness of forces that they are seen as relevant to the security dilemma. Indeed, Ken Booth asserts that strategies 'of non-provocative defence ... seek to deal with the military problem which lies at the heart of the security dilemma'.[56] The acquisition of power projection weapons by ASEAN members and the security dilemma is examined in Chapter 4.

With the end of the Cold War an interest has arisen in the security field with conflicts between different ethnic groups within states. This interest in the 1990s has resulted in the security dilemma being used to help explain the causes of this type of conflict. It is to this latest development that our attention must now turn in the final part of this chapter.

D. Intrastate security dilemma

Brian Job and Barry Buzan have both applied the security dilemma to intra-state strife, while Barry Posen and Stuart Kaufman, amongst others, have attempted to operationalise it with reference to ethnic conflicts in the former Yugoslavia and the republics of the former Soviet

Union.[57] The immediate problem of applying the security dilemma to relations within states is the role of anarchy. Since the anarchical system promotes the self-help behaviour of states in the international system, is the security dilemma applicable to relations within sovereign states? Kaufman recognises this problem by admitting that '[s]trictly speaking, the security dilemma should not apply to contending ethnic groups within a state, because they rarely find themselves in a situation of complete anarchy'.[58] However, he reasons that if the government's authority and territorial control is such that it cannot protect its populace, 'anarchy can be approximated'.[59] This also explains Posen's reference to the collapse of an imperial regime being, 'a problem of emerging anarchy'.[60] They both overcome the problem of anarchy within a sovereign state therefore by applying the security dilemma to states in which there is no effective sovereign. Job's reference to an insecurity dilemma is examined in Chapter 2 since this is an attempt to apply the security dilemma to ethnic relations within sovereign states that have not collapsed.

Barry Posen was the first to utilise the security dilemma concept when examining ethnic conflicts. Posen makes an accurate reference to the security dilemma when he notes that the security dilemma arises when states 'have no expansionist tendencies' (benign intent), but their actions cause 'reactions that, in the end, can make one less secure' (paradoxical policies). He also notes the role of uncertainty when he writes, '[c]ooperation among states…can be difficult because someone else's "cheating" may leave one in a militarily weakened position. All fear betrayal'.[61] However, when applying the concept, although he notes that the participants have reasons to be mistrustful of each other, he highlights the pursuit of policies that cause concern in the other group without linking this specifically to the security dilemma. He therefore concentrates solely on the spiralling process of insecurity and assumes that it is being driven by a security dilemma. However, if the actions are intended to do harm to others, and this generates fear in those others which causes them to take defensive actions, then it is not a security dilemma. This was precisely the point Jervis made when he noted that a similar action–reaction of events could be witnessed in the deterrence model. The existence of malign intent creates a real incompatibility that ensures the defensive actions being taken by the target state/group are not self-defeating or paradoxical. If these actions should deter the aggressor and the aggressor embarks upon more aggressive actions, this has not occurred as a result of the aggressor misperceiving the actions of the target but rather its desire to complete its political goal of conquest. Posen's application of the security dilemma is not therefore aided by his claim that in the Croat/Serb example 'there were plenty of signals of malign intent'.[62] The essence of the security dilemma is the tragedy that unknown to either participant their incompatibility, while appearing real, is actually illusory. Should that incompatibility be real or become real, then while the scenario may indicate a decrease in security for both, it is not a security dilemma that is driving this process. Instead, it is an accurate assessment of the very real danger that the aggressor poses to the other group.

The need to distinguish between conflicts that have occurred as a result of a real incompatibility and those due to an illusory incompatibility becomes essential when understanding Kaufman's use of the security dilemma. Kaufman divides ethnic conflicts into mass-led and elite-led. The difference between these is crucial for the security dilemma. For mass-led, it is their hostility and fear which activates the security dilemma and begins the process of spiralling insecurity. The security dilemma does appear relevant to mass-led ethnic conflicts. In Kaufman's case study, of Nagorno–Karabakh, the historical fears that the Armenians and Azerbaijanis had of one another, led in 1987/88 to a wave of refugees as the minority groups began to feel threatened. The hostility that generated this deterioration in relations was based on the enemy-image the groups had of one another. Neither harboured aggressive designs but because they were uncertain of this, and indeed their history led them to perceive each other as a threat, the actions they took proved self-defeating as they generated a hostility neither Armenian nor Azerbaijani leaders sought. Kaufman also notes how in Moldova demands for Moldovan, or Romanian, to become the official language had the effect of creating a perception of fear amongst the Russian speaking populace. In both cases the deterioration of relations can be seen as a tragedy as the security dilemma took hold as an unintended consequence of actions undertaken by both sides. If it is an illusory incompatibility that is at the heart of the mass-led ethnic conflict, this does not appear to be the case with the elite-led example.

Kaufman distinguishes between the two ethnic conflicts by noting the elite 'intentionally cause both mass hostility and a security dilemma, rather than reacting to them'.[63] In other words, rather than an unintended consequence of an action, the security dilemma in the elite-led example acts as an objective of the leader's policies. Kaufman is explicit in stating that the elite-led security dilemma is caused by individuals seeking to do harm: 'extremist elites begin or provoke violence in order to activate an ethnic security dilemma which in turn generates even more violence'.[64] In his case study of Croatia and Serbia, Kaufman notes that in early 1990 the two groups were living peacefully together, and it was due to the Serbian leader, Slobodan Milosevic, 'promoting popular hatred and fears, chauvinist ideas, and strategic myths' that provoked the violence and, according to Kaufman, a security dilemma.[65] From Kaufman's analysis it is therefore clear that the violence between the Serbs and the Croats was caused by the elite's malign intent, which is crucial, because it means that the deterioration in relations was not due to paradoxical policies *per se* but the machinations of the Serbian leaders. Does the existence of this malign intent ensure that it is not a security dilemma that causes this type of ethnic conflict?

Kaufman's elite-led example distinguishes between the leaders and their people and analyses the deterioration of relations from these two separate perspectives. The role of leaders in the elite-led example therefore adds another dimension to the process of spiralling insecurity. Kaufman highlights how the elite misinform their people and fool them into believing the other group harbours aggressive ambitions: 'leaders spread the key myth that the ethnic group is somehow threatened'.[66] Thus, for the masses the conflict is driven by an illusory incompatibility since they are responding to a bogus threat created by their leaders. Since the threat is bogus, or illusory, does this indicate that the security dilemma is relevant? The answer must be no, because if the opposing group responds to the myth by taking actions to protect itself which in turn, by reinforcing the myth, creates a spiralling process of insecurity as the other responds, what is driving this process is the elite's malign intent. The elite are intentionally causing the fear of their people, which means that the incompatibility at the heart of the conflict is real. Attempts to arrest the deterioration in the relationship by conciliation, which could mitigate a security dilemma, would in this instance reward the aggressor. Thus, while the masses do not harbour malign intent, their leaders do and their political objectives (overthrow of existing regime, territorial expansion) ensure that the incompatibility between the groups remains real. It was noted above that when Jervis warns against assuming 'that the desire for security, rather than expansion, is the prime goal for states', he is echoing Herz's warning that the security dilemma is not at the heart of all conflicts, there also exists sheer political ambition. In this instance it is the sheer political ambition of the leaders that is inducing the conflict, and by misleading their people and causing war they can be considered in Butterfield's words to be great criminals seeking to do deliberate harm.

Kaufman's application of the security dilemma to ethnic conflict reveals the importance of determining the intent of the leaders and their people. If elite individuals deliberately induce conflict via disinformation, then their willingness to use violence against others produces a scenario that is not too dissimilar to Herz highlighting Hitler, not the security dilemma, as responsible for World War II. The existence of such malign intent is problematic for the security dilemma concept. Accordingly, if the elite pursue actions which inadvertently create a perception of threat amongst ethnic groups, the security dilemma could explain a consequential deterioration in relations. This is also true where the actions of one ethnic group inadvertently appear threatening to others. The key is the requirement of an illusory incompatibility (benign intent), since it is from the misperception of threat (uncertainty of intent) that the spiralling process of greater insecurity leads to the tragedy (paradoxical actions) of a conflict neither wanted. Kaufman initially appears to understand this when, in defining the security dilemma, he correctly asserts that the 'key point is that the conflict need not be the result of aggressive intent', instead, 'it is a result of the structure of the situation'.[67] Indeed he perfectly highlights the paradox inherent within the security dilemma when he states a 'security dilemma requires that the fears of extinction be mutual – that actions taken by one side to avert extinction be seen by the other side as threatening extinction for themselves'.[68] In other words, it is the defensive actions which each group takes to protect itself which unintentionally provokes a security dilemma. However, he then claims that if the fear of extinction becomes justified, 'because its existence as a community may really be threatened by the goals of the other', the resulting measures undertaken by each group can still be explained by the security dilemma.[69] This though cannot be true since the incompatibility is real, the measures both parties are pursuing are not paradoxical and spiral prescriptions such as unilateral restraint in arms procurement are potentially suicidal.

The confusion over the security dilemma's application to ethnic conflict is explained by Kaufman when he claims that his use of the concept differs from that of international relations scholars. Kaufman writes:

[T]he neorealist concept of a security dilemma cannot be mechanically applied to ethnic conflict: anarchy and the *possibility* of a security threat are not enough to create a security dilemma between communities which may have been at peace for decades. An ethnic security dilemma requires reciprocal fears of group extinction, and such fears do not arise unless hostile masses define their security in extreme ways, or unless outbidding elites emerge to make the pursuit of such goals into policy (emphasis in original).[70]

For Kaufman such extreme measures can include the belief that security can only be achieved by eliminating others and thus instances of malign intent such as ethnic cleansing can be partly explained by the security dilemma. The problem with Kaufman's use of the security dilemma is that if the suspicion and fear that each group harbours of the other (the *possibility* of a security threat) is not enough to create a security dilemma and that malign intent is required, his application of the security dilemma is the antithesis of what Butterfield and Herz intended. For the originators of the term it is precisely the fear and suspicion that each group harbours of the other which creates pressure to think in zero-sum terms. Malign intent is not required for a vicious and ferocious war to be fought. Hence Butterfield claims

> neither party sees the nature of the predicament he is in...It is...possible for each to feel that the other is wilfully withholding the guarantees that would have enabled him to have a sense of security. The resulting conflict is more likely to be hot with moral indignation – one self-righteousness encountering another – than it would have been if the contest had lain between two hard-headed eighteenth-century masters of *realpolitik*.[71]

The possibility of a security threat may therefore be sufficient on its own to generate a security dilemma. This does not prevent scenarios in which parties define their security in extreme ways, being inapplicable to the security dilemma. After all in Snyder's security dilemma one party requires the other to be insecure for it to be secure, which can be interpreted as an extreme way of defining one's own security. However, it is clear that for Kaufman such extreme measures can include the intent to eradicate the other, but since such a goal represents a real threat it cannot be compatible with the security dilemma. Determining whether the incompatibility is real or illusory is therefore critical in determining the applicability of the security dilemma.

The application of the security dilemma to intra-state conflict, and in particular this issue of communities using extreme measures to acquire security, raises a fundamental issue for the security dilemma. Since the security dilemma is dependent upon determining whether the intent of the participants is malign or benign, how do observers do this? This is particularly vexing and when Butterfield notes that uncertainty arises because it is impossible to look inside the mind of another he is also revealing that it is impossible to know their intentions. Of course it is precisely because determining intentions is difficult that statesmen rarely recognise that they are victims of a security dilemma, and, at least according to Posen, even if they think they are they cannot avoid it because it is too risky to try. Yet, if we are to proceed with the security dilemma, it is necessary to be able to make judgements concerning whether the situation is a tragedy in which two parties desperate to avoid conflict are actually making it more likely, or, whether one party actually wants a conflict.

The answer can be found by referring to Jervis's real and illusory incompatibility of goals. Determining whether the incompatibility of the participants' ambitions are real or illusory is also far from simple but it is easier than determining whether the intentions are malign or not. For instance, and this is examined in more detail in Chapter 3, if a regime seeks to unify a population which contains numerous different ethnic groups by imposing a single identity on them, then, assuming the groups wished to maintain their separate identities, the incompatibility of the regime's policy and the ethnic groups is real. The regime's goal of a mono-ethnic nation-state constitutes a real threat to the ethnic groups' separate identities. Thus, a rise in tension within the state, and the possible desire for secession by the ethnic communities, represents not a misperception of threat as in the spiral model, but rather, the real incompatibility between both participants' goals as in the deterrence model. It is therefore possible to conclude that the security dilemma is not in operation. However, to argue that the regime's intentions were malign would require determining whether the elite knew what impact their policy would have on the ethnic groups. Determining this is not only very difficult, and probably impossible, but perhaps more importantly, unnecessary. The real incompatibility between their goals ensures that the actions both are taking are not self-defeating and thus not a security dilemma. This does not mean that using benign and malign intent as characteristics for the security dilemma is wrong, since in some instances they are synonymous with real and illusory incompatibility; instead, it means that determining whether the participants' ambitions are compatible, or not, is the key.[72]

The recent application of the security dilemma to intra-state conflict is clearly an exciting if not problematic development for the security dilemma. Kaufman's analysis in particular is complex as he attempts to combine the security dilemma with hostile masses and belligerent leaders to understand the causes of ethnic wars. It would appear that mass-led, and in certain circumstances elite-led, ethnic wars can be understood from the perspective of the security dilemma. However, as Kaufman admits, the security dilemma 'cannot be mechanically applied' to all ethnic conflicts, and it is in those instances where the elite intend harm to others that it becomes inapplicable.

Conclusion

Introduced in 1951, the security dilemma in the last twenty years has been subject to reinterpretation and reapplication. The 1980s witnessed the arrival of state-induced security dilemmas by Jack Snyder, although this was not a term he himself used, while the 1990s has seen its application extended to different referent objects for security; societies within states. The security dilemma has thus evolved since its inception, but this evolution can only be useful if the term remains true to its original value. Otherwise it is in danger of becoming a meaningless and ambiguous term associated with any deterioration in relations.

The essence for Butterfield was that war could occur without the intervention of statesmen who seek such an outcome. As Herz recognises, the security dilemma is a tragedy where both sides anxious to avoid war actually pursue the very policies that make war likely. Glenn Snyder's definition of the security dilemma in 1984 highlights how this could occur and it is also a good example of what the term meant before the challenges of the mid-late 1980s and 1990s. Glenn Snyder writes:

> even when no state has any desire to attack others, none can be sure that others' intentions are peaceful, or will remain so; hence each must accumulate power for defence. Since no state can know that the power accumulation of others is defensively motivated only, each must assume that it might be intended for attack. Consequently, each party's power increments are matched by the others, and all wind up with no more security than when the vicious cycle began, along with the costs incurred in having acquired and having to maintain their power.[73]

The three characteristics of the security dilemma are present. None of the parties desired to attack, and their actions were defensively motivated (benign intent). However, they did not know that the others were only acting for defensive reasons (uncertainty of intent), thus their actions only made matters worse (paradoxical). It is with these three characteristics in mind that the subsequent reinterpretations and reapplications of the security dilemma needs to be tested.

It is Jack Snyder's definition of the security dilemma arising when one state requires the insecurity of others which lies at the heart of the subsequent reinterpretations in the literature. Stuart Kaufman's application of the security dilemma to ethnic conflicts, for instance, is based upon Jack Snyder's definition. It is suggested here that, while Jack Snyder's definition can be interpreted as an accurate extension of the concept, it is not without problems. Whether Snyder's definition remains an accurate extension of the security dilemma depends upon the ambition of at least one of the actors. If the ambition entails a threat to a state's territory or an ethnic group's identity the rise in insecurity is not a consequence of the security dilemma. However, where the ambition is hegemony, the security dilemma could explain a rise of insecurity, since such an ambition does not necessarily indicate a threat to neighbouring actors' security; although they may perceive it as such. Snyder's main argument is that in some instances it is not possible to mitigate a security dilemma via spiral prescriptions such as confidence-building measures. In other words simply reducing statesmen's uncertainty is not enough, the goal of hegemony is the cause of the neighbours' insecurity. In this instance it is only possible for all to be secure if the hegemon reinterprets its criteria for achieving security. How this can be achieved is examined in the final section which utilises Jack Snyder's definition of the security dilemma to analyse the ASEAN–China relationship.

Finally, it was noted that the key for the security dilemma's first characteristic is illusory incompatibility, and while this is still difficult to determine, it is easier to determine than malign intent. Ultimately of course, it is only possible for the outside observer to interpret the actions of the parties as accurately as they can and thus this book is about determining whether at the heart of the tensions in Southeast Asia are real or illusory incompatibilities, and in so doing, reveal whether a tragedy is unfolding in the region. The first section focuses on ethnic tensions in Southeast Asia and the application of the security dilemma to internal state security. The second examines intra-ASEAN state relations, and in particular the 'ASEAN Way' as a mitigator of the security dilemma, while the final section utilises Jack Snyder's definition of the security dilemma to analyse the ASEAN–China relationship.

Part I

Intra-state Security Dilemma

2
Third World Security: Security and Insecurity Dilemma

The goal in this first section (Chapters 2 and 3) is to determine if the security dilemma is as applicable to ethnic conflict as has been suggested in recent writings, to examine its application using ethnicity as the security issue, and whether it is possible to mitigate or even escape its detrimental effects. Southeast Asia has a multitude of ethnic tensions that have arisen from the process of state-making and nation-building. In Malaysia there exists tension between the indigenous Malay and the descendants of Chinese and Indian immigrants. In Indonesia similar tensions exist between the indigenous people and the ethnic Chinese, although in this archipelago ethnic tensions also exist between settlers and the indigenous communities of the Outer Islands. In southern Thailand the Patani Malays have pursued a goal of irredentism, while the Moros of Mindanao in the Philippines have sought both autonomy and independence from Manila. In the next chapter a number of these ethnic tensions will be examined to determine if the security dilemma is applicable and what, if any, insights it might offer.

In the previous chapter the application of the security dilemma to ethnic conflict was highlighted. In this chapter this process will be taken a step further by seeking to determine its applicability to ethnic tensions within states that are not in the process of collapsing. In other words, to determine if a security dilemma is in operation and whether it can be mitigated or even escaped before the state collapses. This entails providing an examination of Third World security issues and locating the security dilemma in this literature.

The chapter is divided into two parts: the first (A–C) is specifically concerned with the security dilemma. It addresses the problem of sovereignty; ethnicity as the security issue is examined; and a comparison is provided between Brian Job's insecurity dilemma and the security dilemma. The second part (D) is concerned with mitigating the security dilemma and provides an examination of the difficulties regimes face in state-making and nation-building. In order to mitigate a security dilemma it must be possible for the belligerents to overcome their difficulties without resorting to violence. This second part of the chapter examines the reasons for the regimes' propensity to resort to violence, and seeks to determine if alternatives exist. It is suggested that the means to successful state-making and nation-building are different from the seventeenth and nineteenth century European experience and therefore an alternative does exist. However, before examining whether it is possible to mitigate an intra-state security dilemma it is necessary to determine if it exists at all. Since the security dilemma operates in a self-help environment the issue of sovereignty needs to be addressed: how can there exist an intra-state security dilemma in a sovereign state?

A. The problem of sovereignty

The existence of a sovereign authority is problematic for Barry Posen and Stuart Kaufman because they assume it will negate the self-help environment which is essential for the operation of a security dilemma. Hence they both apply the security dilemma to states in which there is no effective sovereign. This concern with sovereignty has also been raised by Barry Buzan and Ole Waever. They have introduced the idea of societal security, in what has been referred to as the 'Copenhagen school', and within this concept Buzan has made reference to a societal security dilemma.[1] Buzan writes:

> [t]o the extent that tensions over migration, identity and territory occur between societies, we might by analogy with international politics talk about a 'societal security dilemma'. This would imply that societies can experience processes in which perceptions of 'the others' develop into mutually reinforcing 'enemy-pictures' leading to the same kind of negative dialectics as with the security dilemma between states.[2]

He goes on to note that these reinforcing enemy-pictures reduce the security for all involved.

> Societal security dilemmas might explain why some processes of social conflict seem to acquire a dynamic of their own. While initial

conflicts might be explained with diverging interests, from a certain threshold the processes can evolve with a self-sustained internal dynamic, which might end up being very destructive.[3]

Buzan therefore emphasises how, once initiated, a self-reinforcing dynamic that exacerbates the fears each has about the other, can cause the relationship of the parties to deteriorate to such an extent that conflict can occur. So long as this spiral of insecurity is the result of actions intended by both communities for defensive purposes only, and thus a result of paradoxical policies, the security dilemma analogy appears accurate. Why though would Buzan's societies adopt defensive measures if their security was already safeguarded by a governing regime? The sovereignty issue, while acknowledged by Buzan, is not answered:

> Fundamentally, though, the situation at the sub-state level is differ-ent from the situation in the international system, because we gen-erally have at least some state authority and not complete anarchy at the sub-state level.[4]

The answer to the difficulty with sovereign regimes and the security dilemma can be found in Brian Job's edited work, *The Insecurity Dilemma*.[5] The 'in' prefix not only captures the spiralling process of decreasing security inherent within the security dilemma, but it also alludes to where the focus of study is concentrated – *in* the state. For Job, the key to why groups would mimic the self-help international system lies in the type of state in which they inhabit. He suggests that in some Third World states sovereignty does not equate to the regime having effective control over the state institutions which provide secu-rity or well-being for their people. Here Job is referring to what is com-monly known as the weak state. Although the term has been widely used its common distinguishing features are: (1) inadequate infrastruc-tural capacity, (2) poor national identity and social cohesion and, (3) internal security threats. The final feature is often the result of the first two – the ethnic diversity of the state, coupled with the regime's inability to provide for its people, leads to the populace's loyalty being expressed elsewhere. This expression of support for alternatives leads to the perception that the greatest threats to the regime lie within the state. Hence David Steinberg's comment that since 'independence the role of the military in Burma has been less to protect the state against external threats than to put down internal centrifugal tendencies – the inclination of ethnic elements to spin off into independent entities'.[6] The 'weakness' of the state therefore alludes to the population's lack of identity with the state, and not a reference to its military or economic capacity. The stronger the state the more a regime is able to rule by consent; the weaker it is, the more likely coercion will be required to enforce rules. Towards the weaker end of this spectrum the less the regime is seen as a provider of security and the more it is seen as the danger. In these circumstances ethnic groups have no guarantor for their security, they must provide for themselves; they exist in a self-help system.

B. The security issue

The classification of states into weak and strong is most readily associated with Barry Buzan.[7] This distinction has been seized upon by writers of Third World security to reveal the different security concerns of these states in comparison to the First World. In essence, while Third World security is influenced by regional and global actors, the main concern is with internal issues. Thus, for Mohammed Ayoob the security issues of the Third World – which he refers to as their security predicament – are the internal matters of state-making and nation-building.[8] The former concerns the regime's ability to control peripheral communities through the expansion of the state apparatus. The latter is the creation amongst the populace of a common identity. In both cases the barometer of success is the legitimacy the regime is able to achieve amongst the people. Caroline Thomas adds to nation-building other issues, such as food, health, money and trade as she explains the multiple challenges to Third World security.[9] Edward Azar and Chung-in Moon borrow computer language in distinguishing between the tangible assets of economic and military power (hardware) and the equally important but more intangible factors of political context and policy capacity (software). While the hardware factors are important these authors note that the software 'variables are especially germane to the Third World national security context'.[10] Two differences between security dialogue in the West and the Third World become immediately apparent. The first is that security concerns are focused in the state rather than between states, and the second is that Third World security is defined in a broad context, and not purely in military terms. This has important consequences for the application of the internal security dilemma. First, because these states have internal security concerns, an internal security dilemma could occur; and second, the perception of threat could be non-military in character.

The multifarious nature of the security threats facing the populace in Third World states complicates the application of the security dilemma. In the inter-state security dilemma, the security issue has traditionally been one of territory. The threat statesmen perceive concerns their state boundaries and the means adopted to safeguard their territory is military. Hence, the security dilemma is often manifest in an arms build-up, and the literature refers to offensive/defensive weapons postures as a means of mitigating the dilemma's detrimental dynamics.

For the intra-state security dilemma the security issue (from Posen, Kaufman and the Copenhagen school) is ethnicity. Ethnicity refers to an individual's association with others through a shared consciousness that arises from, amongst other things, a common language, religion, lifestyle, physiognomy and history. Ethnicity is a relatively new term first recorded in the *Oxford English Dictionary* of 1953, but it is derived from the much older term, ethnic, which in turn is a derivative of the ancient Greek term, *ethnos*.[11] It can be understood from both a primordialist and situationalist or instrumentalist position. The former defines ethnicity as a given which is conferred on the individual from birth. Not only does this entail the sharing of common genes which engender feelings of common identity, but the primordialist position also includes socialisation attributes such as common language and religion which strengthen the bond between the individual and group. The central issue for primordialists is that an ethnic identity is fixed. Hence David Brown writes the 'primordialist perspective asserts that people are naturally ethnocentric, exhibiting trust and preference for those of their own cultural group while feeling more distant from, and distrustful of, those of other cultural groups'.[12] In this sense, understanding politics in a multi-ethnic state entails an appreciation of the conflicting interests the different groups are pursuing. The situationalist position acknowledges that individuals belong to different ethnic groups, but the individuals do not necessarily recognise them as having political significance. It is only when they feel threatened that the individuals' perception of 'them' (the aggressors) creates a sense of 'us' (ethnic group). Ethnicity is thus a resource that individuals use to protect their interests. In a weak state where the regime might not be trusted to protect individuals, or indeed may be considered the threat to them, the more likely it is that ethnicity will gain political currency as it becomes a tool to protect individuals that have a common bond. While the primordialist and situationalist perspectives are seen as opposed to one another there have been attempts to synthesise the approaches and in practice few scholars adhere strictly to either position.[13]

The dynamics of the intra-state security dilemma arise when one ethnic group fears its identity is being challenged – for Posen and Kaufman this challenge is still military in nature and is manifest by the physical assaults of one ethnic group on another. For the Copenhagen school, the challenge can be more subtle with the group's identity being unravelled by the denial of its culture. Thus Buzan asserts that

> societal identity can be threatened in ways ranging from the suppression of its expression to interference with its ability to repro-duce ... The reproduction of a society can be threatened by sustained application of repressive measures against the expression of its iden-tity. If the institutions that reproduce language and culture are for-bidden to operate, the identity cannot be transmitted effectively from one generation to the next.[14]

The intra-state security dilemma operates therefore when one ethnic group perceives its identity is being challenged by another group. The situation is more complicated when the security dilemma is applied to regime/ethnic minority relations. When a minority group seeks inde-pendence from the regime's rule because it fears its distinctive identity will be lost, the security issue this secessionist ambition raises for the regime is territory. For example, Che Man argues that because the Philippine government would not allow the Moro Muslims of Mindanao to exercise autonomy within the Philippines, 'Moro ... leaders ... took the position that only through separation and independence from the centre would the Muslims be able to preserve their identity.'[15] Thus while for the Moros the issue is their ethnic identity, their secessionist ambitions make the issue one of territory for Manila. Thus for the regime the security issue is likely to be not only about identity (nation-building) but also territory (state-making).

C. Dynamics of internal security: insecurity and/or security dilemma?

Is it possible to apply the security dilemma to internal security issues? In Chapter 1 it is explained that there are three key requirements of a security dilemma: first, an illusory incompatibility (benign intent) between the participants;[16] second, uncertainty regarding their intent which can lead to a misperception of threat; third, the pursuit of para-doxical policies that create greater insecurity resulting in the tragedy of a conflict neither wanted. These requirements need to be evident for the security dilemma to be applicable. Although Brian Job introduces the security dilemma to the internal security of weak states he is explicit in stating that its relevance is minimal. He claims in the 'internal ... circumstances of contemporary Third World states, the security dilemma metaphor and underlying logic do not hold up to scrutiny'.[17] However, Job's reasons for minimising the security dilemma relate more to the differences between Third and First World states than the security dilemma itself. Consequently when he expounds his alternative concept – the insecurity dilemma – the difference is marginal. He writes that within a multi-ethnic state, 'individuals and groups acting against perceived threats to assure their own security or securities consequently create an environment of increased threat and reduced security for most, if not all, others within the borders of the state'.[18] He continues by noting that regimes are preoccupied with their own safety and that it is rational for them to 'utilize scarce resources for military equipment ..., to perceive as threatening opposition movements demanding greater public debate, and to regard as dangerous communal movements that promote alternative identifications and loyalties'.[19] Is there a difference between the insecurity and security dilemma?

There is a difference and it centres on whether the incompatibility between the actors is real or illusory. Rather than focusing on what initiated the perception of threat (the cause), Job focuses on the self-sustaining and paradoxical logic of intra-state violence. Hence Job quotes a conclusion from T. David Mason and Dale Krane that 'presents a striking characterisation of the insecurity dilemma':[20]

> This leads us to the question of why a regime, itself composed of supposedly rational individuals, would pursue a policy of escalating repression if such measures are ultimately counterproductive. We argue that the conditions of structural dependence characterizing these regimes leave them without the institutional machinery, economic resources, or political will to address opposition challengers through more accommodative programs of reform. Thus, escalating repression is perpetuated not because it has a high probability of success but because the weakness of the state precludes its resort to less violent alternatives.[21]

In other words, it is not why this situation occurred that is important, but rather why, despite the self-defeating nature of violence, regimes become locked into using it. This has important ramifications for mitigating the security dilemma and is examined later in the chapter. For now though the key point is that while the security dilemma is concerned with determining if the rise in tension has occurred despite neither participant seeking such an outcome, this is not true for the insecurity dilemma. Although Job notes that regimes are 'preoccupied with their own safety' this is not the same as stating their actions are defensive. The following hypothetical example will help identify the differences between the two dilemmas.

In an attempt to state-make and nation-build, a regime will seek to expand its control over the territory by establishing regional bureaucracies and creating amongst the populace a common affinity. This expansion of control could be perceived as a threat by the peripheral communities to their authority and to their identity. Consequently, the regime's actions could have the effect of strengthening the group's identity and thereby highlighting the differences rather than the similarities amongst the population. Instead of creating a nation-state the regime could have sparked off demands for autonomy. So far the example appears to be both an insecurity and security dilemma; indeed it is possible for both to operate at the same time. However, at this point a question needs to be raised to determine if it is a security dilemma. Do the regime's state-making and nation-building policies constitute a real threat to the peripheral communities? In other words, are the peripheral communities right to perceive a threat, or are their fears and suspicions based upon a misperception? This is vital for the security dilemma since it is concerned with the cause of the tension. Hence Herbert Butterfield's remark about war not requiring the intervention of great criminals, or John Herz's emphasis on the incompatibility between political ambition and the security dilemma when he dismisses the security dilemma as a cause of the Second World War. Randall Schweller perfectly captures this vital characteristic:

> When the goal of one or more states is something other than mutual security, conflict is not only apparent but real; and because it is real, the resulting insecurity cannot be attributed to the security dilemma/spiral model of conflict. States acquire more arms not because they misperceive the security efforts of other benign states but because aggressive states truly wish to harm them.[22]

For the insecurity dilemma though the goal of the participants does not matter since in Mason and Krane's 'striking characterisation' the ambition of the regime is not in question. The insecurity dilemma is simply concerned with highlighting, first, how the regime's actions are paradoxical since its state-making and nation-building programme have had the opposite effect to that intended, and second, the hopelessness of the regime's position since there appear to be no satisfactory solutions to its problems. This though is not enough for the security dilemma because it does not reveal what initiated the process. If the regime sought to nation-build for instance by assimilating all the different ethnic groups into the dominant ethnic group, or creating an overarching identity through acculturation, then this clearly entails a real threat to their identities. The peripheral communities would be faced with a real threat to their identity and thus the actions they take to defend their identity are not paradoxical. If it was possible for the elite of the minority group to look inside the minds of the regime's elite, it would reveal not a misunderstanding, instead, it would confirm their worst fears. Of course determining illusory incompatibility is far from easy and this is noted by both Barry Buzan and Myron Weiner. The former writes, '[e]valuating what is, and what is not, a threat, to whom, in what ways and over what time-scale can be a tricky business';[23] while Weiner notes 'what constitutes a threat is a matter of perception, which differs from one society to another'.[24] Yet despite these problems Weiner asserts, '[w]e...need to distinguish between real and reasonably perceived threats, on the one hand, and paranoid notions of threat or mass anxieties, on the other'.[25]

Determining whether the incompatibility between the regime and the ethnic group is illusory or not, is dependent not just on the goals of the regime but also the goals of the ethnic group. Attempts to promote the group's self-identity are not in themselves incompatible with the notion of belonging to a wider community or nation, although it was anticipated that a consequence of modernity would be the consignment of ethnic diversity to the history books as people's ethnicity lessened. Ethnic identification was expected to wither as modern communications and transport networks integrated and assimilated the people into one nation.[26] Ethnic identification however has proven to be resilient; the challenge for nation-builders today is to seek a strong nation with ethnic diversity. According to Brown, Southeast Asian states, '[i]nstead of trying to eradicate or restructure ethnic affiliations...have attempted in very different ways to accommodate, manage or manipulate them so as to try to turn ethnicity from a potential problem into a potential resource'.[27] This approach will be examined in the next chapter; for now though it is claimed that attempts to maintain cultural values, such as language and religion, need not be incompatible with the regime's nation-building programme. However, an ethnic group's promotion of its own identity could be perceived by the regime as a threat to its right to rule. If no such objective was sought by the group then the regime's reaction, which could be extremely brutal, is based on a misperception. The security dilemma would appear to be relevant since the threat perceived by the regime is an unintended consequence of the ethnic group's actions, and the regime's response could become self-defeating since by acting in a hostile fashion it is alienating the group, increasing the group's self-identity and possibly generating calls for secession.[28] If this last event were to occur then the incompatibility between the two would have become real, since secession is incompatible with state-making and nation-building, and the security dilemma would no longer be applicable. The actions undertaken by the regime and ethnic group would be designed to counter each other's ambitions and, thus, at the heart of the tension or violence would lie a real, not an illusory, incompatibility that had arisen due to an unintended consequence of their actions.

The relationship between secessionist demands and the security dilemma is an extremely important one. If the group desires secession because it does not identify itself with the other groups in the state then the security dilemma is not applicable. However, if the group's demand for secession has occurred because it was prevented from expressing its own identity, then the security dilemma might help to explain the dynamics that led to the demand for secession. The security dilemma cannot therefore help to explain the dynamics behind the secessionist demands of the independence movement in East Timor. However, the support for an independence movement in Irian Jaya – led by the Free Papua Movement (OPM) – could have its roots in the Indonesian government's policy of transmigration.[29] The policy of transmigration and the issue of migration as a cause of the security dilemma is examined in the next chapter. For now though the security dilemma can be seen to be applicable in some circumstances, but it cannot explain all deteriorating relations amongst the population nor between the regime and elements within the population. Regimes must therefore determine if actions undertaken by ethnic groups to maintain their identity constitute a real threat to their authority/legitimacy or whether they are simply designed to preserve the group's cultural distinctiveness within the state.

The insecurity dilemma, because it is concerned with the cycle of repression, is not dependent on illusory incompatibility for its applicability. Instead it focuses on why the policy of repression occurs and the difficulties of overcoming the regime's propensity to resort to violence as a means of state-making and nation-building. The conclusion Job highlights by Mason and Krane not only helps to distinguish between the insecurity and security dilemma, but it also reveals the difficulty of overcoming these dilemmas. Mason and Krane suggest that the circumstances in which the regime is attempting to rule explains why it embarks upon paradoxical policies of repression. In other words the structure within the state, its weakness, is an important explanatory factor behind a deterioration in regime/populace relations. Buzan suggests that an analogy with the traditional security dilemma 'implies that we can look for confidence-building measures which might modify or neutralise the societal security dilemma'.[30] However, if the regime is locked into a policy of repression and less violent alternatives are precluded, the pursuit of confidence-building measures appears problematic. Therefore, trying to determine whether it is possible to mitigate an intra-state security dilemma requires examining the claim that regimes resort to violence because of the state's weakness.

D. Mitigating the intra-state security dilemma

At the core of the security dilemma lies the uncertainty actors have about each other's intentions. If this uncertainty could be removed then the dynamics of the security dilemma, which lead to the pursuit of self-defeating policies, would be negated. Hence Buzan's interest in confidence-building measures noted above. With intra-state security dilemmas, however, an initial hurdle needs to be overcome before the question of removing uncertainty can be answered. This hurdle is the regime's propensity to resort to violence to coerce the population into one nation-state, an outcome that can occur regardless of whether it is a security dilemma generating the rise in tension. Is it inevitable that regimes in weak states will resort to violence as their legitimacy is challenged?

Combining the work of Mason and Krane with Mohammed Ayoob's reference to a security predicament reveals why a regime resorts to violence against its own people. The underlying condition that leads to regime-orchestrated violence, according to Mason and Krane, is the economic structure of the state. They emphasise how the conversion from subsistence agriculture to export-earning cash crops in many Third World countries transforms and disrupts the people's way of life. The peasants lose their land as large commercial estates which can produce the quantities of crops required for export flourish. This can result in growing unrest amongst the rural population as their living standards decline. Jonathan Rigg notes this effect during the colonial period on the peasants of Southeast Asia, when he writes:

> Families that previously might have been able to assure their subsistence either by farming communal lands or by clearing forest at the frontiers in farmland expansion were forced to provide wage labour for the farms of landowners or on commercial plantations. Peasant discontent rose accordingly and was expressed in a series of riots and disturbances in Java, Malaya, Sarawak, and the Philippines.[31]

The rural population, having become landless wage labourers, become dependent upon the vagaries of the international market for their economic security. The combination of an increasing rural population and the poor terms of trade that confront the producers of primary products, erodes the peasant's economic well-being and leads in many Third World countries to urban migration. Urbanisation has not solved their economic plight and with the creation of shanty towns, which generally have no drainage or running water, their plight could be said to have deteriorated further. When the states of Southeast Asia enjoyed economic prosperity, such problems were minimised. However, in the wake of the economic crisis, because few Asian societies have welfare support, the urban populations in Southeast Asia are now also faced with hunger and poverty. According to the United Nations Children's Fund (UNICEF) the level of malnutrition in under 5-year-olds in Southeast Asia is 30 per cent, a figure comparable to that of Africa. In Thailand, some 4 million people have lost their jobs, while in Indonesia the figure is nearer 20 million and it is estimated that 80 million Indonesians live below the poverty line.[32] The response from the region's regimes has been limited. They agree with the sentiments of Singapore's Information Minister, George Yeo, who has warned: 'If governments try to rescue all who are weak, even the strong may perish ... Those who seek an easy way out are less likely to survive. We may be entering a new time of troubles. If so, there will be a great culling, whether we like it or not'.[33] Plans to cut wages and welfare benefits are being considered throughout the region. Mason and Krane claim that in 'the absence of state action to remedy their economic distress, nonelites turn to alternative institutions in search of some form of relief'.[34] While these alternatives might be in a welfare capacity, such as health and hygiene, literacy and child care, these economic self-help functions provide the impetus for the politically charged demands of policy change and reform.[35] In the Malaysian political crisis in late 1998 when the Malaysian Prime Minister, Dr Mahathir Mohamad, first sacked and then arrested his deputy, Anwar Ibrahim, a dozen NGOs joined forces with two political parties to create the Coalition for People's Democracy.[36] In the aftermath of the May 1998 attacks on ethnic Chinese in Indonesia, the Perkumpulan Masyarakat Surakarta (PMS), a social-welfare organisation established in the 1930s, began calling for reforms on citizenship rules, education and the lifting of restrictions on cultural activities. Rachmat Santoso, a PMS leader, said that now the consciousness-raising process has begun, 'it won't be difficult to advise them to rise up'.[37] The regime can thus find itself facing an opposition movement that has the support of the masses. The enormous lifestyle changes that modernisation has brought in the Third World could create perceptions of threat that generate a reactive response along ethnic lines.[38] In Malaysia, the Islamic missionary movement, Al-Arqam, was initially tolerated as a non-political vehicle for Islamic resurgence, but by 1994, it was considered a political challenge to the ruling regime and its leaders were placed in detention.[39]

A regime faced with a disillusioned populace and one that is dividing along ethnic lines can either try to accommodate their demands, or rely on coercion to intimidate the masses and deny opposition groups their base of support. The former would help reduce the likelihood of a security dilemma, while the latter would exacerbate it. Mason and Krane's analysis is that the regime will almost inevitably choose coercion. They argue that many regimes in the Third World either have close ties to the military or are the military, thus ensuring that they have the capacity for coercion or repression.[40] Hence, they claim:

> Coercion is the response for which the requisite institutional machinery (i.e., the security forces) is the most extensive and well-established in the authoritarian state. The ideology of the military is such that political tranquillity is presumed to be a prerequisite for economic development. On this basis the military often comes to serve as the ultimate arbiter of political authority in the system. Hence, the almost reflexive response to opposition challenges is to increase the level of officially sanctioned violence directed against the opposition leaders and their actual, or suspected, or potential supporters.[41]

The implication that the regime will deem anything which threatens its 'tranquillity' as a threat, and as such can be dealt with accordingly, is that intra-state security dilemmas are quite possible. Regimes which interpret the most ambiguous signals as indications of malign intent are the most susceptible to the security dilemma. In addition to the role of the military, Mason and Krane also argue that because the regime will represent a segment of the population that has profited during its tenure, the regime's supporters will have little interest in redistributing wealth or political power. Indeed, they suggest that should the regime seek accommodation with an opposition group it could be replaced through a coup. Hence their conclusion that even though repression might not solve the regime's difficulties, and indeed could make them worse, such actions are still preferred.

In Southeast Asia, the regimes' responses have been a mixture of violence directed against those seeking reform, and attempts to steer a middle path between the demands for change and the needs of the regime's supporters. In Indonesia, the Habibie regime responded to students protesting that political reforms were not being implemented, by resorting to violence when in November 1998 the army killed eight students.[42] In Malaysia, when Mahathir removed his nearest political rival, Anwar Ibrahim, Kuala Lumpur witnessed riots with police firing water cannons and tear gas at demonstrators.[43] In Thailand, Chuan Leekpai's regime is, according to Michael Vatikiotis, finding that a 'compromise [is needed] to get things done', and consequently, 'the new constitution's promises of more power to the people are being watered down in follow-up legislation'.[44] These responses to calls for reform have led even reform-minded politicians, such as Thailand's Foreign Minister Surin Pitsuwan, to note that while 'change will come ... it will be incremental'.[45]

Ayoob's security predicament complements Mason and Krane's analysis by focusing on the difficulties Third World regimes confront in state-making. He arrives at the same conclusion – that regimes are insecure because there exist alternatives vying for the population's loyalty – but he does so by focusing on the key security issues facing Third World regimes: state-making, which entails the regime achieving political legitimacy amongst the populace; and nation-building, which entails the creation amongst the populace of common cultural traits which in turn produces a sense of community and solidarity. The importance of these two is endorsed by Thomas when she claims for security to be achieved, '[p]olitical allegiance must be transferred from lower levels of group identity to the national system, and governmental authority must achieve legitimacy in the eyes of the population'.[46] It is the failure to achieve either of these that lies at the core of the Third World's continuing security problems. The lack of Mobutu

Sese Seko's political legitimacy was revealed in 1997 by the popular support enjoyed by Laurent Kabila when he ousted Mobutu's regime in Zaire. The tragedy in neighbouring Rwanda is a graphic representation of the failure of nation-building.

According to Ayoob three conditions need to be met for state-making to occur. First, the acquisition of territory (war function); second, the maintenance of order in the territory (policing function); and third, the ability to extract resources from the people (taxation). The means the regime uses to accomplish these objectives acts as a barometer for measuring the stage of state-making that the regime has attained. The more developed the state the less the regime relies on coercion to accomplish these objectives; in Buzan's terminology it becomes stronger. Ayoob's argument is that all states proceed through a state-making process and eventually emerge into nation-states.[47] He argues that Third World states, having gained independence after colonisation in the mid- to late twentieth century, are at an early stage of the state-making process. They are undergoing a similar experience to that of the European states between the seventeenth and nineteenth centuries.[48] Drawing on the work of Charles Tilly, Ayoob notes that in Europe, state-making 'went through a long period of gestation' and that the problems Third World states face today 'assume inflated dimensions only when compared with the "finished" products in Western Europe and North America'.[49] In essence, the regimes' willingness to resort to violence can be explained by their early stage in the state-making process. Indeed, Ayoob claims that there are factors which make Third World state-making much harder to achieve today than during the European experience.

Although Ayoob highlights the limited time Third World regimes have to state-make, which is an important issue, the crux is the politicisation of the population. Ayoob concurs with Mason and Krane that modernisation (urbanisation, literacy, internal migration) has played a role in the politicisation of the population. He views modernisation as exacerbating the differences within the state that began under colonialism because it widens the gap between the rich and poor communities. The modernisation of the state, therefore, not only exacerbates tensions between the regime and the people but also communities within the population. The politicisation of the population has resulted in both a desire for political participation and the demands for a more equitable distribution of the state's economic wealth. Thus, unlike European states where 'state-makers constructed, then imposed, strong national governments before mass politics', in the Third World, 'these two processes tend to occur together'.[50] Third World regimes are therefore faced with demands for political pluralism and are expected to be responsive to the economic demands of their people; factors that were not prevalent in European state-making. State-making thus becomes harder because a politically active populace is more likely to question the legitimacy of the regime.

The difficulties in creating a modern nation-state are also exacerbated by, first, the expectation that this will be achieved in a much shorter time period than required by European states, and second, because international norms safeguarding the state, 'contribute to creating and augmenting internal discontent within Third World states by forcing all the diverse and dissatisfied elements within it...remaining within [its] boundaries'.[51] The inviolability of state borders, in other words, has maintained such weak states as Lebanon and Somalia, and consequently kept the people within the state, when in the past they simply would have ceased to exist and the disaffected groups would have formed or joined other states. The issue of time refers not to why regimes resort to force, after all Ayoob's argument is that European state-making involved violence, but rather, whether the propensity for violence prevents the state-making process progressing. Hence Ayoob writes:

> When spread over a period of time and essentially localized regionally and socially, state-induced violence and counterviolence could give the appearance of a succession of manageable crises in the drawn-out process of state building.
>
> However, given the short amount of time at the disposal of state makers in the Third World and the consequent acceleration in their state-making efforts, crises erupt simultaneously, become unmanageable as they overload the political and military capabilities of the state, and lead to a cumulation of crises that further erodes the legitimacy of the fragile post-colonial state.[52]

Ayoob, Mason and Krane therefore explain Third World regimes' resort to violence as a consequence of their weak structure. Although they approach the issue from an economic perspective the reasons Mason and Krane provide for regime orchestrated violence are the same as Ayoob; it is a consequence of their early stage of state-making when the challenge to the regime's legitimacy is at its peak. Legitimacy in the sense of 'whether citizens are loyal and willingly support state policies – whether they accept the authority of the state and believe existing institutions are in some sense appropriate'.[53] The key to whether a regime will seek alternatives to violence depends therefore on its legitimacy, the more illegitimate the regime the more likely internal security threats will be met by violence. Mason and Krane are pessimistic about regimes resorting to less violent alternatives, but if the intra-state security dilemma is to be mitigated then such alternatives must be available, as well as agreeable, to the regime and its supporters, and acceptable to the population.

The case postulated is that the consequences of modernisation and the difficulties of state-making and nation-building have exacerbated the societal and economic differences within Third World states. The regimes in power have lost their legitimacy as alternative sources for the people's loyalty have emerged. The lack of political and social cohesion reveals the weakness of the state. In response to the challenge the regime perceives to its authority from these alternatives vying for the people's support, the regime becomes focused on its own security. With the militarisation of the political process, regimes resort to violence to maintain their position of power.[54] This abuse of power worsens the situation as the regime becomes the main threat to its populace's security rather than its guardian. The outcome is a spiral of increasing insecurity; the regime's attempts to maintain power alienate the population and undermine state security by depleting the state's resources. The answer to whether such violence is inevitable, given that it has been argued that regime-orchestrated violence is a consequence of the state's structural weakness, would appear to be an unequivocal yes. However, since the end of the Cold War there are signs that this might not necessarily be so.

The emergence of ethnic nationalism in the 1990s, which has been encouraged by the international community's willingness to admit new members,[55] coupled to the rise in interest in human rights issues, has significantly altered the methods of successful state-making.[56] Ayoob argues that the rising tide of ethnic nationalism will cause the collapse of the state unless the regimes take preventive action. In particular he claims that the European experience of state-making, in which the regimes coerced their populations, must be weighed against other political realities of the late twentieth century. These political realities are the notions of democratisation and human rights. These are increasingly being demanded by the peoples of the Third World, and the international community is encouraging their adoption.[57] Ayoob asserts categorically:

> In the climate of these changed domestic and international attitudes, the move toward democratization is no longer merely a laudable

goal for states in the Third World; it has become a political precondition for establishing legitimate state structures and regimes that enjoy the acquiescence, if not the enthusiastic support, of their populations.[58]

For those regimes that continue to rely upon coercion and violence Ayoob believes the state will disintegrate into anarchy; 'repression alone is no longer sufficient to maintain the fragile fabric of political unity within Third World states and to attain the goals of the state-making process'.[59] In other words, it is in the regime's self-interest to adopt alternative methods of state-making other than the violent repression of its population.

The collapse of the Suharto regime in Indonesia in the face of student protests, which were galvanised by the economic crisis sweeping through Southeast Asia, confirms Ayoob's argument that repression alone is no longer sufficient as a means of successful state-making and nation-building. The latter was tragically highlighted by the May 1998 attacks on ethnic Chinese leading many to flee Indonesia.[60] Tentative steps towards political reform can, however, be witnessed in China, although Beijing's acceptance of the need to introduce political reform in conjunction with economic reform as it seeks to strengthen the state, is still at an early stage.[61] Researchers at the Chinese Academy of Social Sciences have, for example, been commissioned by the Communist Party to examine the operation of presidential and democratic systems throughout the world. In addition, a more open attitude is prevailing with regard to criticism directed at state corruption, as epitomised by the publications from the Chinese Academy of Social Sciences.[62] The increasing number of self-help organisations in China also indicates the emergence of a civil society, although where such organisations are perceived as an alternative foci of authority the communist regime has outlawed their operation, as in the case of the Falun Gong sect.[63]

The argument that democratisation and respect for human rights have become necessary components in the state-making process aids the process of security dilemma mitigation.[64] Democratisation, by creating an inclusive means of governance which enables each ethnic group to influence the political process, and human rights, which if implemented safeguard ethnic differences, can reduce the uncertainty each has of the other which underlies their suspicion and fears. In the next chapter, power-sharing and ethnic reconstruction are examined as methods of mitigating and even escaping the intra-state security dilemma. To what extent the states of Southeast Asia can be considered democratic and respectful of human rights is dependent upon the interpretation placed on Asian values. Thus, Clark Neher and Ross Marlay note that while 'Confucianism emphasizes harmony, stability, and consensus, attitudes that may enable a government to weather the social and economic storms of modernization ... [it] also stresses hierarchy and reverence for those in power, values that seem to support authoritarianism'.[65] Yet, for those that subscribe to 'Asian-style democracy' it is the consensus-building and greater importance of community rather than individual rights which ensures that all have an input into the process, and that when a decision is reached it is to benefit the majority. Donald McCloud writes, '[i]n the eyes of Westerners collective decision-making may readily appear to be authoritarian, but ... consensus-building *requires* participation' (emphasis in original).[66] It is the inclusion of different ethnic groups in the political process that aids security dilemma mitigation, hence Renée de Nevers' statement that in Malaysia, 'voting districts were designed in many cases to require candidates to gain multi-ethnic support to ensure victory, thus mitigating minority fears about being excluded from political power. The Malaysian example illustrates the possibility of finding solutions to complex problems.'[67] The extent to which Malaysia provides an inclusive means of governance is examined in the next chapter.

The acceptance of democracy though is preconditioned on the regime recognising that it supports and does not undermine the state-making process. Hence Myron Weiner's warning that in India, 'faced with the choice of exercising coercive authority to maintain a single country or remaining democratic, most of the elite would choose the former over the latter'.[68] The Rangoon regime has likewise shown little enthusiasm for democratisation as the means to achieve state-making and nation-building in Burma. The first, crucial step, therefore, in mitigating an intra-state security dilemma is the realisation and acceptance by the governing regime that its legitimacy can only be assured in the long term by turning its subjects into citizens.

Mitigating the security dilemma is not, however, solely dependent on the actions of the regime, but also on the actions of the ethnic groups within the population. Where an ethnic group desires secession methods of security dilemma mitigation would be inappropriate, since this objective indicates a real incompatibility between the regime and ethnic group. However, if the group desired political autonomy within the state then this might be an acceptable solution. It is this attempt to differentiate self-determination from secession that leads the Carnegie Endowment to claim:

> The principle of self-determination is best viewed as entitling a people to choose its political allegiance, to influence the political order under which it lives, and to preserve its cultural, ethnic, historical, or territorial identity. Often, although not always, these objectives can be achieved with less than full independence.[69]

The role of democratisation and respect for human rights are obviously important factors in enabling this type of solution to intra-state security dilemmas. While democratisation is certainly not a cure for all incidences of ethnic conflict, Ayoob is right when he claims: '[o]pening up avenues of political participation to all or most ethnic groups in a Third World state offers disgruntled segments of society the prospect that self-determination can take place within an existing state rather than being achieved only by destroying that state'.[70]

The availability of alternative, peaceful, methods for a regime to state-make and nation-build is only the first, albeit important, step towards mitigation and escape. Overcoming the suspicion and fear that each will harbour about the other's intent, in other words their uncertainty, depends upon how the process of democratisation is implemented.[71] However, for now it is sufficient to determine that victims of intra-state security dilemmas are not doomed to their tragedy with no hope of escape.

Conclusion

This chapter has sought to develop the idea of an internal security dilemma by applying it to sovereign states. It has examined whether the security dilemma can operate within a sovereign state, the differences between the insecurity and security dilemma have been explored and the problems of mitigation have been raised. The chapter has identified ethnicity as well as territory as the security issue for the intra-state security dilemma, and in so doing has provided an insight into the security issues of the Third World.

The application of the security dilemma to developing states immediately raises the issue of whether a sovereign body negates the self-help environment in which the security dilemma flourishes. It is argued that it is possible for the security dilemma to be applicable to intra-state strife because in weak states the regime's sovereignty is compromised. The regime does not command the loyalty of all of its people, indeed there might be a number of competing foci of authority. This can create the perception that the greatest dangers to the regime are internal. For the different groups within the state the regime could pose the greatest threat to their security – rather than being the provider of security – thus they exist in a self-help environment. The issue of sovereignty, at least in weak states, does not therefore negate the operation of the security dilemma.

The deterioration of relations between ethnic groups and the regime and between each other does not, however, indicate that a security dilemma is present. The essence of the security dilemma is that it explains why participants fall victim to an event both wished to avoid. Herbert Butterfield and John Herz each highlight this tragedy and Robert Jervis concurs that the security dilemma explains something unwanted when he states the 'unintended and undesired consequences of actions meant to be defensive constitutes the security dilemma'.[72] It is then a tragedy where the efforts of the participants to maintain their security have the unintended effect of making others insecure. For example, if the composition of the regime represents just one ethnic group in a multi-ethnic state, the regime can easily fall foul of the security dilemma if the other groups perceive they are biased towards their own group. Horowitz warns of this when he writes, 'groups have been given so much security as to make others restless. Ethnic allocations that convince one group of a regime's benign intentions have served to persuade others of its unfairness.'[73] Hence in the case of Burma, Tin Maung Maung Than notes, 'ethnic dissidents identify the military leadership with the majority Bamar (Burman), and this, in turn, raises suspicions that a hidden agenda for perpetuating ethnic hegemony is part of [the regime's] conception of security'.[74]

The security dilemma is often manifest in international relations with an arms build-up as the states, convinced the other intends them harm, increase their ability to defend themselves. This action, however, just fuels their own insecurity since the other does not intend them harm and is itself arming because it feels threatened by the weapons they are procuring. In other words, both are pursuing self-defeating or paradoxical policies. In the internal security of the Third World such paradoxical polices have also been highlighted. The regimes of the Third World are attempting to state-make and nation-build in territories inherited after decolonisation which were an artificial construction that grouped together different ethnic groups. During the early stages of state-making when the regime's sovereign authority is being imposed on the population, the state structure is weak. With a population that has little in common there is the possibility the state will collapse. During this time, the regime is likely to be highly insecure and regard attempts by different groups to maintain their separate identities as a challenge to its authority and legitimacy. Regimes are likely to resort to violence to coerce their disparate people into one nation. This is likely because the weakness of the state precludes the use of a legitimate judicial or political alternative and often the regime has become militarised. The danger for the regime is that this action can alienate the population since far from being their guardian the regime becomes the main threat to their security. Regime-orchestrated violence can thus have the unintended and paradoxical affect of bringing about exactly that which it was supposed to prevent – calls for secession. Thus, Mason writes, 'the calculus of fear induced by repression makes inevitable the very revolution that the state seeks to preempt'.[75]

The reasons behind the violence orchestrated by a regime and its obsession with internal security threats dictates much of the writings on Third World security. In particular, Job's insecurity dilemma focuses on the rising tension and possible outbreak of secessionist demands that can result from a regime's use of violence. While Ayoob, noting the composition of the regime, claims 'that while Third World societies are overwhelmingly multiethnic in their composition, many Third World elites deny this reality and attempt to construct monoethnic states dominated by a single ethnolinguistic or ethnoreligious group'.[76] The consequence of this is that others feel unfairly treated by the regime and so seek alternatives to provide for them. While this is relevant for the security dilemma it is essential that at the heart of the deterioration is an illusory incompatibility. The applicability of the security dilemma therefore becomes dependent upon the ambitions of the regime and the ethnic groups within the state. Where the regime explicitly pursues assimilation – as in the case of Indonesia towards its Chinese community – or a peripheral community is actively engaged in pursuing seccession – as with the Moro Islamic Liberation Front (MILF) in the Philippines – the security dilemma is not appropriate, since the goals pursued by both parties are incompatible. However, if the regime is committed to 'unity in diversity', then ethnic tensions could be explained by the security dilemma since the fear the ethnic minority perceives from the regime concerning its identity, is based upon an illusory incompatibility. Likewise, if the ethnic groups are seeking to assert their own cultures and identities and are persecuted for this because the regime perceives it as a threat, the security dilemma could be applicable even if this persecution later leads to secessionist demands.

Applying the security dilemma to weak states entails an appreciation of the problems facing the incumbent regime in its twin programmes of state-making and nation-building. This does not of course entail approval of its actions, but rather just an awareness of why leaders of such regimes use violence against their own people. While Mason and Krane's analysis suggests that the regime's propensity to use violence indicates that mitigating or escaping an intra-state security dilemma could prove problematic, developments in the 1990s imply a more optimistic conclusion. Ayoob asserts that the Third World 'state-building requirement must ... be weighed against other political realities of the late twentieth century. These include the global dissemination of the ideas of democracy and human rights, including group rights, and the changed international sensibility toward these principles in the political lives of states, including those in the Third World.'[77] To determine to what extent these ideas have helped to diffuse intra-state security dilemmas in Southeast Asia, and indeed, whether intra-state security dilemmas exist at all in the region, is the task of the next chapter.

3
Ethnic Tensions and the Security Dilemma in Southeast Asia

The purpose of this chapter is to determine the applicability of the security dilemma to ethnic tensions within Southeast Asia and the prospects of mitigating its effects. The chapter does not provide an analysis of all ethnic tensions in the region because such an undertaking would be beyond the scope of one chapter. Rather than examining each ASEAN member separately the analysis will focus on three case studies involving ethnic conflict: ethnocratic regimes; self-determination; migration. In all three case studies the focus is on the existence of the three characteristics of the security dilemma in the relations between ethnic groups, and also between ethnic groups and the regime. Is their fear of losing their identity based upon an illusory incompatibility? Is their fear a misperception based upon uncertainty of the other's intent? Are their solutions paradoxical and result in making matters worse by creating a real threat to their ethnicity? This section will then be followed with an examination of power-sharing and ethnic reconstruction to determine if these explain the apparent success of some ASEAN states in mitigating the intra-state security dilemma. However, because the security dilemma operates in a self-help environment, it is first necessary to determine whether the ASEAN members are weak states.

Since the security dilemma operates in a self-help environment it was noted in the previous chapter that so long as the state was weak (it lacked legitimacy in the eyes of the people), the regime, instead of being the provider of security, could become the main danger. With no guarantor for their security the ethnic groups would have to rely upon their own efforts to safeguard their security, and thus they could be considered to exist in a self-help environment. Buzan suggests that states can be plotted along a spectrum with the strongest at one end and the weakest at the other. At the extremes, states are either socially cohesive (strong) or have collapsed (weak). Examples of the latter include Lebanon, Somalia and the former Yugoslavia. Amongst the ASEAN members while there are no states at either extreme they all lie within the weakest half of Buzan's spectrum. Muthiah Alagappa writes, '[m]any states in the region still belong to the category of weak states. Their fragile nature (political and economic) gives rise to a range of rather complex domestic conflicts which centre on authority and legitimacy, political participation, ethnicity, religion, distributive justice and other related issues'.[1]

Evidence of their weakness can be gauged from the population's perception of the state. Towards the weakest end lies a recent addition to ASEAN's membership, Burma, in which the ethnic minorities, such as the Karen separatist community, desire independence. In Indonesia and the Philippines there also exist minorities which wish either to secede (East Timor in Indonesia) or to have substantial political autonomy (Mindanao in the Philippines) and consequently they too can be considered weak.[2] In Thailand, the diffidence of the northern hill tribes towards Bangkok, the Karens on the Burma-Thai border, and the irredentist desire amongst the Patani Malay, keep Thailand weak. Even amongst the strongest states in ASEAN, Malaysia and Singapore, evidence can be garnered to highlight their weakness. In these cases it is not so much the people's perception of the state that provides the evidence, but rather the actions of the ruling regime. In Malaysia, because the regime is aware that issues can give rise to ethnic tension which could pose a serious threat to state security, state leaders often highlight the need for careful policy implementation. Such warnings would not be needed in a strong state. An example of this occurred in July 1997 with the implementation of Islamic law and the conviction of three Muslim beauty contestants in Selangor. The then Deputy Prime Minister, Datuk Anwar Ibrahim, stated that 'in a multi-faceted society we must be careful in implementing [Islamic] law' and he stressed that if it is done in a forceful manner it would result in unrest and revolt by the people.[3]

In Singapore, evidence of the state's weakness is likewise found from state leaders; although because Singapore is the strongest ASEAN member such evidence usually only surfaces during election time when racial issues might be used for political gain. This was particularly evident in the 1997 election with the hounding of opposition candidate Tang Liang Hong, whom PAP leaders accused of 'threatening the delicate harmony between the island's Chinese, Malay and Indian communities'.[4] Given that the PAP could not lose this election it seems odd that a regime would go to such lengths, which included upsetting Malaysia, unless it felt the security of the state could be threatened by Tang's campaigning.[5] The PAP's concern with Tang, coupled with concern about the populace's seeming ignorance of Singapore's history, reveals that Singapore's 'weakness' stems from its early stage of nation-building.[6] Worried that Singaporeans lack a sense of national identity, the regime responded with the opening of an exhibition – *The Singapore Story: Overcoming the Odds* – and the creation of 'Shared Values'.[7]

Noting these states are weak does not mean they are about to collapse as ethnic conflict rages across Southeast Asia. However, the economic crisis that began in 1997 is beginning to have political/social consequences. In Malaysia, the sacking and arrest of Anwar Ibrahim led to violent clashes between protesters and riot police in September 1998, while poverty in Bangkok is causing a rise in crime, drug-dealing and other social ills.[8] Within all of these states ethnic tension lies just beneath the political surface, and even before the Indonesian riots of May 1998, the violence in Aceh and the 'spice islands', the archipelago state often erupted into violence.[9] Is the security dilemma applicable to ethnic tensions in ASEAN?

A. Intra-state security dilemmas within ASEAN members

1 Ethnocratic regimes

The term ethnocratic regime signifies that one ethnic group has gained control of the state machinery and is using this to maintain its ethnic identity at the expense of the other groups within the state. The controlling ethnic group achieves this position of power by, first, recruiting only members of its ethnic group to positions of power within the state machinery, such as the civil service and armed forces. Second, the national identity of the population is determined by the cultural attributes of the dominant ethnic group, although as David Brown cautions, such 'ethnic particularism will not usually be made explicit, but will emerge clothed in the language of universalism'.[10] This domination of the national identity is achieved in particular with the adoption of the governing group's language. Finally, the institutions of the state, such as the constitution and laws, will favour and reinforce the monopolisation of power by the dominant ethnic group. This description is not one that governing regimes are likely to fit absolutely; rather, it is one they manifest in varying degrees. Thus, while in Malaysia the regime is a ruling coalition representing the different ethnic groups, it can still be considered ethnocratic because the dominant party represents the Malays and the constitution grants the Malays a 'special position' which, amongst other things, gives them special access to government employment. The regimes of Southeast Asia are ethnocratic to varying degrees, with Burma dominated by the Burman, Thailand by the Thais, Malaysia by the Malays and, at least until recently, Indonesia by the Javanese.[11] The key for the security dilemma is that the mono-ethnic control of a plural ethnic society can create fear in others that their identities are being assimilated, and therefore lost. Brown even suggests that 'where effective assimilation is not feasible in practice, state penetration is seen by peripheral communities to be assimilationist in intent'.[12] The extent to which the intra-state security dilemma is applicable to ethnocratic regimes will now be examined in Burma and Malaysia.

Burma

On 4 January 1948 Burma (now also known as Myanmar) gained independence from Britain and from the very outset the regime has been dominated by the majority ethnic Burmans (also known as Bama/Bamar). Burma is a multiethnic state which is also home to the Karen, Shan, Arakanese, Kachin, Chin and Mon, and, at least superficially, does not appear to be run by an ethnocratic regime since the constitution safeguards the rights of the state's various ethnic groups and the national slogan is 'unity in diversity'. However, according to David Steinberg, 'all the systems in Burma that allow growth, development and mobility are those dominated by the Burman cultural tradition', and this, 'has led to considerable local resentment'. Steinberg asserts:

> Minority cultures and languages are relegated to one's home and cannot be used for other than local purposes. Education is in Burm[an]; the symbols of the state and deployment of power are Burman ... 'The Burmese Way to Socialism' might more accurately be termed the 'The Burman Way to Socialism', because it reflects Burman cultural, political, and nationalistic norms.[13]

The first government of Burma was dominated by the Anti-Fascist People's Freedom League (AFPFL) and its leader, U Nu, favoured the 'submersion of local identities and mutual mistrust in favour of creating a new identity equally shared by all and based on new community values and ideals'.[14] Unfortunately these 'new' values were actually Burman thus the AFPFL's espousal of new values did not actually mean the acculturation of the different ethnic groups into Burmese but rather their assimilation into Burman. The creation of a Burman national identity is manifest in the 1952 decision that all government business was to be conducted in the Burman language, Burmese history was taught from the perspective of Burman nationalism and the sole language used in education was Burman.[15] Despite the changing regimes in Burma – which since 1962 has been ruled by the military in the guise of the Burmese Socialist Programme Party (BSPP), the State Law and Order Restoration Council (SLORC) and is currently known as the State Peace and Development Council (SPDC) – the Burmanisation of Burma has continued because the regime has remained dominated by Burmans. The result of this concentration of power in the hands of Burmans was the emergence of separatist movements, even prior to Burma's independence, amongst the ethnic minorities.[16] Can this development be understood from the perspective of the security dilemma?

Initially the case of Burma looks like an intra-state security dilemma. The regime has sought to create a Burmese nation but an unintended consequence of the regime's assimilationist policies has been the exacerbation of separatist demands amongst the state's ethnic minorities. In other words, the regime's policies have paradoxically resulted in dividing rather than uniting the people of Burma. However, on closer inspection Burma does not match the characteristics of the security dilemma. The very nature of assimilationist policies is that they replace the identities of the different ethnic groups with a new communal identity. U Nu considered national unity and minority rights to be incompatible and he explicitly stated that 'as long as we allow this spectre of minority rights to continue in our midst, so long shall our efforts to achieve unity and solidarity be of no avail'.[17]

The assimilationist policies of the Burman regime were thus a real challenge to the ethnic identity of the minority groups, and in the case of the Shan they actually helped develop the concept of a Shan consciousness even though the Shan at this stage had political autonomy within Burma.[18] The subsequent removal of this autonomy by the regime and the growth of Shan identity led to the first military clashes between the *Noon Sukhan* (Shan State Independence Army) and the Burmese army in 1959. Despite a cease-fire agreement reached in 1989 Shan separatism was taken up by the drug baron, Khun Sa, and although in 1996 his forces were defeated by the military regime, Shan separatists are still active.[19] The oldest ethnic clash lies with the Karen, whose ethnic identity had already developed from a local village level to a pan-ethnic Karen consciousness by 1948.[20] Indeed, relations between the Karen and Burman, and the hostility and suspicion which marked it, can be traced back to the British colonisation of the region in the nineteenth century. During 1942 the Burman dominated Burmese Independence Army (BIA) ran amok in some Karen communities, ensuring, according to Clive Christie, that 'ethnic reconciliation and belated nation-building could not ... overcome the now entrenched suspicions of the Karens'.[21] Faced with domination by and assimilation by the Burmans, the Karens responded with the creation of the Karen National Union (KNU) and its military arm, the Karen National Defence Organisation (KNDO), subsequently renamed the Karen National Liberation Army (KNLA). The Karen continue to fight against the Burman regime, but since the fall of their central headquarters at Manerplaw in early 1995 they no longer represent a serious threat to the regime's survival.

The key for the security dilemma is that these nationalist movements have not resulted from a misperception of intent, but rather the accurate interpretation of what the regime's assimilationist policy meant for the continuing survival of their ethnic identities. Silverstein captures the real incompatibility between the regimes and ethnic group's goals when he writes:

> What moved them were their common fears of Burmanization, loss of cultural identity, interference in their affairs by the national government and a belief that the Burmans were creating an internal colonial system in which they would not share the wealth of the country.[22]

Thus, while for the regime their policies for nation-building have paradoxically made matters worse, the situation is not a security dilemma because the cause of the ethnic conflicts in Burma are the real incompatibilities between the regime's policies and the ethnic group's desires to maintain their ethnic identity. It is the regime's Burmanisation of the people that lies at the heart of the problems. Hence, Silverstein claims, '[t]his is and has been the dilemma in Burmese federalism and its solution is necessary before genuine national unity can emerge'.[23]

Malaysia

Formed in 1963 with the amalgamation of Malaya and the territories of Sabah, Sarawak and Singapore (the latter was subsequently expelled in 1965), Malaysia is home to many ethnic communities including the indigenous Malay *bumiputeras* and the descendants of Chinese and Indian immigrants who settled in Malaya during British colonial rule.[24] Ever since independence from the British in 1957, Malaya and then

Malaysia has been governed by a coalition government with parties representing the different ethnic communities: the dominant party is the United Malays National Organisation (UMNO), while the Chinese are represented mainly by the Malaysian Chinese Association (MCA) and the Gerakan, and the Indians by the Malaysian Indian Congress (MIC). Originally called the Alliance the coalition government became known as *Barisan Nasional* (BN) in 1974. Malaysia would not appear to be a clear instance of ethnocratic rule, but it is simply because of a constitution which enshrines the 'special position' of the Malays and the domination by UMNO of the BN coalition. Although Malaysian ethnic tensions have not resulted in separatist demands such as in Burma, ethnic relations dominate the Malaysian political process.

Milton Esman comments that in Malaysia the 'polity [is] structured explicitly along ethnic lines of cleavage ... [v]irtually every problem that [the] government encountered, even those that on the surface appeared ethnically neutral, proved to have competitive ethnic implications'.[25] On 13 May 1969, ethnic riots broke out in Kuala Lumpur. The communal violence between Malays and Chinese lasted five days and according to official figures resulted in 196 fatalities. Eighteen years later in 1987 the UMNO leadership of Dr Mahathir Mohamad was challenged from within UMNO by Tengku Razaleigh. UMNO split into Mahathir's team A and Razaleigh's team B and both teams 'began rapidly to compete for Malay support by vaguely demeaning the Chinese and proposing restrictive legislation upon Chinese businesses and cultural activities'.[26] Both teams held rallies in provocative locations – team A in a Chinese part of Kuala Lumpur and team B in the focal point of the 1969 riots. William Case writes that, '[e]thnic tensions rose to the boiling point and set off panic buying of foodstuffs, a phenomenon widely viewed after 1969 as preliminary to dreaded communal bloodletting'.[27] Mahathir invoked the Internal Security Act to arrest over 100 Malaysians and stability was restored.[28] Can the ethnic tensions of Malaysia be understood from the perspective of the security dilemma?

A consequence of Britain's management of Malaya during colonialism was that the Malay population lagged behind the economic and educational advancement of the competitive Chinese and Indian communities, which the British had encouraged to emigrate to Malaya. By 1931 the population census revealed that the Malays only accounted for 44 per cent of the total population, thus leaving them outnumbered by the immigrants.[29] The census also revealed that the number of Chinese born in Malaya had risen to 29 per cent from 8 per cent in 1911: born in Malaya these Chinese considered the country their home, creating the emergence of a permanent Chinese presence. The realisation that this Chinese presence was not going to be of a transient nature, was one reason which led to the emergence of a Malay ethnic identity. Crawford Young describes this emergence as a defensive action against the 'Chinese challenge' and consequently, 'running through Malay nationalism is a note of fear and frustration regarding their relationship with the immigrant communities, above all the industrious and frugal Chinese'. Thus, prior to independence ethnic divisions in Malaya were being demarcated by the indigenous Malay people fearing that they would be left behind in 'rural stagnation' by the active and vibrant Chinese community.[30]

In order to redress the economic balance and to ensure that Malaya, and subsequently Malaysia, is governed by the indigenous people, UMNO has pursued a policy of positive discrimination in favour of the *bumiputeras*.[31] The constitution explicitly grants special status to the Malays with positive discrimination operating in higher education, government employment and economic opportunities. English was replaced by Malay as the national language while the symbols of the state are Malay with Islam the state religion. The consequence of this long term policy has been the perception amongst the ethnic minorities that they are second-class citizens. This has been particularly evident for the Chinese in higher education and the acquisition of shares.

In order to increase Malay enrolment in universities, the regime has favoured Malay applications at the expense of other ethnic groups. This restriction on Chinese students enrolling in university education has been bitterly resented by the Chinese community. By 1977 it has been suggested that 75 per cent of new students were Malays and many Chinese families were sending their children abroad because of the discriminatory policies.[32] This also led to a call for a privately funded Chinese university – Merdeka University – but this was rejected by UMNO in 1978 on the grounds that by teaching through the medium of Chinese it would conflict with the goals of a unified national system of education.[33]

In share ownership the regime has sought to increase Malay activity in the economy by enabling Malays to purchase shares at below market prices. The intention was to reserve 30 per cent of stocks for Malay ownership. However, Malays instead of holding on to the shares have sold them at market prices thus receiving a windfall profit, and by keeping the Malay share ownership below 30 per cent continue to remain eligible for shares at preferential rates. By 1990, Malay share ownership had risen to 20.3 per cent, although 'only 8.2 per cent was owned directly by Malay individuals, the rest being owned either through unit trust schemes or by state agencies'.[34] There exists in Malaysia, although its intensity has declined, ethnic tension amongst the Malays and non-Malays. The Malays perceive that they are economically inferior to the Chinese and consequently have a feeling of insecurity which can become quite intense. The Chinese likewise are insecure, but in their case it is because they fear that rather than being content with equality, the Malays will maintain their special position to the detriment of the Chinese.

The Malays fear that they were about to lose their special privileges enshrined in the constitution and lose political control of *their* country to the Chinese, and the Chinese grievance that they were second class citizens became so intense in the late 1960s that it ignited the race riots of 13 May 1969.[35] Throughout the 1960s communal polarisation was on the increase as the Malays became aggrieved at not sharing in the modest economic growth Malaysia enjoyed, while the Chinese blamed Malay political obstacles from preventing them achieving greater gains.[36] Malay disillusionment was further compounded by UMNO's leader, Tunku Abdul Rahman, appearing to appease the Chinese community by compromising on the National Language Act of 1967. James Jesudason asserts, 'the government was surprisingly restrained in its vanguard ethnic role...the high expectations the Malays had of "their" government helping them vigorously failed to be realized'.[37]

By the 1969 election, political parties outside the Alliance coalition were gaining support as the Parti Islam Se-Malaysia (PAS) focused on Malay grievances and the Democratic Action Party (DAP) highlighted the inferior political and cultural status of the Chinese. The Alliance responded by also focusing on communal issues leading Lee Teik Soon to claim the 'unwritten law regarding communal issues was violated by both the Alliance and Opposition parties when they indulged in open, public and heated debate over such subjects'.[38] Although the Alliance won the election, its majority had been severely curtailed and the 'Malays' fear of Chinese domination increased sharply as the election results were announced'.[39] The success of the DAP led some Malays to fear another state election would be called resulting in greater Chinese gains. Fear was also evident in the Chinese community when the MCA withdrew from the Cabinet. With Chinese youths shouting 'Malays out! The Malays are finished! The Chinese are going to run the country!', Malay fear became exacerbated until it manifest itself as violence with the Malays turning on the Chinese and Indian communities.[40]

The Malays had lost faith in the regime safeguarding their 'special position' while the Chinese did not believe the authorities were either able or willing to protect them in the face of Malay violence. John Funston asserts that the intensity of the violence embarked upon by the Malays indicated a Malay perception that the Chinese represented a real threat to their security. He writes, '[c]haracteristically, such outbursts occur when the very identity if not existence of the community is felt to be threatened ... [The] Malays perceived a direct threat to their identity and retaliated with the fanaticism of the religiously possessed in a holy war'.[41] The security dilemma can be seen in operation. Both communities began to conceive of one another as a threat and, with the Malays and Chinese losing faith in the regime to provide for their security, began to take measures to defend themselves. A spiral of insecurity developed with their perception of threat leading to defensive measures (supporting communally based parties) which had the paradoxical affect of generating fear in the other. This fear reached such a crescendo that it erupted in ethnic violence. Eighteen years later similar dynamics could be seen at work again.

After the 1987 UMNO leadership tussle between Mahathir and Razaleigh the issue which gave rise to the greatest ethnic tension was a government decision to appoint 54 non-Mandarin speaking Chinese to positions within Chinese-medium primary schools. To the Chinese this symbolised a systematic programme by UMNO to undermine their language, and in response the MCA in conjunction with the DAP threatened a school boycott in four west coast states between 15–17 October. This collaboration between the MCA and DAP was seen by UMNO as a clear breach of BN discipline and tension rose. According to Suhaini Aznam the school issue 'reflected the extent to which ethnic relations [had] deteriorated ... Each race appears to think that every small concession will be seen by the other as a sign of weakness, and worse, will trigger more demands, leading to further concessions'.[42] Fear can cloud accurate threat perception and can lead to the belief that resolve is required since compromise can be seen as a sign of weakness.

Tensions reached a peak with a UMNO Youth rally calling for the resignation of Lee Kim Sai, the Labour Minister and deputy president of the MCA. It appeared as though Malaysia was again going to be wracked by ethnic violence, and once again the dynamics of the security dilemma can be seen at work. In particular, the misperception of threat, since despite the primacy of Malay culture the regime has sought not to undermine Chinese culture but rather maintain a diversity of cultures in Malaysia. For example, rather than trying to undermine

Chinese language provision, Mahathir, prior to the 1990 election, provided additional grants to Chinese primary schools and lifted restrictions on cultural events such as the Chinese lion dance while also asserting that his government was committed to multi-culturalism.

Although these measures were clearly designed to woo Chinese voters, Harold Crouch asserts, 'they were significant concessions in a symbolic sense that made Chinese feel that their cultural identity was not being ignored'.[43] Indeed, when these communities have felt their identity threatened both the MIC and the MCA have at times proven successful in modifying UMNO's policies. In 1979 the MCA was able to persuade UMNO to increase non-Malay university admission by 2 per cent per annum, until Malay and non-Malay recruitment was proportionate to the ethnic diversity of the population.[44]

Yet, the fear the ethnic communities harbour of one another can cause worst-case thinking. An issue as seemingly harmless as shop signposts can become an important issue of ethnicity as it becomes magnified far beyond the immediate concerns involved. During the 1970s and 1980s Chinese businesses sporting signs in Chinese were required to either have Malay lettering larger than the Chinese characters or no Chinese characters at all. The reason was that for Malays 'many urban areas seemed alien, like Hong Kong'. According to Donald Horowitz this issue resulted in a number of dangerous flare-ups and resulted in the prime minister becoming involved.[45] In 1997 when it was announced that Islamic studies was to become a compulsory subject at university there was an outcry, with the DAP releasing a statement 'saying it was shocked that the MCA...was not consulted'.[46] In fact the compulsory subject was 'Islamic studies and Asian civilisations' but the Asian civilisation component had not been included in the initial announcement. With such suspicion it is easy to see how incidents can occur as insecurities create hostilities along ethnic lines even though neither's ethnic identity is under threat. What is interesting about the Malaysian case is that the security dilemma's operation has lessened since its heyday in the late 1960s. We will return to consider Malaysia again later in this chapter when the discussion focuses on mitigating an ethnic security dilemma.

2 Self-determination

The desire for ethnic groups to determine their own fate, rather than have others deciding for them, creates a 'them' and 'us' dichotomy which gives rise to the security dilemma. The demands by a minority for greater autonomy within a state could lead the regime to perceive a threat to the state's territorial boundaries whereas in fact secession was not the objective. The regime's attempts to prevent this perceived secession attempt could have the paradoxical effect of altering the minority's goal of autonomy within the state to autonomy from the state. In other words, the regime may cause the very outcome it was trying to prevent. The relationship between the intra-state security dilemma and secession was examined in the previous chapter. It is sufficient here to state that the issue of incompatibility focuses on the maintenance of identity for the minority group and state's inviolable boundaries for the regime. The case-study for self-determination will draw upon two different examples within Thailand rather than between two different countries as in the previous case-study.

Isan

In the 1960s there emerged in the Northeastern region of Thailand an Isan ethnic identity. In his fieldwork, Charles Keyes discovered that in addition to their local distinctiveness from one another, the people of the Northeast were developing a pan-ethnic identity in contrast to the central Thais. He writes:

> within recent years the term Isan, already used by people of other regions to indicate the people of the Northeast, has been taken up by a growing segment of the northeastern population to indicate their own ethnic identity. Northeasterners have begun to speak of themselves as being *khon isan* or *phu isan* ('Isan people'), as using *phasa isan* (lit. Isan language) and living in *phak isan* ('Isan region'). The increasing usage of 'Isan' by Northeasterners bespeaks their growing sense of regional/ethnic identity.[47]

This ethno-regional consciousness emerged, according to Brown, because of economic, educational and migration factors.[48] He highlights how the Thai regime concentrated the economic wealth in Bangkok, though this was not always a conscious policy of the regime, and thereby not only caused a relative deprivation of the Northeast in comparison to other areas, but also an absolute deprivation. The latter claim is contentious, but Brown suggests that official figures claiming a dramatic reduction in those living below the poverty line conflict with independent reports.[49] In addition to economic factors Brown adds migration and education. He concurs with Keyes' analysis that the migration of northeastern workers to Bangkok, and the discrimination they suffered on arrival, promoted a communal consciousness amongst the immigrants. Keyes writes:

> From his experiences in Bangkok the returned migrant carried home with him feelings of class and ethnic discrimination directed towards him as a Northeasterner by Central Thai inhabitants of Bangkok and an enhanced awareness of the common culture and problems which all Northeasterners share ... [T]he pattern of increasing temporary migration of northeastern villagers to Bangkok beginning in the post-war period greatly spurred the development of 'we-they' attitudes among Northeasterners.[50]

This awareness of their differences from the Thais was also manifest in education policy. The Thai authorities considered education to be a means of creating national integration and imposed an educational system on the Northeast in which the Thai language was the sole medium. In order for northeasterners to progress they therefore needed to work in the Thai language. This had the effect of reinforcing the inferior status of the northeasterners with Thai associated with government and high prestige, while their own language they came to perceive as 'a hay-haw language'.[51] The Isan identity emerged therefore as a response to another ethnic group. Brown writes, 'it constitutes a distinctive ethnic consciousness defined in terms of distance from the "dominating other", the Central Thais'.[52]

Between the mid-1960s and 1980s the Thai authorities were faced with a communist insurgency based in the Northeast region. To what extent the workings of the security dilemma can be seen to have been active in the rise of tension between the Central Thais and Isan now becomes the focus of study. The crucial criterion concerns the Isan's objectives; if they supported the communist uprising as a means of establishing a separate state then clearly the security dilemma is not applicable. However, if they sought autonomy within Thailand and the Thai authorities mistakenly saw the communist uprising as a method of articulating a secessionist objective, then the security dilemma could be applicable.

Keyes' fieldwork on Isan migration to Bangkok revealed that the northeastern peasants conceived of the Central Thais as superior and consequently they were held in admiration.[53] Brown interprets this as significant because he writes:

> it implies that the political consciousness of Northeasterners would be unlikely to take an overtly separatist direction which would ensure exclusion from the potential benefits of Bangkok. Rather, the

experience of economic and cultural discrimination implied that the goal of Northeasterners would be that of gaining respect from the Central Thais as a distinct, autonomous and equal constituent community of Thailand.[54]

Keyes also notes that while northeasterners had a growing perception of being Isan this did not manifest itself as not wanting to be a Thai citizen. Indeed quite the opposite. Keyes found that villagers wanted to remain in Thailand and appreciated that in order to advance as individuals they needed to adopt the 'Thai way'. However, they were prepared to 'utilize an Isan identity for purposes of expressing feelings of distrust, resentment, and antipathy towards the Central Thai'.[55] This though did not mean they wanted to secede or join Laos. Keyes is quite emphatic on the issue and states categorically, '[r]ather than leading Northeasterners to seek a separate political destiny, the uses of Isan regionalism have been directed towards improving the status of the Isan people *within* the national order' (emphasis in original).[56]

The Isan objective was not therefore likely to be secession. However, Thai governments branded Isan political activists as separatists seeking unification with Laos. This was probably due to the activities of the communists, the porous nature of the Thai-Laos border and the number of opposition MPs in the Northeast region. For instance in the late 1940s the Thai military regime of Phibun Songkram accused Northeastern MPs of supporting the idea of a Southeast Asian Union, an idea associated with Pridi Phanomyong, the ousted leader. This accusation led to the deaths of four MPs. By the late 1950s the Northeast was regarded as a security threat with communist insurgents from Laos and Vietnam being supported, as far as the Thai government were concerned, by 'fifth columnists' in the Northeast. Brown is adamant, however, that 'there is little evidence of [an Isan secessionist] movement ... even less ... mass support for it ... [nor is there] a link between Thai communism and Isan separatism'.[57] An incompatibility between Thai state-making and Isan objectives would appear to be illusory.

The uncertainty of the Thai regime towards the aspirations of the Isan led therefore to the perception of threat and the regime's actions had the paradoxical effect of making the situation worse. Keyes notes that the death of the four MPs had lasting repercussions for the Thai–Isan relationship. He states:

> these four men became symbols of the growing sentiments shared by a large part of the northeastern population that they were discriminated against as a whole by the Central Thai and central

government. The death of these prominent northeastern leaders was a major catalyst in the development of Isan regional political identity and purpose for it demonstrated most dramatically the attitudes of the central government towards those who were identified with Isan political aspirations.[58]

He goes on to note how having assumed the worst about the Isan the Thai regime began to interpret any action from the Northeast as threatening. Keyes asserts:

It was believed that the success of the Viet Cong and/or Pathet Lao would bring hostile and expansionist governments to power near the borders of Thailand. If some of the regional opposition in the Isan region was sympathetic to or controlled by these powers, then Thailand itself would be threatened by internal insurrection or external threat supported by a 'fifth column', in the exposed Northeast. All northeastern political dissent, since it was not permitted to be channelled within legitimate forums, was viewed by the Thai government as part of a larger Communist-led conspiracy to overthrow the pro-Western government of Thailand. Consequently, such dissent must, in the government's belief, be ferreted out and eliminated.[59]

In December 1961 over one hundred people were arrested in Sakon Nakhon and Udon because the government accused them of supporting 'the cause of Communist separationists who want to effect secession of the Northeast from the rest of the Kingdom'.[60] These harassing tactics and the use of violence by the Thai regime in the Northeast region had the effect of mobilising Isan support for the Communist Party of Thailand (CPT) since this was the only method of articulating Isan demands left available to them. Ironically, for the Isan, the CPT leadership was unwilling to recognise them as a distinctive ethnic minority, preferring instead to mobilise amongst the Isan a class consciousness. Consequently, the CPT failed to be a vehicle for Isan regional autonomy. This explains why the CPT failed to gain the support of the majority of Isan. The Isan demands for regional autonomy have dissipated and the reasons for this will be examined in the second half of this chapter. For now though it would appear that the Thai regime's uncertainty concerning Isan intentions led them to believe that the Isan were a threat to the Thai state. This belief had the paradoxical effect of heightening Isan identity and pushing the people towards the CPT; a tragedy unfolded as Thai actions were bringing about exactly that which they sought to avoid.

Patani Malays

The Patani Malays live in Southern Thailand on the border with Malaysia and, unlike the Isan, this Muslim community has a clear ethnic distinctiveness from the Central Thais. Their identity is based on three pillars: the seventeenth/early eighteenth century Patani kingdom; Malay race and Islam. The Patani kingdom represents a golden era for the Patani Malays when they were regarded as a centre of Islamic scholarship of comparable worth to that of the Sultanate of Aceh. Throughout the seventeenth century, however, the Patani kingdom faced threats to its independence from the Buddhist kingdoms to the north and by the late eighteenth century they were ruled by the Thais. According to W.K. Che Man, since then their 'basic concern ... has been to ensure their survival as a distinct Muslim community'.[61] The arrival of British colonial rule in Malaya resulted in the southern states of the Patani Kingdom (Kelantan, Trengganu, Kedah and Perlis) being divided from those in Thailand (known at this time as Siam). This artificial divide not only lies behind the Patani Malay's irredentist ambitions, but also the Thai regime's concerns about Patani Malay loyalty to Thailand. Consequently, the Thai regime sought strict central control of the Muslim population – manifest in taxation policies but also the imposition of Siamese education and language – which in turn hardened the Patani Malays' resistance to the assimilationist policies of Bangkok. This paradox is captured in Che Man's statement that '[a]s efforts were made by the Thai government to assimilate [the Patani Malays], resentment developed into political resistance and [a] separatist movement', which in turn led to, 'sporadic insurrections and a series of abortive revolts'.[62]

The assimilationist policies of the Central Thais were accelerated throughout the 1930s and climaxed with the military regime of Phibun. Clive Christie asserts that

> the policy of Phibun's government combined an emphasis on Thai racial identity and unity, with forced-pace modernization. In 1939, Siam was renamed *Thailand*, thereby highlighting the one-ness of Thai ethnic and national identity. Pan-Thai rhetoric encouraged the irredentist dream of bringing the whole Thai family ... within one state.
>
> Although this policy was not aimed solely at the Muslim Malays of South Thailand, it clearly constituted a direct threat to the very foundations of their ethnic and religious identity [emphasis in original].[63]

With the Patani Malays failure to rejoin their Malay brethren in Malaya after World War II, their ambitions have oscillated between irredentism and independence. It would, therefore, appear as though the Patani Malays have been engaged in a struggle with the Thai regime over maintaining their separate identity, while the Thai regime's state-making and nation-building programme is incompatible with the irredentist ambitions of the Patani Malays. Thus, although Che Man notes that while the gap between the Thai and Muslim communities remain, 'their mutual misunderstandings and prejudices continue', it does not appear that underlying this ethnic tension is a situation created by the defensive actions of both parties.[64] Instead, it appears to be a clash over the real incompatibility of their different objectives.

3 Migration

The movement of people from one area to another can obviously have the effect of bringing two or more different ethnic groups into contact. The influx of large-scale immigration can easily generate fears amongst the indigenous population that they will be politically and culturally overwhelmed by the immigrants' arrival. This might not happen of course, it is quite plausible that the new ethnic group will be welcomed by the indigenous population. According to the World Bank, Indonesia's 'transmigration programs have brought enough benefits to the [outer] regions in terms of infrastructure, employment, markets and labour to be generally welcome, and the provinces themselves have sponsored or assisted resettlement from Java and Bali'.[65] This though is a generous interpretation of the transmigration programme, and in most cases the arrival of immigrants has been a cause of trouble. For example, the ill-feeling between locals and settlers, along with frustration over the economic crisis and resentment about the disparity of wealth, is regarded as a cause of the violence that engulfed the island of Ambon in early 1999.[66] Weiner argues that generally the more homogeneous the society the more likely immigrants will be conceived of as a threat.[67] Barry Buzan concurs by arguing, 'threat works on the societal level when the incoming population is of a different cultural or ethnic stock from those already resident. It is amplified when migrants seek to maintain their identity rather than adapting to that prevailing in their adopted country'.[68] In this final case-study the key is to distinguish between ethnic tensions that have arisen because there exists a real threat to the group's identity due to migration, and those that are based on an illusory incompatibility. The security dilemma is thus applicable in situations where the arrival of a different ethnic group is perceived as threatening by the indigenous population even though no harm to the native identity is intended.

Indonesia's transmigration programme

In Southeast Asia the rationale for government-sponsored large-scale migration of people is clear. The region has increasing population density in some areas while other areas are sparsely populated and underdeveloped. Land settlement schemes have been implemented in Malaysia, Thailand and the Philippines. However, it is the Indonesian transmigration programme that because of the numbers involved is by far the most significant. Indonesia is the fifth most populated country in the world with over 200 million inhabitants. The distribution of this population throughout the archipelago is very uneven with almost 60 per cent concentrated on the islands of Java, Madura, Bali and Lombok which in turn only account for 7 per cent of Indonesia's land area. The settlement of people throughout the myriad of islands that compose Indonesia can be traced back to the Dutch colonisation programme of 1905 but it was in 1950 that transmigration became an essential feature of Indonesia's development strategy. Government sources reveal seven reasons behind the transmigration programme. They are: improvement of living standards; regional development; even population distribution; equal development throughout Indonesia; utilisation of natural resources and human labour; integrity and unity of the nation; strengthening of defence and national security. On these criteria, the transmigration programme has been largely unsuccessful, especially with regard to demographic change with Java's population increase exceeding the number of people emigrating.[69] Our concern, however, is with the goal of uniting the nation and whether this poses a real threat to the identity of Indonesia's ethnic minorities (assimilation) or whether, if it is perceived as a threat, it is an illusory one (an overarching Indonesian identity complemented by local identities).

Since the transmigration programme is a policy tool of the Indonesian government the intent behind the migration of people and the effect this has for the indigenous people is perhaps easier to discern than if the migration was unauthorised. However, the analysis of the intended affects of transmigration on the identities of the local population is inconclusive. Marcus Colchester considers transmigration as a real threat. He writes, '[t]ransmigration, far from being a humanitarian exercise, is really a political programme designed to extend government control over the peripheral islands through the elimination of ethnic diversity. Transmigration has become one of the government's

key means for assimilating tribal people'.[70] He argues that 'cultural pluralism does not exist in Indonesia, and local claims for minor degrees
of regional or even cultural autonomy are often interpreted by the
authorities as being fundamentally anti-Indonesian'.[71] Colchester supports this interpretation of the transmigration programme by quoting
the following from the minister of transmigration in 1985, Martono:

> On 28 October 1928, a youth congress was held concluding that we
> are one nation, the Indonesian nation; we have one native country,
> Indonesia; one language, the Indonesian language. By way of
> Transmigration, we will try to realize what has been pledged, to
> integrate all the ethnic groups into one nation, the Indonesian
> nation … The different ethnic groups will in the long run disappear
> because of integration.[72]

Not all commentators however view the transmigration process in
this way. Catherine Caulfield claims that the threat to ethnic identity
is either intended or not depending upon where the migrants are emigrating. She states that the

> real motive for the program, many believe, is 'Javanization'. The
> indigenous population of many of the islands under Indonesian rule
> (notably Kalimantan, Irian Jaya, and Timor) have rebellious tenden-
> cies. They have their own cultures, languages, and religions and do
> not want to be part of Indonesia. Many people on these islands bit-
> terly deprecate transmigration as a move to swamp them with peo-
> ple who share an ethnic and religious identity with Indonesia's
> military rulers.[73]

For Caulfield therefore the migration of people from the populated
islands of Indonesia to the Outer Islands is a real threat to the indigenous people's identity. However, she then notes that this is not always
the case, and indeed, indicates how the two communities can become
antagonistic towards one another although neither intends to challenge the other's identity. Caulfield continues by stating that even

> where the intention of the program is not to subordinate the native
> community, local people often resent the transmigrants for the facil-
> ities and assistance they get from the government. The need for the
> settlers to develop a sense of community in order to help one
> another over the hard times conflicts with the goal of integration

with the native population. The government now has a policy of allocating 10 per cent of the places in each settlement to local people, but that will only draw the line between natives and settlers at a different point, not eliminate it.[74]

In other words, to consider the entire transmigration programme as a policy of ethnic cleansing is wrong. Caulfield's conclusion gains support from Jonathan Rigg who concurs by noting, '[i]t is no doubt true that at times the authorities have been rather heavy-handed in their dealings with local peoples, but to see behind every transmigration policy directive some insidious attempt at ethnocide is taking these fears to extreme'.[75]

Although the Indonesian regime may not in all cases seek the elimination of tribal identities, its very policy of development is having this affect. Hence the comment by Michael Vatikiotis, 'that Jakarta's homogenising approach to development does pose a threat to the preferred lifestyle and culture of the Irianese', and the statement from the Alliance of the Indigenous People of the Archipelago – formed at the first indigenous conference held in Indonesia in March 1999 – that the country's ethnic groups had been 'systematically victimised in the name of economic development'.[76] As Indonesia attempts to develop the Outer Islands by utilising the natural resources, so these development projects have a huge impact on the local inhabitants and therefore constitute a real threat to the indigenous people's ability to maintain their ethnicity. In some cases the government's policies have strengthened the indigenous identity. Dewi Fortuna Anwar writes, '[t]he central government's policies on migration and resource exploitation underscore the political unrest that has periodically erupted in West Irian. The intrusion of the modern economic sector into Indonesia's most undeveloped province has clearly disrupted the traditional mode of living of the Irianese, stimulating support for the separatist movement.'[77] The transmigration policy is also the root cause of the violence between the local Dayak population and the migrants from Madura that erupted in early 1997 and again in 1999 in Kalimantan, the Indonesian part of Borneo. The disturbances required the intervention of Indonesian forces to quell the troubles and according to reports over 300 people died in 1997.[78] In other instances, the indigenous people have not resisted, but rather than adopting an Indonesian identity they have found themselves caught between alienation from their old ways and alienation from the new – a state of anomie manifest by such social ills as drunkenness, prostitution and crime.[79]

The problems of development for indigenous people is not of course limited to Indonesia. In Sarawak the indigenous Penan community has resorted to violence against the logging companies to protect its rainforests and way of life; while for some of the Dayak communities that inhabit this part of Borneo, the remnants of their culture are strictly for the tourists.[80] In the Philippines too the impact of development has eroded the cultural beliefs of tribal groups. Focusing on the Batak community on Palawan Island, James Eder argues that development programmes have not only eroded the Batak ethnic identity but have also hindered their ability to acculturate.[81] Rigg concurs with Eder by stating, 'as the culture of hunter-gatherers has become eroded, so there has arisen the possibility, in some cases the reality, of culture extinction. Some tribal groups have – culturally – disappeared entirely'.[82]

In Indonesia, transmigration, since it is a tool of development, links migration with development issues. It is a tragedy that the forces of modernisation make change inevitable, but this tragedy has not occurred because both the regime and the ethnic groups have brought about something they wished to avoid.[83] Transmigration does constitute a real threat to the tribal people's way of life, and therefore, the security dilemma is not applicable to the ethnic tensions that it causes.

Summary

It would appear that as with the inter-state security dilemma the intra-state version is applicable in some instances but not in others. This might seem a less than insightful conclusion, but the literature applying the security dilemma to ethnic conflict treats the dilemma as omnipresent. Hence Chaim Kaufmann's assertion, that a 'problem that must be overcome by any remedy for severe ethnic conflict is the security dilemma'. Indeed, Kaufmann's next claim that the security dilemma will operate '[r]egardless of the origins of the ethnic strife', indicates that Kaufmann's interpretation of the security dilemma suffers from the same shortcomings noted in Chapter 1 with Barry Posen and Stuart Kaufman's interpretation.[84] That is, by arguing the security dilemma will operate because 'no group can provide for its own security without threatening the security of others', Kaufmann is falling into the trap of not seeking to determine whether the group's security requirements are compatible or not.[85] Yet this is critically important, as Charles Glaser notes, 'the security dilemma is the key to understanding how … [actors] with fundamentally compatible goals still end up in competition and at war'.[86] It is the misinterpretation of a security threat and the response this generates which gives rise to the security dilemma.[87] Thus it is argued that in Malaysia and the Thai/Isan relationship, the uncertainty each community harboured about the other's intentions generated a security dilemma because it appears that their fears were based upon an illusory incompatibility. Whereas in Burma and the Outer Islands of Indonesia it appears that the concerns of the minority groups are well founded, and that their ethnic identities are being challenged. It is this real threat that negates the application of the security dilemma and makes the latter cases examples of Robert Jervis's deterrence model.

B. Mitigating an intra-state security dilemma

The traditional inter-state security dilemma operates because ambiguous foreign policy actions or military force deployments/postures create the perception of threat. If statesmen could either remove their uncertainty concerning the foreign policy action, or interpret the force characteristics accurately, the security dilemma would not operate. The latter means of mitigating and ultimately escaping the security dilemma are associated with Robert Jervis and his seminal piece, 'Cooperation Under the Security Dilemma'.[88] In essence, Jervis argues that if the weapons that states procure for defence are incapable of offensive actions, then neighbouring states need not fear their deployment, and therefore, the security dilemma will not operate. Jervis's article has been particularly influential in the literature that utilises the security dilemma in conjunction with ethnic conflict. The first article associating ethnic conflict with the security dilemma, Barry Posen's 'The Security Dilemma and Ethnic Conflict', interprets the security dilemma's operation entirely from the perspective of offensive/defensive force postures.[89] Posen's piece has inspired a number of articles linking the security dilemma to ethnic conflict and these were analysed in Chapter 1. This recent literature, however, contains two limitations regarding its relevance to the present discussion.

The first is that because it retains the focus on the military aspect of security it remains locked into the offensive/defensive attributes of the security dilemma equation. Thus, a number of commentators highlight Posen's argument that pockets of one ethnic minority surrounded by another, or even worse, the intermingling of ethnic groups, heightens the security dilemma because it is harder to defend the group, and thus ethnic groups need to rely on offence for their security. Hence Chaim Kaufmann's assertion that, 'offense has an advantage over defense in inter-community conflict, especially when settlement patterns are inter-mingled, because isolated pockets are harder to hold than to take'.[90] Consequently, Kaufmann asserts that 'the security dilemma is reduced by physical separation of the rival groups'.[91] The belief that separating rival groups will reduce the security dilemma is, however, extremely dubious since they will remain uncertain of one another's intentions. Indeed, separating the ethnic groups does not 'solve' the conflict although it might stop the fighting. With the issue that caused the conflict left unresolved and both groups highly suspicious of one another, the chance of a security dilemma operating between them is high, not low. The reason Kaufmann arrives at the reverse conclusion is because he focuses on the offensive/defensive element instead of uncertainty concerning intentions. Since our focus is on identity as the security issue it is the latter, uncertainty, that is more appropriate. To mitigate and ultimately to escape the security dilemma requires removing the uncertainty the actors have about the other's intentions, and this requires something other than the separation of ethnic groups.

The second problem with the current literature is that the focus is on ethnic war and how the security dilemma helps to explain the deterioration in relations between the ethnic groups during the war. Hence, for Kaufmann separation becomes the key because '[o]nce a majority of either group comes to believe that the killing of noncombatants of their own group is not considered a crime by the other, they cannot accept any governing arrangement that could be captured by the enemy group and used against them'.[92] In other words, self-determination becomes an essential feature of any peace arrangement. However, using the security dilemma in war, as opposed to explaining the cause and escalation of tension leading to war, corrupts the term and leads to wholly implausible statements. The security dilemma is premised on the threat each perceives being illusory. Thus, David Lake and Donald Rothchild write, the 'dilemma follows from the inability of the two sides to observe each other's intentions directly; if each party knew the other was arming for strictly defensive purposes, the potential spiral would be cut short. But because states cannot know the intentions of others with certainty', they embark upon paradoxical policies that make matters worse.[93] Thus, Kaufmann's claim that '[u]nder conditions of anarchy, each group's mobilization constitutes a real threat to the security of others', does not support his claim that the security dilemma is active. Indeed, given that the security dilemma is premised on illusory incompatibility, it cannot be active when war has broken out, since this act in itself indicates that a real incompatibility must now exist. The security dilemma can explain why a war occurred but not the antagonists' feelings of fear during the war. Hence, the focus for Robert Jervis, when he writes 'the security dilemma can not only create conflicts and tensions but also provides the dynamics triggering war', is on the events leading up to the outbreak of hostility rather than on events during the war itself.[94]

Kaufmann does highlight alternatives to separation for achieving ethnic peace and two of these (power-sharing, reconstruction of ethnic identities) are relevant because they can reduce the actors' uncertainty of each other's intentions. Because Kaufmann is examining ethnic war, he dismisses these alternatives; but because we are interested in the situation prior to the outbreak of war they hold out the promise of mitigating and escaping the security dilemma.[95]

1 Power-sharing

The usefulness of power-sharing to ethnic conflict is self-explanatory. If ethnic elites adhere to an agreement where each group has influence over government policy, then their uncertainty about the intent that lies behind that policy is, at worst, minimised, and at best, removed. The centrality of uncertainty is the focal point for Lake and Rothchild since it exists at the heart of the three elements they consider give rise to ethnic conflict: information failures, credible commitments and the security dilemma. Although they distinguish the latter from the others, the other two are actually essential features of the security dilemma; a point the authors acknowledge.[96] Both information failure and credible commitment refer to the problem of uncertainty. The former refers to ethnic groups not knowing the intentions of others and having to distinguish between groups which seek nothing more than their own security and those that are aggressive. Credible commitment highlights the uncertainty that comes with the passage of time; is their commitment to an agreement credible or will today's friend be tomorrow's enemy? In classic security dilemma terminology, Lake and Rothchild highlight the problems of determining intent and conclude ethnic conflict cannot be escaped, it can only be mitigated. They write:

> Information is costly to acquire and, as a result, there is always some uncertainty about the intentions of other groups. Groups compensate for their information limitations by acting on the basis of prior beliefs about the likely preferences of others. These beliefs are formed through historical experience ... and represent each group's

best guess about the other's intentions. Groups then update these beliefs as new information becomes available to them. Nonetheless, information is always incomplete and groups are forever uncertain about each other's purposes. Conflict, then, always remains possible in ethnic interactions.
Problems of credible commitment in ethnic relations are universal. Concerned that the balance of power may tip against them or that the other may have hostile intentions, groups worry that agreements made today will not be honored tomorrow ...
To provoke conflict, one group need not believe that the other really is aggressive, only fear that it might be. With incomplete information, even small changes in beliefs about the intentions of the other group can generate massive violence.[97]

Borrowing from international relations, Lake and Rothchild focus on confidence-building measures and they highlight 'four major trust-building mechanisms for helping ethnic minorities deal with perceived insecurity'.[98] They are: demonstrations of respect; elections; regional autonomy and federalism; and power-sharing. Although Lake and Rothchild distinguish power-sharing from the other three, these can be seen as elements within power-sharing. For instance, demonstrations of respect, which refers to ethnic groups acknowledging each other's ethnicity as sacrosanct, is an essential forerunner to successful power-sharing. Likewise, regional autonomy and elections must safeguard the ethnic pluralism of government control otherwise power-sharing would collapse. Since power-sharing entails the discussion of the different wants and needs of each group it helps to reduce information failure and because the outcome of the discussion is agreed to by all it makes the commitment more credible. The willingness of ethnic groups to share power is therefore a major step towards removing the uncertainty that lies at the core of the security dilemma.
It was noted above that the intra-state security dilemma was applicable to the relationship between the Malay *bumiputeras* and the Chinese and Indian communities in Malaysia. To what extent power-sharing, with its emphasis on lessening uncertainty, has mitigated this ethnic security dilemma will now become the focus of attention. The coalition regime formed from the main ethnic parties, as well as smaller parties including those representing the interests of Sabah and Sarawak, appears to be a clear case of power-sharing. However, it has already been noted that Malaysia can be considered an ethnocratic

regime because of the dominance enjoyed by the Malays. It is certainly the case that UMNO is the dominant party in the BN and consequently Malaysia's executive authority lies with the Malay leadership. Despite this, the other parties, in particular the MCA, do enjoy a degree of influence over government policy, and whilst power is not evenly shared, it is nevertheless shared. This influence has ensured Chinese businesses receive government contracts, the percentage of non-Malays entering university rose to 45 per cent in the 1980s, Chinese and Tamil language primary schools are government funded, a private Chinese college was approved in 1997, and the Chinese and Indian communities can practise their customs and religion.[99] This, albeit unequal, power-sharing of the coalition has been a durable feature of Malaysian politics since independence for four broad reasons.

First, and perhaps most importantly, non-Malays account for 40 per cent of the Malaysian population. This acts as a check against UMNO imposing a Malay regime since such action would not only cause massive 'social upheaval and ... risk ... civil war but could [cause] economic disruption if Chinese skills were withdrawn'.[100] The percentage of non-Malays also means that the BN requires the support of non-Malay voters to secure a majority in parliament, and UMNO also requires non-Malay support to win some constituencies where the PAS support is strong.[101] Therefore, UMNO leaders have sought to portray themselves as defenders of non-Malay as well as Malay interests. Thus, the ethnic division of Malaysia makes a coalition regime, in which 'the non-Malay partners ... are more than token representatives', a crucial element in reducing uncertainty and allaying fear amongst the ethnic communities.[102]

The second reason relates to the economic policies and economic prosperity enjoyed by Malaysians. Although the wealth generated by Malaysia's economic growth has not been evenly distributed amongst the population, all the different classes and ethnic communities have benefited. There is a general level of satisfaction amongst the rural population where the incidence of poverty has declined, the material aspirations of the urban middle-classes have been satisfied and a Malay business culture has developed. These achievements have not been gained at the expense of the non-Malays, with the Chinese continuing to be the main business group, and according to Crouch, they constitute 'a significant bulwark against movement toward Malay-dominated authoritarianism'.[103] The economic prosperity of Malaysia has therefore created a population which is supportive of the power-sharing arrangement and returned the BN to power with its largest ever post-independence victory in the 1995 election.

The third reason is concerned with aspects of British rule. Case argues that during the colonial period the membership of the Malay state councils was broadened to include ethnic Chinese. These Chinese were concerned with various business interests including tariffs and the immigration of coolies and Case argues, 'they learned swiftly to collaborate with the rulers in mutually beneficial ways'.[104] Thus although the British favoured the Malays with some limited political responsibility, they did not obstruct Chinese participation. Thus, with independence the ethnic bargain was struck in the Merdeka Constitution. This has been interpreted to mean that Malay leaders would have the greater share of political power, and would award state licences and contracts to Chinese business, while the Chinese would have unfettered access to economic opportunities – although not to the detriment of Malay economic aspirations – and have an influence in political decision-making through the MCA.[105]

The final reason for Malaysia's power-sharing arrangement is more contentious and refers to 'Asian values' and Asian-style democracy. The debate concerning Asian values or the 'Asian Way' emerged during 1992 and 1993 while the economies of Southeast Asia were growing at phenomenal rates and the talk was of the 'East Asian Miracle'. Regional leaders such as Mahathir and Singapore's Lee Kuan Yew have noted the role of Asian values in explaining the region's success. It was argued that Asia offered an alternative model to development which would avoid the moral decay and lack of social discipline that accompanied the Western model. The problem with these claims is that the evidence from the region, even prior to the economic collapse which revealed the depth and pervasiveness of cronyism, was that Asia also suffered from the social ills attributed to the West. If Western cities were degenerate centres of drugs and prostitution then they were no worse than Bangkok, Jakarta, Manila, etc. The debates concerning Asian values encompass a wide range of issues (primacy of the family, respect for authority and education, the rights of the community over the individual), in this instance our interest concerns the emphasis on consensus-building because this can reduce uncertainty and thus aid the mitigation of the security dilemma.

Renée de Nevers claims, 'democratization has the potential to help mitigate ethnic tension by allowing for the establishment of an inclusive means of governance to address the needs of all ethnic groups in the state'.[106] However, Asian-style democracy as practised in Malaysia, as well as in other states in Southeast Asia, is more akin to authoritarianism than Western liberal democracy. Despite the veneer of democracy Malaysian politics operates along authoritarian lines. For instance, although in Malaysia elections are held regularly, the electoral system favours the Malay community and UMNO is almost guaranteed to be the dominant party.[107] The BN coalition has made use of the Internal Security Act, the Sedition Act and the Official Secrets Act to detain without trial government critics and to deter public debate. The media is government controlled and the two key political posts in UMNO and therefore Malaysia, the president and deputy president, are no longer contested.[108] Crouch claims that in 'each election the government was returned to power with substantial majorities through a combination of genuine popularity, manipulation of the electoral system and authoritarian controls'.[109] Thus, for James Putzel, 'Asian democracy, defined in opposition to Western liberal democracy, has been used to legitimize … Malaysia's increasingly authoritarian regime.'[110] Despite this, it is argued by Southeast Asian scholars and leaders that because of Asian values this political process is inclusive and therefore democratic.

The existence of Asian values is however contentious with some commentators noting that the diverse ethnicity of Asia prevents the people having similar values, while others see such values as little more than a creation by the elites to maintain their hold on power.[111] Interpreted this way, such Asian values as consensus-building and communitarian rights, instead of individual rights, mask one party, or one man's rule, and stifle the opposition. However, while it might be the case that elites have referred to Asian values to justify their actions, this can only be possible if the people in these states have an affinity with those values. Donald McCloud is in no doubt that they exist, as he asserts, 'the origin of this philosophical view matters less than does the recognition that this concept of the primacy of the community over the individual permeates every aspect of life in Southeast Asia and creates for the average citizen there a completely different pattern of thoughts and expectations than that of the average citizen in the West'.[112] The argument is not so much about whether such values exist, as to whether they are distorted when applied at the state level. Thus, while it is true that Confucianism stresses hierarchy and reverence for those in authority, this is balanced by the leaders being virtuous and leading by moral example. So while much is made of Asian values emphasising harmony, stability and consensus, it is the apparent lack of virtuous rule by such ex-Asian leaders as Indonesia's President Suharto and the Philippine President, Ferdinand Marcos, which gives rise to the cynical view that Asian values are distorted by Southeast Asian elites to restrict political activity in their country. In Malaysia it would appear that consensus-building is grounded in both Malay and Confucian values. Both highlight the central authority of a ruler while noting that this authority is dependent upon a just and fair treatment of his citizens and consultation with local elites. The *Malay Annals* warn, '[s]ubjects are like roots and the ruler is like the tree; without roots the tree cannot stand upright'.[113] Thus, the building of consensus and respect for the masses remain essential elements in present Malaysian politics: the 'Barisan way'. Case writes, 'even as UMNO proclaim[s] before [the] Malay...its defence of their birthright, it trie[s] to persuade the Chinese and Indians that it responsibly check[s] Malay chauvinism. The institutional basis for striking this balance – redressing Malay grievances while at some level respecting non-Malay identities and property rights – [is], of course the consultative "Barisan way"'.[114] The success of this power-sharing is marked in the stability that has emerged since the 1969 riots, but this does not mean the security dilemma has been escaped. The fear and suspicion that each community has of the other remains and could be exacerbated by any rise in Islamic influence or as a consequence of economic hardship. Nevertheless there has been a decline in the levels of suspicion between the ethnic communities within Malaysia, and this is examined further in the following section.

2   Reconstructing ethnic identities

If power-sharing can mitigate the intra-state security dilemma then reconstructing ethnic identities holds out the promise of escaping it. It was noted in the previous chapter that ethnicity can be both primordialist (you are who you are because of the group you were born into and the social learning that you received; it is both nature and nurture) and situationalist (your identity is heightened as a consequence of the circumstances in which you find yourself). These appear to be incompatible since the primordialist is a given while the situationalist is dependent, and thereby constructed, upon the present event. However, as Brown argues, 'ethnicity appears to exhibit both primordialist and situationalist attributes...It is in part generated by the political and socio-economic structure of the society, but it is also in part a "given" which plays a causal role; it is neither fully determined by the cultural structure of society, nor is it a totally elastic response to situational variations.'[115] Therefore, while some cultural attributes remain fixed, individuals can reconstruct their ethnic identity with the acquisition of other attributes. The need to learn a different language in school has been noted as a tool exercised by the regime to acculturate or assimilate the different ethnic groups into one nation. This attempt to reconstruct identities lies behind the Burman's goal of creating a Burmese nation and Colchester's interpretation of Indonesia's transmigration programme in the Outer Islands.

The case for reconstructing ethnic identities, and thereby creating an inclusive identity that all ethnic groups adopt, is simple: if individuals within ethnic groups have affinity because they share common values, then the creation of an identity that all groups share should engender affinity and reduce any antagonism they feel towards one another. In Burma and Thailand this did not work because the minority groups interpreted the actions of the majority as replacing their ethnic identity; and, thus, far from uniting the nation they had the affect of strengthening the minority group's separate identity. In the case of the Shan, Karen and Patani Malay the interpretation was accurate and the deterioration between these minorities and the majority Burman and Thai was a result of the real incompatibility between the regime's assimilationist goals and the desire of the minorities to maintain their ethnicity. In the Northeastern region of Thailand the activities of the Thais created a communal Isan identity amongst the local people although this was not the Thai intention. It was postulated above, that the security dilemma could be seen at work in the deterioration in the Thai/Isan relationship. By the mid-1980s with the CPT defeated the regime's relationship with its Northeastern region dramatically improved. Indeed, recent Thai governments have owed their victory to the support they have received from the Northeast.[116] Can this improvement be understood from the perspective of ethnic identity reconstruction?

A number of factors help to explain the improvement in relations between the people of the Northeast and the Thai regime. The broad reason lay in the growing sense of confidence in Bangkok. Thongchai Winichakul writes:

With the end of internal insurgency and of the Cold War in the 1980s, neighbouring states became dependent on Thailand in one way or another. The Thai state was secure. Besides, Thailand emerged economically stronger than before. Not only had the security paranoia which had haunted the Thai elite since the birth of the nation subsided, but Thailand could be aggressive. Within this context the diversity of the Thai people and culture was tolerable.[117]

The specific reason behind the improvement was the Thai regime's 'recognition that economic deprivation was a root cause of the communist insurrection, and that the CPT could not be defeated solely by military means'.[118] Although the region still remains the poorest in Thailand – impoverished Northeasterners are known for selling their votes at election time – the Thai regime has succeeded in increasing investment in the region. What though of political Isan ethnic consciousness? Three reasons present themselves as explaining the collapse of the Isan desire for political autonomy. The first was the CPT's failure to act as a vehicle for that ambition. The second was that the Thai regime had removed the resources upon which a separate Isan regional movement could have grown, such as indigenous elites. The third relates to the Isan ethnic identity. Although the people of the Northeast are recognised by the Thai as a distinct community, according to Brown, 'they [see] Isan as referring intrinsically to a low-status subgroup of the Thai people rather than to a non-Thai category'.[119] This notion of inferiority, combined with the Isan identifying themselves as Thai rather than Lao, limited the extent to which an Isan identity could harness a desire for political autonomy. The Isan identity remains and is now seen as a local identity compatible with a Thai national identity. The Governor of Surin, a province in the Northeast, stated in 1990:

> As we all agree, culture is a factor which unifies our nation. In Thailand now we have the main culture [*watthanatham lak*] we all adhere to. But the sub-cultures [*watthanatham yoi*], which are identities of particular localities, continue to exist without being harmful to the harmony of the nation.[120]

The security dilemma therefore was escaped because ultimately Isan ethnicity was unable to maintain a political significance for the people. With the CPT failing to provide the organisational base for autonomy demands, subsequent generations, since the heyday of Isan political ethnic consciousness of the 1960s, have treated Isan as identifying them with their geographical location in Northeast Thailand.

The ethnic reconstruction in the Northeast of Thailand does not, however, help us understand how an intra-state security dilemma can be mitigated or escaped. Using the inter-state security dilemma as an analogy, in this case, the security dilemma would have been escaped because one of the states would simply have sought a union, or in Deutsch's terms an amalgamated security community, with the other.

Returning to Malaysia and Mahathir's 'Vision 2020' may however be more revealing.

In 1991 Mahathir announced his Vision 2020 which seeks an ambitious goal of a fully industrialised and true Malaysian nation (*Bangsa Malaysia*) by that date.[121] *Bangsa Malaysia* is couched in deliberately vague terms so as to not upset the ethnic communities. Thus, it is 'an inclusive concept, based upon loyalty to the country, its constitution and its language'.[122] The idea expounds the goal of a Nation-State in which people have different cultures, values and religions. In other words, while the communities maintain their separate identities, they also share an overarching identity of being Malaysian. What is interesting is that rather than being a clear case of regime-inspired ethnic reconstruction (known as social engineering), Vision 2020 also appears to be a reaction to Malaysian societal changes. A number of commentators have noted that because of the NEP, class divisions have increased within the ethnic communities. Consequently, poor Chinese and poor Malays have more in common with each other than they do with their wealthy compatriots and vice-versa. In the business community, Jesudason argues that 'with the expansion of Malay capitalism, internal competition within the Malay business class has increased, making it difficult for Malays to have a unified conception of their economic interests against the other groups. This development in turn has eroded an important social basis of ethnic conflict'.[123] Consequently, he argues that while conflict along ethnic lines cannot be ruled out, if conflict does occur it is equally likely to be Malay 'lower-class resentment ... directed towards corporate and capitalist co-ethnics as towards the Chinese businessmen'.[124]

While it is too soon to argue that these changes will lessen ethnic uncertainty about each group's intentions, they could in the long term – by the year 2020 maybe – create an overarching Malaysian identity that will contain values Malay, Chinese and Indians will have an affinity with. It is as yet too soon to know what affect the recent economic crisis will have on this development. K.S. Nathan has warned that it 'could undermine the effort of the incumbent political leadership to forge a national community that transcends ethnic divides'.[125] Despite this it was noticeable that in the political crisis of September 1998, when Mahathir sacked and then arrested his Deputy Prime Minister Anwar Ibrahim, the subsequent developments did not become ethnically polarised. Indeed, on 27 September, PAS and DAP held a joint meeting criticising the government's detention of Anwar under the Internal Security Act, and on 4 April 1999 Anwar's wife, Wan Azizah

Wan Ismail, launched the multi-ethnic National Justice Party. This is in marked contrast to the rise of ethnic tension that coincided with the 1987 UMNO political crisis. It is possible that Malaysian ethnic reconstruction could escape the Malaysian intra-state security dilemma, although it is at an early stage and the impact of the economic crisis with its attendant social/political effects are as yet unknown.

Conclusion

For Lake and Rothchild the operation of the security dilemma means there is no escape from ethnic conflict. They write, '[t]here is no form of insurance sufficient to protect against the dilemmas that produce collective fears and violence. We can only hope to contain ethnic fears, not permanently eliminate them.'[126] This pessimistic view is countered by Kaufmann's optimistic opinion that escape is possible – and indeed he asserts, 'lasting peace requires [the] removal of the security dilemma'.[127] It is suggested in this chapter that escape is possible although not by separation but rather ethnic reconstruction. The argument is not too dissimilar to the early modernisation theories that considered ethnic identity would wither away.[128] The argument is not that they will wither, but rather over a prolonged period of time their identity will be complemented by a national identity, as with the Isan. Thus, the Chinese and Indians in Malaysia are Chinese Malaysians and Indian Malaysians. While it is too soon to suggest these labels indicate the emergence of a Malaysian Malaysia, a term too readily associated with the unhappy merger with Singapore to be revived, Mahathir's Vision 2020 is a tentative step in this direction. The key difference between this and the early modernisation theories is that rather than assuming the different groups will reject their traditions and replace them with new shared values, it is argued that prolonged inter-ethnic contact will lessen fears about one another and create shared values in conjunction with traditional values. In Great Britain, for example, the majority of the Welsh, Scots and English maintain their separate identities but complement them with a British identity.

Achieving ethnic reconstruction can be realised with power-sharing. Power-sharing by enabling the groups to influence or determine policy reduces their uncertainty concerning the policies' likely impact on their ethnicity. Power-sharing can, however, do more than this since if it is successful the ethnic elites may realise that cooperation can lead to stability which can bring mutual benefits. The enjoyment of these benefits could in turn engender affinity and shared values. It is argued that despite Malay domination in Malaysia this Southeast Asian country is a good example of power-sharing. The influence of the MCA and the MIC are able to exert in the BN, provides protection for their ethnic groups by limiting the impact of policies which could appear threatening. The benefits in material wealth, education and health which have marked Malaya/Malaysia since independence have been achieved because the coalition regime has maintained stability. It is too soon to know what impact the economic crisis will have on these developments, although initial signs are promising that the security dilemma will continue to be ameliorated and ultimately escaped. Some observers believe that the reform movement in Malaysia could over time transform Malaysia's communal politics into a pluralist democracy, the attainment of which would indicate the end of ethnicity as a political value in Malaysian politics, and consequently the escape of the ethnic security dilemma.[129]

Of course highlighting the prospects of mitigating and escaping an intra-state security dilemma presumes such a thing exists. According to the recent application of the security dilemma to ethnic conflict it would appear to be relevant, but, as explained in the previous two chapters and again noted in this chapter, there are shortcomings with the interpretation given by Stuart Kaufman, Chaim Kaufmann, Posen, Lake and Rothchild. In essence because they associate the security dilemma with any rise in tension they apply it to circumstances in which there exists a real incompatibility and the policies chosen are not paradoxical. With reference to Robert Jervis's deterrence and spiral models of conflict these authors therefore see the security dilemma applicable to both, whereas it is only applicable to the spiral model. Hence Randall Schweller's comment that 'because it is real, the resulting insecurity cannot be attributed to the security dilemma/spiral model of conflict'.[130] The security dilemma is not applicable to all instances of inter-state conflict, and likewise, the intra-state security dilemma is not applicable to all ethnic conflict. Indeed, as this chapter has indicated, it is necessary to assess each case individually. This means that the intra-state security dilemma is not as flexible as the insecurity dilemma, but unlike the latter, because the intra-state security dilemma reveals misperception it also reveals possible solutions. Thus, although it might not be as useful as some analysts would like, it nevertheless can be applied in Southeast Asia and be understood as a cause of the ethnic tensions in Malaysia.

Part II
Inter-state Security Dilemma

4
ASEAN's Security Dilemma

Currently, there does not exist a clear and present danger to ASEAN to delineate the purpose of [collective] power. As a consequence, the rationale for corporate interests to take precedence over state interests has declined within the ASEAN region; and the gradual 'decompression' of historical antagonisms, territorial claims, centre-periphery tensions, ethnic conflict, religious fundamentalism, and inter-state leadership rivalries, all of which had previously been frozen by the dynamics of bipolar politics, are potent forces imping-ing on state interests. In short, states within ASEAN are potential adversaries despite pretensions of being a 'security community', a viewpoint reinforced by the significant increase in defence expendi-ture among its members in the post-Cold War setting.[1]

The economic crisis gripping the region in the late 1990s may have curtailed concerns regarding an ASEAN arms race, but it has only exac-erbated the developments noted above by Hari Singh. This chapter takes the discussion on the security dilemma away from internal con-cerns and places it in its more traditional setting of inter-state rela-tions. The purpose of the chapter is twofold. First, to ascertain the applicability of the security dilemma to the evolving post-Cold War relationship amongst the ASEAN members, and to determine whether its operation lay behind the acquisition of power-projection weapons by the ASEAN states before the economic crisis erupted. Second, to examine the 'ASEAN way' as a mitigator of the security dilemma and determine whether in the late 1990s these norms of behaviour are themselves the subject of change.

The chapter is divided into four sections. The first explores the diffi-culties in applying the security dilemma to relations between weak states. The second focuses on the three characteristics of the security dilemma to determine if uncertainty, illusory incompatibility and paradoxical actions are in evidence. The third examines the ASEAN security complex to reveal the workings of the 'ASEAN way', and in so doing locates these norms of behaviour in relation to common security and security regimes. The final section provides an analysis of challenges to the 'ASEAN way' and what this might mean for the security dilemma.

A. The re-emergence of the sovereignty problem

It was noted in Chapter 2 that Brian Job did not consider the security dilemma relevant to Third World internal security issues. It is also evident that Job does not consider the security dilemma relevant to external security matters either. He argues that because weak states are concerned with their internal security, neighbouring weak states do not pose a security threat to one another and therefore the dynamics of the security dilemma will not operate. It is an argument that finds favour with Nicola Baker and Leonard Sebastian although they disagree with Job's findings regarding the relevance of the security dilemma to internal matters. They argue that weak states in the Asia-Pacific region were faced with internal security dilemmas during the Cold War and it was because of these that they 'were subject to a very weakened form of the external security dilemma'.[2] The argument that weak states are concerned with internal security matters and thus do not pose a threat to one another, combined with international law, which Job asserts protects state sovereignty, leads him to claim 'the assumptions of the traditional security dilemma metaphor are violated – states are preoccupied with internal rather than external security, and weak states have a guaranteed existence in what is supposedly an anarchic international environment'.[3] The argument that states are protected by the conventions of the current international society has also been noted by Peter Jackson. Jackson, who labels weak states quasi-states, contends that their statehood is protected:

> unlike Hobbes' realist scenario, the quasi-state cannot logically collapse into a state of nature because its sovereignty is derived not internally from empirical statehood but externally from the states-system whose members have evidently decided and are resolved that [their] jurisdiction shall not disappear.[4]

Consequently, the security dilemma does not operate because state 'survival is guaranteed not by their own efforts or those of their allies but by the new democratic post-colonial international society'.[5] In essence, these states do not exist in a self-help environment and therefore the security dilemma does not operate.

This argument though appears to be flawed on both counts. First, internal security issues can give rise to external security problems and interference. It was noted in the previous chapter that minority groups in Southeast Asia straddle international borders. This can have the effect of involving outside powers in a state's internal affairs. For instance, the use of violence by the regime in Burma against Karen separatists has resulted in the violation of Thai territory by Burmese forces. In May 1989 these incursions led to a direct military clash between Thai and Burmese troops while the latter were seeking to destroy a Karen base. The incident led the Karen living in Thailand to accuse the Thai government of complicity in allowing the attack, and when the Thai government offered to help negotiate between the Rangoon regime and the Karen separatists they were accused by Burma of interference in an internal matter.[6] Thus, a security issue within Burma led not only to Thai interest in Burmese affairs, but also led to criticism of the Thai government by their own people.

Border violations by either the Burmese army or the pro-Rangoon Democratic Karen Buddhist Army have continued throughout the 1990s. In March 1998 clashes occurred between Thai forces and pro-Rangoon guerrillas when the guerrilla forces attacked a Karen refugee camp. The incident led to the Thai Prime Minister, Chuan Leekpai, warning that if 'more border violations take place and cause damage, Thai forces are authorised to retaliate to the full extent'.[7] The treatment of the Patani Malays in southern Thailand by the Thai regime has also complicated Thailand's relations with Malaysia and led to some Malaysians providing support for the Patani separatists.[8] Therefore, while it is right to note the primacy of internal over external security issues in the Third World, because the former can give rise to the latter, neighbouring weak states do need to be aware of the possibility of security threats emanating from across the border. Of course this need not occur if the second reason cited – sovereignty safeguarded by international norms – negates the need for statesmen to fear others' intentions.

The second issue of international law and the norms of current international society governing state relations preventing the emergence of a security dilemma is however tenuous. Job cites the example of the international community rallying behind Kuwait in 1990–91 and expelling the Iraqi occupiers as supporting this case. However, paradoxically, this example highlights the failure of the norms governing international society to prevent the annexation in the first place. In the summer of 1990 Kuwait faced a real external threat from its neighbour, and while this is not an example of a security dilemma, it nevertheless highlights not the protection of state sovereignty by international society but rather its failure: Iraq was not deterred from annexing Kuwait. With regard to the subsequent reinstatement of Kuwaiti sovereignty, this has not always been guaranteed by the international community as evidenced by the occupation of East Timor by Indonesia.

International norms of behaviour may have lessened the use of violence by states, but they have not yet created an international security community and consequently statesmen still rely upon their own efforts in what remains a self-help environment. The security dilemma is thus not negated in the Third World as a consequence of either the primacy of internal security matters or international law. However, this does not mean that it automatically operates to the detriment of state relations. Whether it is active among the ASEAN members now becomes the issue for examination. However, before this a precondition needs to be noted.

The case that Third World states are concerned with internal matters could lead to the perception that they have little external security relations. Without external relations the security dilemma cannot operate. While it might be true that some regions have few external relations, it is not true of Southeast Asia where since independence, amity, in the guise of ASEAN and its forerunners ASA (Association of South-East Asia) and Maphilindo, and enmity, in the guise of *Konfrontasi* (Confrontation), have ensured that the region represents a security complex.[9] Details of an ASEAN security complex are provided below; at this stage it is sufficient to note that officials of ASEAN members meet under the association's auspices on average two hundred times a year.[10] They engage in dialogue over a vast array of issues in multilateral fora as well as bilaterally; it is a region in which there is much international interaction.

B. Three characteristics

Before determining if evidence of the three characteristics can be found it is helpful to recall their relationship to one another. It is because of the uncertainty statesmen have of each other's intentions that they take defensive actions to protect their state. However, because the other did not harbour malign intent – the incompatibility the statesmen perceive to exist is illusory – this defensive action has the paradoxical effect of creating concern in the other that it intends them harm. The outcome, which is a deterioration in relations, is a tragedy because neither sought to harm the other; they are both status quo powers. All three characteristics (uncertainty, illusory incompatibility, paradox) need to be in evidence otherwise a spiral of insecurity driven by the security dilemma will not occur.

The existence of one of these characteristics on its own does not indicate the security dilemma is in operation, all three need to be in evidence. If, for example, the other did intend harm – it was a revisionist power – then while uncertainty may exist the defensive actions are not paradoxical. The factors driving the insecurity the statesmen feel is not a tragedy over illusory incompatibility but rather the political machinations of the other. Thus, uncertainty although a necessary condition for a security dilemma is not a sufficient characteristic on its own to account for a security dilemma. Likewise, if faced by a revisionist power a status quo state embarks upon conciliatory policies, these actions are likely to be paradoxical as they make the goal of the revisionist easier to obtain, but they are not symptomatic of a security dilemma. It is the combination of the three characteristics that make the security dilemma operate. Can these three characteristics be seen in ASEAN relations during the 1990s?

1 Uncertainty

The lack of certainty in the anarchic nature of state relations means that statesmen remain unsure of their neighbours' intentions. Even if they believe that their neighbours' intentions are benign towards them now, this might change in the future and consequently prudence dictates that planning for the worst outcome is the most sensible option. When a region undergoes a dramatic change, as occurred in Southeast Asia after the Cold War, then uncertainty can rise as statesmen reassess their objectives. This need not result in a security dilemma and a deterioration of relations. Indeed, it could be the harbinger of peaceful relations. Whatever the effect such change has, it will certainly increase the degree of uncertainty among the interested parties.

One of the key consequences of the Cold War's conclusion is the declining engagement of the superpowers in Southeast Asia. Although the superpowers had been involved in the region prior to the Vietnamese invasion of Kampuchea, this act strengthened their role. The Soviet Union was able to gain influence by supplying Vietnam with military aid and providing Hanoi with security guarantees vis-à-vis China. While for the United States the Vietnamese invasion resulted in various defence arrangements with the ASEAN powers.[11] With the collapse of Soviet power and support – the bulk of which began to be scaled down from 1986 – Vietnam reversed its antagonistic relations with its Southeast Asian neighbours; a process that culminated in the most tangible difference between the Cold War and post-Cold War Southeast Asian security complexes with Vietnam's accession to ASEAN in 1995. The Russian presence has continued to be marginalised and with it Moscow's influence.

The United States military presence has also diminished although as the sole remaining superpower it still wields considerable influence in the region. This diminishing military presence, epitomised by the closure of Subic Bay and Clark airfield in the Philippines, has to some extent been off set by the conclusion of arrangements between the United States Navy and a number of the ASEAN countries for joint military exercises and access to port facilities.[12] Indeed, the US re-established military ties with the Philippines in 1999 with the ratification of a Visiting Forces Agreement by the Philippine Senate. The deployment of two American carrier groups off Taiwan's coast during the 1996 Taiwanese presidential election in response to Chinese military exercises, was a potent reminder that not only does the US possess the largest Pacific fleet but that it still retains interests in East Asia.

Nevertheless, the closure of Subic Bay in December 1992 marked for the first time in 45 years that the US did not have a base in Southeast Asia. In addition it is not clear that the United States would provide security guarantees for ASEAN. The United States has indicated that it would not interfere if China used force against the Philippines in the South China Sea, and relations between Indonesia and United States have fluctuated with concern over human rights violations leading to military exercises being suspended and arms sales cancelled.

The declining military presence of the two Cold War superpowers removes the dominating framework of external influence in Southeast Asian security. The 1990s thus began as a decade of uncertainty with ASEAN facing the challenge of a new security environment. Would past differences, frozen by the Cold War, thaw and re-emerge causing disharmony among the ASEAN membership? Would China emerge to fill the vacuum left by the declining superpower presence? With such uncertainties, the prospects of a security dilemma forming in the 1990s cannot be dismissed. The existence of a security dilemma between ASEAN and China will be examined in the next chapter; this chapter is concerned with intra-ASEAN relations.

Perhaps the greatest area of uncertainty within ASEAN lies in the relationship between the essentially Chinese city-state of Singapore and its Muslim neighbours to the north (Malaysia) and south (Indonesia). Singapore's expulsion from the Malaysian Federation in 1965, its small size and its ethnic demography created, according to Michael Leifer, 'an acute sense of vulnerability' in the mindsets of Singapore's decision-makers.[13] This insecurity was initially manifest by an abrasive approach in foreign relations that Leifer refers to as the 'poison-shrimp' policy – by making Singapore indigestible adversaries would be deterred from attacking. This sense of insecurity in their new-found sovereign statehood led the authorities to react negatively when they perceived others were acting in their internal affairs.

Thus, when the authorities in Singapore hanged two Indonesian marines in 1968 for acts of terrorism, they ignored the personal pleas of clemency from President Suharto. This indifference to the wishes of Indonesia, while legitimate, aggravated the situation. The hanging was followed in Jakarta by riots and vandalism directed against the Singapore embassy and local Chinese community. A similiar incident occurred in May 1995 when Filipino maid, Flor Contemplacion, was hanged for murder by the Singapore authorities despite the efforts of the then Philippine President, Fidel Ramos, to refer the matter to a third-party. The action resulted in Singapore-Philippine relations deteriorating and led to the resignation of the Philippine Foreign Minister, Roberto Romulo.[14]

Although relations between Singapore and Indonesia improved after 1968, Singapore's former Prime Minister and now Senior Minister, Lee Kuan Yew, did not make his first official visit to Jakarta until 1973. Despite the improvement in relations Singapore was the only ASEAN member initially not to support Indonesia's annexation of East Timor. Even in the 1990s when Singapore-Indonesia relations were good, suspicion remained in the relationship. It was Singapore's growing concern about the development of nuclear power in Indonesia which eventually led them to agree to the Southeast Asian Nuclear Weapons Free Zone (SEANWFZ).

In the aftermath of the fall of Suharto, the Singapore-Indonesian relationship has again deteriorated. The appointment of B.J. Habibie as President was not welcomed in Singapore. Habibie's plan to develop a cargo airport only 20 kilometres from Singapore and his pro-Muslim sentiments led to a difficult relationship with Singapore. Lee's comment that the fall in the value of the Indonesian rupiah was not unrelated to Habibie's appointment as Vice-President was indicative of the troubled relationship. Singapore's ambivalence towards Indonesia while they waited to see who would emerge as the new Indonesian President, was viewed by some in Jakarta as indifference to Indonesia's plight. Presidential aide, Dewi Fortuna Anwar, for example, commented, 'Who needs fair-weather friends who are by our side only when times are good?'[15] With the vote for independence in East Timor acting as a catalyst for Achenese demands for independence, Singapore's current concern focuses on whether the new President, Abdurrahman Wahid, and the Vice-President, Megawati Sukarnoputri, can prevent Indonesia imploding.

Unlike the Singapore-Indonesia relationship, the Chinese-city state's relationship with Malaysia has remained strained ever since independence and is consequently marked by suspicion. The reasons are numerous, focusing on the ethnic mix in both countries and their fractious experience when Singapore was part of the Malaysian Federation between 1963 and 1965.[16] They have since continued to respond aggressively to internal developments in each other's country. In November 1986 when the Israeli President, Chaim Herzog, visited Singapore the Muslim population of Malaysia responded by burning the Singapore flag and effigies of Lee Kuan Yew, while Lee's description of the Malaysian state of Johor as an area of known criminality resulted in a diplomatic furore in 1997.

Their history and ethnic demography have led both to view developments within the other as impinging upon their security. For instance the restrictions placed on Malays in the Singapore Armed Forces (SAF) is intended, according to Lee Hsien Loong, to 'avoid dividing soldiers' loyalties between their 'nation' (Singapore) and their religion (Islam)'.[17] Indeed, Singapore's defence strategy is based on deterring an attack from Malaysia and, because of its small size and its dependency on Malaysia for its water and food supplies, launching a pre-emptive strike and penetration of Malaysian territory if a Malaysian attack is thought likely.[18] This does not mean that war is likely, although the assertion by Malaysia's ex-Defence Minister Syed Hamid Albar that 'Malaysia has never considered such a possibility' is disingenuous.[19] Whatever the prospect of war, it is clear is that suspicion continues to mar the Singapore-Malaysia relationship. This was given ample evidence with the arrest of nine spies in Malaysia in 1989 for selling military secrets to an ASEAN member,[20] and in 1998 the relationship dipped to a low not witnessed for many years.

The relationship deteriorated in 1998 with both sides failing to reach a formal agreement on the supply of water from Malaysia to Singapore;

the location of customs, immigration and quaratine (CIQ) facilities on the railway line in Singapore; investments promised to one another failed to materialise and Singapore refused to lift a rule which prevented Malaysian workers in Singapore withdrawing their provident fund savings (a pension scheme) until they reached the age of 55, a rule which does not apply to any other foreign worker. Lee published his memoirs which revealed the distrust between the United Malays National Organisation and the People's Action Party during Singapore's membership of the Malaysian Federation, and the resentment he felt about Singapore's expulsion. His view that the 'basic factors or problems that troubled us in the past have not changed' reflects the failure of the two states to improve their relations.[21] In September, Malaysia rescinded the agreements allowing Singapore's air force access to Malaysian air space, Mahathir spoke about Malaysia taking 'back our territory bit by bit', and in October Singapore increased its defence preparations.[22] The Malaysian decision to withdraw from the 1998 Five Power Defence Arrangements (FPDA) exercise, in part due to the poor state of Malaysia-Singapore relations, epitomises the suspicion and distrust which continues to mar this relationship in the heart of Southeast Asia.[23]

Although there is no official leader among the ASEAN members, for the first thirty years of its life Indonesia considered itself first among equals. It is not by chance that the ASEAN Secretariat is located in Jakarta and that the first meeting of the ASEAN Heads of State was convened in Bali. This self-perception as the region's great power manifested itself during Sukarno's rule in an assertive and confrontational foreign policy. Free from colonial rule, Sukarno sought to limit external influence and responded to Malaysia's creation (interpreted as a form of imperialism by Sukarno) by declaring *Konfrontasi*. The replacement of Sukarno with Suharto in 1966 introduced a new approach to achieving and maintaining Indonesia's regional supremacy. Suharto adopted a cooperative approach and used ASEAN as a vehicle for enhancing Indonesia's status.

Indonesia's position was accepted by the other powers because Suharto did not impose Indonesian interests to the detriment of their interests. Thus, while ASEAN's Zone of Peace, Freedom and Neutrality (ZOPFAN) declaration supported Indonesia's goal of limiting the influence of external powers in the region, the defence ties of the other ASEAN states with external powers were not challenged despite the apparent contradiction. With the retreat of the superpowers at the end of the Cold War there was some concern among the ASEAN membership regarding Indonesia's willingness to continue to contain itself, or whether it would seek to gain regional supremacy at the expense of Asian sensibilities. Such perceptions were probably coloured by Malaysia's historical (pre-colonial) experience with Indonesia. Muthiah Alagappa notes that '[i]t may…be possible to link some aspects of the international behaviour of contemporary Indonesia and Malaysia and the tensions in their bilateral relationship to the historical rivalries and tensions between Javanese (Majapahit) and Malay (Malacca, Sri Vijaya) kingdoms and the attempt by the former to control the latter'.[24]

Prior to the upheavals of the late 1990s, which saw the resignation of Suharto, the short-lived presidency of B.J. Habibie and the election of Abdurrahman Wahid, Indonesia's lasting internal political stability had generated greater self-confidence. Suharto's first concern on assuming power in the mid-1960s was with internal development, and in his 1990 national address he argued that such development now permitted Indonesia to act in world affairs. He attended his first non-aligned heads of government meeting since 1970 in Belgrade in 1989 and was elected chairman in 1991. This greater international role, Michael Vatikiotis suggests, raised concern in neighbouring states since the 'region's previous experience of Indonesia articulating a more active foreign policy was not a happy one, and this perception seems to have survived the end of the Sukarno era'.[25] Within ASEAN, Indonesia became more forceful with its rejection of Malaysia's East Asian Economic Group (EAEG) proposal and the Singaporean initiative of inviting major powers to accede to the Treaty of Amity and Cooperation.[26] Hari Singh suggests that Indonesia's more assertive approach was one of the reasons which lay behind ASEAN's desire to admit Vietnam in 1995. He writes, 'Hanoi's balancing role in the context of intra-ASEAN threat perceptions must also be acknowledged.'[27] This does not mean that Indonesia was about to embark upon anything like *Konfrontasi* again, however, with greater self-confidence being exhibited by Malaysia, with their charismatic leader Mahathir Mohamad, and Singapore, how intra-ASEAN power relations between these three would develop was uncertain. The effect on Indonesia of the East Asian economic crisis has nevertheless been so severe that concerns regarding a self-confident, assertive power have dissipated. Indeed, it is the prospect of Indonesia imploding that raises security concerns amongst its neighbours in the latter 1990s. The immediate concerns focus on the safety of the four important shipping lanes (the straits of Malacca, Sunda, Lombok, Ombai and Savu) and the wave of refugees seeking asylum. With Jakarta concentrating on the state's internal security problems, neighbouring powers' suspicions of Indonesia's ambitions in the region have declined. Uncertainty remains, however, while the outcome of the economic crisis, and its attendant political and social effects, remain unknown.

Uncertainty also marks Thai-Malaysia relations concerning the activities of terrorists on their border. During the Cold War, the activities of the Communist Party of Malaya (CPM) were aided, according to Kuala Lumpur, by the lack of assistance forthcoming from Bangkok when the communists were operating from bases in Southern Thailand. This suspicion gains credence because, Leifer argues, the Thai government perceived the CPM's activities 'as a useful obstacle to Muslim separatism or Malay irredentism' among its Patani Malay population in the south.[28] With the collapse of the CPM and the demands of independence from the Muslims lessening, talks began in April 1993 within the framework of the Committee to Review Border Cooperation to solve the border issue. However, in August and September 1993 a series of arson attacks on schools, the killing of two Thai soldiers and an attack on a train by the Patani United Liberation Organisation acted as stark reminders that the Thai-Malaysian border remains a bone of contention.[29] This combined with the tensions over violations of territorial waters by fishing vessels led Wilfried Herrmann to note, 'Thai experts consider Malaysia to be the main security-political/military threat in their short-term situation assessment.'[30]

While it remains very unlikely that Thai-Malaysia relations would deteriorate to such an extent that Bangkok and Kuala Lumpur would begin to view one another as a serious security threat, the potential for armed clashes is very real. In response to the sinking of a Thai trawler by the Malaysian navy on 6 November 1995, the then Thai Defence Minister and now former Thai Prime Minister, General Chavalit Yongchaiyudh, warned that Thailand might have to retaliate, while it was also announced that a flotilla of trawlers led by 'three fisheries department vessels' would enter Malaysian waters in protest at the Malaysian action.[31] The incident did not lead to a further deterioration of Thai-Malaysian relations, but it acts as a reminder that border disputes, whether at sea or on land, have the potential to escalate when the parties to the dispute are uncertain of the other's intentions.

Thailand's relations with other ASEAN members in continental Southeast Asia are also marred by uncertainty and mistrust. In this instance, such suspicions have their roots (beginning in the fourteenth century) in the historical struggles for domination among the expansionist Thai (Ayuthia), Vietnamese and Burmese kingdoms at the expense of the Khmer (Cambodian) empire and the Laotian kingdom.

The legacy of these clashes is that Thailand and Vietnam view one another as rivals and compete for power at the expense of Laos and Cambodia, while Thailand's relations with Burma remain strained because of Rangoon's infiltration of Thai territory when it attacks the Karens based along the border. Alagappa notes that because of the region's early history, '[d]eep resentment and distrust characterises relations among all these countries'.[32]

Intra-mural disharmony exists therefore within ASEAN, not because there exists the fear of an impending intra-ASEAN war, but rather because of the uncertainty the states have about future relations with one another. This uncertainty focuses not only on unresolved problems from the Cold War, but also on new contentious maritime boundaries generated by the 1982 international law of the sea which came into force on the 16 November 1994. This provides a 200 nautical mile Exclusive Economic Zone (EEZ) for coastal states, which in the South China Sea has created overlapping sea claims. The most notorious are amongst a myriad of islands and reefs collectively known as the Spratlys. The conflicting claims in the South China Sea are not just among ASEAN members, but they also involve China; the South China Sea dispute is therefore examined in the following chapter.

Uncertainty is thus prevalent among ASEAN members because of territorial disputes and ethnic differences. The existence of conflicting territorial disputes however immediately raises a query over the security dilemma's applicability. If states hold conflicting territorial claims how can the incompatibility of their goals be illusory?

2   Illusory incompatibility?

For both Herbert Butterfield and John Herz the essence of the security dilemma is that it is a tragedy in which both parties perceive the incompatibility of their objectives to be real, when in fact the incompatibility is illusory. Applying this to territorial disputes requires a closer examination of the participant's objectives. The existence of the dispute signals the existence of the incompatibility, and since both claim the territory at one level this difference is real. However, the intensity of the dispute may be sufficiently low that neither participant considers the use of force a realistic option with which to solve it. In the short term both claimants are thus status quo; neither harbours a desire to force the issue and decide the fate of the territorial dispute. However, neither claimant can be sure that this present state of affairs will last, and in the future one of them may seek a solution on its terms. The acquisition of weapons by one of the claimants, or a more bellicose approach in state relations, could therefore raise concern in the other that this indicates the emergence of a revisionist goal. If this assumption is false (it remains a status quo power) and both engage in tit-for-tat actions that appear to confirm the other's worst fears, then despite the existence of a real incompatibility over the disputed territory, the security dilemma is operating. It operates because although the participants maintain their claim to the territory they do not seek to alter the present situation, and thus the perception created by the actions taken are based on an illusory incompatibility.

The Malaysia-Philippine dispute over the state of Sabah on the island of Borneo is a good example of how a security dilemma could operate even when both parties claim the same territory. The Philippines claim Sabah on historical grounds arguing that British occupation, in the guise of the British North Borneo Company, did not entail the transfer of sovereignty.[33] For Kuala Lumpur, Sabah's accession to the Federation of Malaysia in 1963 ensures it belongs to Malaysia. The issue, while not resulting in conflict between the two states, remains unresolved. It periodically flares up with the most serious incidents occurring in the late 1960s, notably the Corregidor Affair, and it wasn't until the removal of Philippine President Marcos in 1986 that the strain in the relations caused by the Corregidor Affair began to subside.[34] In May 1993 Philippine President Ramos reiterated that Manila had not given up its claim, while in November 1998 Kuala Lumpur sought assurances from Manila that the Estrada administration would not revive the Philippine claim after a task force was established to review the Sabah issue.[35] While the Philippines gave assurances that the claim was not a priority, the claim has not been abrogated and Sabah remains a disputed territory.

Despite the longevity of the dispute the prospect of war occurring between the Philippines and Malaysia is remote. Nevertheless, should Malaysia-Philippine relations deteriorate for other reasons – for instance, Manila suspects that Muslims in Sabah are supporting the Muslim separatists in Mindanao – then Malaysian concerns regarding Philippine intentions over Sabah could arise. The refusal of Manila to drop the Sabah claim could exacerbate worst-case thinking in Kuala Lumpur leading to a deterioration in relations even though the Philippines may have no intention of annexing Sabah.

The perception that ASEAN members are status quo powers but could harbour revisionist ambitions in the future captures the condition of many intra-ASEAN security relations. An outline of territorial disputes among ASEAN members is given in Table 4.1.[36] The key for the

Table 4.1   Territorial claims among ASEAN members

---
* Philippine claim to the Malaysian state of Sabah
* Competing claims to the islands and reefs in the Spratlys involving Vietnam, Brunei, Malaysia and the Philippines
* Boundary dispute between Indonesia and Vietnam on the demarcation line on the continental shelf near the Natuna Island
* Border dispute between Vietnam and Cambodia
* Boundary dispute between Malaysia and Vietnam on their off-shore demarcation line
* Malaysian-Singapore dispute over the ownership of the Pulau Batu Putih island
* Competing claims by Malaysia and Indonesia to the islands of Sipadan, Sebatik and Ligitan as well as the border between Sarawak and Kalimantan on the island of Borneo
* Border dispute between Malaysia and Thailand
* Border dispute between Thailand and Burma

Source: Desmond Ball, 'Arms and Affluence: Military Acquisitions in the Asia-Pacific Region', *International Security*, 18/3 (Winter 1993/94), p. 88.

security dilemma is that although these are areas of real incompatibility the likelihood of force being used to solve them is low. Therefore, the acquisition of military forces by one of the disputants does not necessarily indicate an attempt to acquire the territory. However, the very existence of the dispute could raise concern that the acquisition of military equipment, if not purchased for that immediate goal, could still be used in the future if a revisionist ambition was adopted. If a build-up of arms was to follow as each believed the other had adopted a revisionist goal, or would once it had the military capability to take the disputed territory, but they were in fact only arming in response to one another, then the spiral of insecurity would be based upon an illusory incompatibility – they remained status quo powers.

Desmond Ball refers to this when he writes, 'there remains much fertile ground for regional conflict [but] ... most of these issues are unlikely to lead to inter-state conflict ... Nevertheless, all of them remain sources of tension, suspicion, and misunderstanding. In all cases, the parties concerned maintain at least a "watching brief" on the issues.'[37] Amitav Acharya concurs that the likelihood of inter-state conflict is low, and while noting that 'recent concerns about a regional arms race among ASEAN states may be somewhat overstated', nevertheless warns, 'the unresolved intra-ASEAN territorial disputes cannot be discounted as one of the factors behind the massive increase in defence expenditures and weapons acquisition by its member-states'.[38]

The existence of territorial disputes, and thus at one level a real incompatibility, does not negate the applicability of the security dilemma because the dispute can be between two status quo powers. The existence of a quiescent territorial claim could therefore generate a security dilemma, since neither is actively seeking to change the status quo but the existence of the claim could lead to actions being interpreted to that affect. Among the ASEAN membership there is uncertainty and, it is argued, illusory incompatibility. However, the security dilemma is also dependent upon actions being taken which prove self-defeating, or paradoxical, for it be active. This is often manifest in an arms build-up and this is the next area of investigation.

3 Paradoxical actions

This third and final characteristic of the security dilemma occurs because of the other two. The actors' uncertainties lead them to take actions which, because both are acting for defensive reasons only, make the situation worse by creating for the other an image of aggressive intent. In inter-state relations these paradoxical or self-defeating actions are usually manifest by an arms build-up. The acquisition of military equipment does not though automatically initiate a security dilemma. If the weapons are deployed in a discernibly defensive force posture then the other state need not fear their procurement since they are incapable of offensive action; the security dilemma is avoided. However, even if the weapons procured have an offensive capability and are deployed in such a manner to highlight that capability this does not automatically mean that a security dilemma is in operation. If the equipment is procured for domestic reasons – modernisation, internal suppression, prestige, corruption – rather than because the state is suspicious of its neighbour's intentions, then the weapons procurement does not indicate a security dilemma is in operation; they could though instigate a security dilemma if they give rise to suspicion in neighbouring states. It is not therefore sufficient simply to note that an arms build-up is occurring, it is necessary to determine the reasons behind the arms build-up and whether the military postures adopted indicate an offensive capability.

Prior to the recent economic crisis in Southeast Asia, the rate of arms accumulation in the region rose in the aftermath of the Cold War. There was a real increase in expenditure between 1985 and 1996 by Indonesia of US$1,402 million, by Malaysia of US$1,133 million, by the Philippines of US$810 million, by Singapore of US$2,337 million and Thailand of US$1,653 million. One of the latest recruits to ASEAN,

Burma, increased its defence expenditure between 1985 and 1996 by US$729 million. There was a rise in the delivery of arms to East Asia from 11.9 per cent in 1987 to 23 per cent in 1996 of all weapon transfers in the world. Only the Middle East in 1996 received more weapons. Spending US$700 million each in 1996, Thailand and Indonesia were the largest arms purchasers in Southeast Asia; which for Indonesia amounted to a rise of US$530 million from 1995.[39] Both states were the hardest hit by the economic crisis, however, and this severely curtailed their procurement programmes. Indonesia postponed indefinitely its procurement plans, while the Thai government sought another buyer for the F/A-18 Hornet jet fighters it ordered from the US.[40]

The economic crisis has affected the other states in the region to a lesser extent. Malaysia has deferred its modernisation programme to the year 2000, and while it has announced its intention to purchase two frigates it has put on hold plans to buy submarines and attack helicopters.[41] Singapore meanwhile has begun to take delivery of advanced F-16 fighters from the US and has no plans to curtail its order of 30 planes, indeed its defence budget in February 1998 raised defence spending from 4.4 per cent of GDP to 4.6 per cent.[42] The Philippines has also announced a S$13 billion modernisation programme including the purchase of 24 multi-role fighter aircraft and 7 patrol vessels, although this procurement programme is highly dependent on an economic upturn.[43] The region, therefore, clearly witnessed an arms build-up in the early to mid-1990s before the 'tiger economies' were humbled by the region's economic crisis. Why did these states in the 1990s increase their defence expenditures, and why did they buy sophisticated power projection forces? Did the reasons include fear and suspicion of their neighbours' intentions?

The reasons for the arms build-up in Southeast Asia were multifarious. Ball highlights thirteen factors – economic growth and increasing resources for defence spending; the requirements of enhanced self-reliance; the drawdown of the US presence and capabilities; fears about Japan and China; regional conflict among Southeast Asian states; requirements for protecting EEZ; broadening regional security concerns; prestige; technology acquisition; corruption; supply-side pressures; pre-emption of international restraints on arms transfers; arms race dynamics – which explain the arms acquisitions in East Asia. The economic growth in the region, combined with the availability of military equipment as weapon manufacturers sought new markets with the end of the Cold War, were undoubtedly the key conditions for enabling the arms build-up to occur. The declining US presence coupled with fears about their Southeast Asian neighbours and the growing interest of China and Japan in the region, as well as the types of equipment needed to protect EEZs, are the factors of relevance to the emergence of a security dilemma. The issue of corruption and prestige are factors that help to explain specific purchases, such as Thailand's aircraft carrier the *Chakri Naruebet*, while the existence of an arms race could signify that a security dilemma is in operation.[44]

Writing in 1993, Ball highlights the wealth of the ASEAN states and their need to provide for themselves as the US presence declined as the key factors behind the arms build-up. Indeed, he notes factors 'such as threat perceptions or arms race dynamics, have generally been less determinate than other considerations'.[45] It is a conclusion that Mak and Hamzah concur with when in 1995 they wrote, '[d]efence spending in the post-Cold War situation, at least among the ASEAN countries, is more resource driven rather than driven by specific threat perceptions'.[46] These conclusions are important because in the early 1990s it was difficult to discern which factors were the more important.[47] By 1997 Chien-pin Li concluded that corruption and state-subsidised defence industries were the main determinants, which combined with Ball and Mak/Hamzah indicate that the arms build-up did not indicate paradoxical policies and was thus not a manifestation of a security dilemma.[48] The sudden postponement and cancellation of orders by some ASEAN members in the wake of the economic crisis confirms the importance of economic growth in enabling the arms build-up to occur.

However, Chien-pin Li cautions that although they might be procured for internal reasons weapons can still be used against external neighbours; while Ball and Mak/Hamzah despite highlighting the resource factors also focus on the factors that are more pertinent to the security dilemma. Mak and Hamzah note how with the end of the Cold War, uncertainty has come to dominate contingency planning in the region. With regard to Singapore the possibility of regime change in Indonesia – which duly occurred in 1998 – and Malaysia, where Islamic groups are gaining popular support, could foretell a worsening of relations. They write, 'Singapore's defence planning is increasingly based on meeting the unpredictable'.[49] In Malaysia, Mak and Hamzah quote the former defence chief, General Abdul Rahman, explaining that modernising the military was necessary because 'no one knew who would become the country's enemies and threaten its sovereignty'. They conclude that although a hostile arms race is not occurring, one 'powered by the dictates of contingency planning, or uncertainty-based planning' is in operation.[50] They quote David Denoon who captures perfectly how such an arms race can instigate a security dilemma because with contingency planning, 'there is no obvious boundary between taking prudent steps to prepare for future challenges and taking actions that could be perceived as threatening others and thus stimulate hostile responses'.[51] Thus, although Mak and Hamzah consider resource factors the primary reason behind the arms build-up, they also note that contingency planning on the worst-case scenario was prevalent.

The danger of the security dilemma arising because of the increasing attempts by the ASEAN states to achieve greater self-reliance is noted by Malcolm Chalmers. He writes:

> when four or more, roughly equivalent, military powers in a region seek self-reliance – that is, the ability to defend themselves without help – they cannot all attain it simultaneously. If one country seeks to maximise its own security…it will generate increased concerns amongst its neighbours, and will tend to provoke countervailing action. Even where, as is the case at present, ASEAN political leaders have no reason to fear their existing counterparts, they still harbour concerns about future political trends. Signs of arms builds in neighbouring states will, therefore, tend to encourage precautionary build-ups in response.[52]

Ball also notes that their need for self-reliance, or self-help, was engineering an arms build-up with three worrying developments. First, the lack of transparency in the region created an 'atmosphere of uncertainty and some lack of trust'. Second, the lack of any clear threat resulted in justification of weapon procurements 'simply not ring[ing] true … [and] leading to misunderstandings and unanticipated and unfortunate reactions'; and finally, the type of equipment the states were purchasing.[53] This latter point is particularly important for the security dilemma. Even in an atmosphere of uncertainty and suspicion the security dilemma will not operate if the armaments of the other do not pose a threat. However, if they are power-projection forces with offensive capabilities then clearly they could pose a threat. With the creation of EEZs the ASEAN members were busy acquiring the type of power-projection capabilities they needed to provide surveillance and protection for their new resources. Some of these purchases are outlined in Table 4.2, although a caveat should be added that some of these planned acquisitions have been postponed because of the economic crisis. The fact these purchases may not occur is less important than the fact these weapons possess offensive capabilities, since it is this capability that can drive the security dilemma. The table therefore

Table 4.2   Planned ASEAN weapon acquisitions

- *Indonesia* has rebuilt its air and naval capabilities with the acquisition of 12 F-16 fighter aircraft, and in August 1997 Jakarta ordered 12 Russian SU-30Ks. In addition it is set to acquire 40 Hawk combat-capable training aircraft from the UK by 1999, over half of which have been delivered. In addition to the purchase of 39 ships from the East German navy in 1992 nine minesweepers and five submarines have been ordered for delivery in 1997 and 1998.
- *Malaysia* is likewise improving its air and naval capabilities. It has acquired 200 fighter aircraft from the US (F-18s), the UK (Hawk) and Russia (MiG-29s) while it has also received frigates and submarines. For reconnaissance they have purchased Beechcraft B200T maritime patrol aircraft from the United States.
- *The Philippines* are seeking to acquire 24 fighter jets and are considering the F/A-18 Hornet and F-16 from the US, the Mirage 2000 from France, the Kfir 2000 from Israel, the MiG-29 from Russia and the Swedish designed Grippen. They are also seeking to acquire three frigates and six corvettes.
- *Singapore* has purchased a squadron of F-16 fighter aircraft, and four submarines from Sweden. A variety of helicopters have been ordered as have minehunters.
- *Thailand* has ordered 18 A-7 fighter aircraft from the US as well as F-16s and British vertical take-off Harriers. It has acquired frigates as well as its aircraft carrier.
- *Vietnam* has ordered 12 SU-27s from Russia and 6 MiG-21Bs from the Ukraine.

Source: Mark J. Valencia, 'Asia, the Law of the Sea and international relations', *International Affairs*, 73/2 (April 1997), p. 267. *The Military Balance 1997/98* (IISS). Malcolm Chalmers and Owen Greene, *Taking Stock: The UN Register After Two Years* (Bradford Arms Register Studies No. 5, Westview Press, 1995). *The Straits Times*, 28 April 1998.

includes those acquisitions that have been postponed because the key factor is that the planned acquisitions possessed offensive capabilities.

The acquisition of such sophisticated aircraft as the F-16/18, SU-27/30 and MiG-29s with their array of air-to-air and air-to-surface missiles, plus maritime craft equipped with anti-ship missiles, would provide these ASEAN states not only with the capability to protect their territory but also to attack the territory of their neighbours. Hence, Chalmers' assertion that 'the new weapon systems of regional states can be used – and are designed to be used – in attacks on the territory (at sea or on land) of neighbouring states'.[54] These are therefore the type of armaments that could trigger counter-acquisitions and provide a tangible manifestation of the security dilemma. For Ball the most worrying are the fighter plane purchases because the 'quantitative and qualitative enhancements of air power are perhaps the most likely to trigger unanticipated and undesired arms acquisition competitions'.[55]

It is unclear if this began to occur among all the ASEAN members by the mid-1990s. There are particular instances where weapon purchases appeared to be designed to counter those of neighbouring states. Singapore's interest in acquiring the Patriot air defence system is widely believed to be because Indonesia showed an interest in acquiring Scud missiles. The Thai decision to purchase F-16s seems to have been prompted by Singapore's decision to do the same, while Bangkok's interest in the Tornado fighter aircraft began after Malaysia considered acquiring the European plane. The sale of the United States AIM-120A AMRAAM (advanced medium-range air-to-air missile system) to Thailand was justified on the grounds that Malaysia's MiG-29s were equipped with similar weapons. However, in the Thai case it is difficult to discern if countering neighbours' acquisitions is the key reason behind the purchases, with both prestige and corruption allegedly important determining factors.[56]

It is a worrying development that in the most strained intra-ASEAN relationship, according to Tim Huxley, arm procurements by Singapore and Malaysia can be understood as countering one another. Writing before the economic crisis, Huxley states that 'many recent and potential improvements in the Malaysian armed forces' capabilities are almost certainly intended as counters to developments in the Singapore Armed Forces. A prime example is the new Malaysian emphasis on air defence, which is essentially a belated response to the Singapore air force's ability to devastate the Malaysian air force and command facilities in the first few hours of any conflict between the two countries.'[57] His analysis that the Malaysian intention to procure MiG-29s 'may provide a justification for Singapore's air force to follow up its long-standing interest in the F-18' indicated the initial operation of an arms race and a manifestation of a security dilemma.[58]

Summary

Prior to the economic crisis intra-ASEAN relations would appear to have been ripe for a security dilemma. The uncertainty of the post-Cold War era with the United States military presence on the decline, combined with territorial disputes left unresolved from the Cold War and new maritime disputes emerging, mixed with the acquisition of sophisticated military equipment, create fertile grounds for the seeds of the security dilemma to grow. Yet, for ASEAN as a whole the security dilemma operates in only a mild form, and only in the Singapore-Malaysia relationship does it operate with any degree of severity and even here the intensity varies. Consequently, ASEAN has been variously described by

Barry Buzan as representing a security regime, quasi-security community and a security community.[59] It is therefore necessary to examine the ASEAN security complex to determine how, given the existence of the security dilemma's three characteristics, the region has managed to mitigate its detrimental effects by becoming a security regime.

C. The ASEAN security complex: the 'ASEAN way'

The term 'security complex' has been coined by Barry Buzan to refer to a region where states 'primary security concerns link together sufficiently closely that their national securities cannot realistically be considered apart from one another'.[60] Within a security complex the relations between its members can be plotted along a spectrum depending upon the levels of amity and enmity exhibited. For Buzan, amity refers to the 'expectation of protection or support', while enmity refers to relationships beset 'by suspicion and fear'.[61] Where the states' security interdependence is marked by enmity, Buzan refers to the security complex at this extreme end of the spectrum as Raimo Väyrynen's conflict formation. Towards amity lies a security regime, while at the amity extreme end of the spectrum is Karl Deutsch's security community.[62] This ties in with the security dilemma, with it operating strongest with high levels of enmity and gradually weakening as amity becomes the dominating force. Determining therefore where along this spectrum the ASEAN security complex lies will help to ascertain the severity of the security dilemma.

The relationship between security regimes, communities and the security dilemma focuses on the removal of the uncertainty that leads to worst-case thinking by establishing norms of behaviour. In a security regime the key element is that the norms and rules which constrain and guide state behaviour entail more than the following of short-term interest. Statesmen are prepared to accept short-term losses on the understanding that, in moments of relative weakness, they will not be taken advantage of (that is, other states will be restrained), that other states will also endure moments of relative weakness (that is, the roles will be reversed and reciprocation will occur), and that ultimately their security will improve. The extent to which these norms of behaviour will affect the security dilemma's operation depends upon the scale of the regime. If the regime operates on specific sub-issues in the states' security relationship then its ameliorating effects will be slight, although success on one issue could lead to security regimes being created on others, thus having a greater impact on the security dilemma.

A security regime encompassing more security issues, especially if it is institutionalised with procedures for punishing defection, will have a much greater impact on reducing state uncertainty and mistrust. When norms are established about abolishing the use of force as an instrument for settling disputes the regime becomes a security community. In a security community the security dilemma cannot operate because there exists 'a real assurance that the members of that community will not fight each other physically, but will settle their disputes in some other way'.[63] In this respect, the members of the European Union form a security community since it is inconceivable that force would be used to settle disputes that arise among its membership. Therefore, if the ASEAN security complex lies towards the amity end of Buzan's spectrum determining whether it is a security regime or security community will reveal whether the security dilemma could operate. This section is concerned with ASEAN prior to the challenges of economic crisis and membership expansion that occurred in the late 1990s.

From its inception in 1967, ASEAN has provided a security function, although not in a military sense because the founders (Indonesia, Malaysia, Singapore, Thailand and the Philippines) were aware that this could lend credence to the charge that ASEAN was a replacement for the defunct Western-inspired military alliance SEATO (South-East Asian Treaty Organisation). Acharya writes that ASEAN was created with an awareness that a military alliance 'was likely to invite counter-measures from…China and the Soviet Union, thereby intensifying Great Power rivalry in the region and aggravating the sense of insecurity felt by the ASEAN states'.[64] This awareness, that an explicit security function in the form of a military alliance would be counter-productive, bodes well for ASEAN leaders recognising the dynamics of a security dilemma. The lack of a commonly perceived external threat, and the various tensions that existed and continue to exist among the members, also made a military alliance problematic.

A military security function would also be inappropriate, since the security issues facing these states in the 1960s were largely internal with the regimes occupied with achieving regime and state legitimacy in the face of communist insurgency and ethnic secessionist demands. A military alliance among states that possessed few capabilities to aid one another would be both unhelpful and counter-productive. Thus, the primary functions of ASEAN are 'to accelerate the economic growth, social progress and cultural development in the region' which would promote peace and create a stable region by reducing the internal threats of communism and separatism.[65] Specifically, ASEAN was created to stabilise the region after *Konfrontasi* and the Malaysia-Philippine dispute over Sabah, and it is no coincidence that ASEAN's inaugural meeting was in Bangkok since Thailand had not become involved in *Konfrontasi*, and had tried to mediate between Malaysia and Indonesia and also between Malaysia and the Philippines over Sabah.

The extent to which the security approach adopted by ASEAN creates a series of norms that constrain and guide state behaviour will reveal whether ASEAN is a security regime. The success of the ASEAN membership in achieving security can be explained by their adoption of an approach that has similar characteristics to that of common security.[66] Common security was a label used by the Palme Commission in the early 1980s to identify a cooperative approach to security which recognises that the security of states is interdependent and that only when statesmen conceive of security as a shared goal – as opposed to achieving security at one another's expense – can states acquire security. For the Palme Commission the existence of nuclear weapons was central for making the interdependence of state security explicit; Washington's security was dependent upon restraint in Moscow and vice-versa. In Southeast Asia such weapons are not in the states' armouries, instead, the interdependence of their security was made explicit by the existence of common problems that required collective action to overcome them. The two common security problems that the members faced were internal threats to the regimes in power and the involvement of extra-regional powers in the region. Only by acting in concert could the ASEAN states solve these security threats.

The security approach adopted by ASEAN to overcome these common problems was termed 'regional resilience' by ex-Indonesian President Suharto, and is dervied from Indonesia's national resilience. National resilience refers to the security of the nation emerging from the strength of national development. Thus, national resilience covers all aspects of nation-building – ideological, political, economic, social, cultural – and identifies the security of the state being dependent upon the loyalty of the population to that state. By focusing on internal issues and addressing the dangers of subversion, the state remains a viable entity and prevents the contagion of communist insurgency and ethnic separatism from infecting neighbouring states. Consequently, if all states adopted national resilience they would provide regional stability (regional resilience). Regional resilience has been likened to a chain in which the chain derives its strength from its constituent parts.

Regional resilience would likewise support national resilience by creating stable external relations which would enable the regimes to concentrate on national development. Michael Leifer captures the logic of the process when he writes, '[b]y cultivating intra-mural accord and so reducing threats among themselves, the ASEAN states would be able to devote themselves through the instrumentality of economic development to the common cause of political stability'.[67] ASEAN publicly endorsed regional resilience in the 1976 Treaty of Amity and Cooperation in Southeast Asia (TAC) and the 1971 Zone of Peace, Freedom and Neutrality (ZOPFAN).[68] The TAC also reaffirmed the ASEAN principles enshrined in the 1967 Bangkok Declaration (mutual respect for political independence, territorial integrity, and national identity; non-interference in the internal affairs of one another; peaceful settlement of disputes; renunciation of the threat or use of force; and effective cooperation), as well as establishing a High Council to settle disputes among its membership; it also contains the provision that ASEAN is open to accession by other states in Southeast Asia.

The adoption of regional resilience is thus an acknowledgement that because one member's problems can affect its neighbours, the security of all members is indivisible. Only by adopting a common security approach (regional resilience) could they address these common problems; in essence this has become an agreement by the ASEAN members not to interfere in one another's internal concerns in the knowledge that this would be reciprocated. Hence, Malcolm Chalmers' statement that 'common security took the form of a strong norm of non-interference in each other's internal affairs'.[69] Non-interference was a trademark of ASEAN throughout the Cold War and thus when Indonesia annexed East Timor and was subjected to a hostile resolution in the General Assembly of the United Nations in December 1975, ASEAN members supported Indonesia's position.[70]

Regional resilience is also linked to the problems of extra-regional power involvement in Southeast Asia. The involvement of outside powers in the region led Southeast Asia to become a battleground where these extra-regional powers could pursue their ambitions to the detriment of the regional states' development. By acting in concert the ASEAN members could limit or at least influence this outside interference. The ZOPFAN declaration emphasised the role of regional resilience in maintaining security by calling on ASEAN members to neutralise the region from outside interference. However, the members' lack of military capability to protect themselves from attack resulted in many, with the exception of Indonesia, retaining external security ties with Western powers. ZOPFAN was not a statement of fact but rather an objective to be achieved through the realisation of national and regional resilience.

With ZOPFAN a goal for the future, the members of ASEAN discovered that by working in concert their combined voices gave them the ability to control the involvement of extra-regional powers in Southeast Asia. This was manifest during Vietnam's occupation of Cambodia, when ASEAN members, by acting in concert, were able to keep the Cambodian crisis on the international agenda and set the agenda.[71] Using their membership of the United Nations; the Organisation of Islamic Conference; the Commonwealth; their bilateral ties with, amongst others, the United States, the European Community and Japan; as well as other states through ASEAN's Post-Ministerial Conference (PMC), the members were able to mobilise international support. They initiated a UN-sponsored international conference on Kampuchea (ICK) in July 1981; they denied the Vietnamese-installed regime – the People's Republic of Kampuchea (PRK) – international recognition from most states, including the United States and United Kingdom; they preserved the ousted regime's – Government of Democratic Kampuchea (DK) – seat in the United Nations; they sponsored each year UN resolutions against Vietnam, and by creating a coalition of the three opposition groups to the PRK – the Coalition Government of Democratic Kampuchea (CGDK) – ASEAN was able to maintain international support for the ousted and despicable Khmer Rouge regime. In addition to these diplomatic efforts, ASEAN also provided the Khmer Rouge with military assistance to prevent the PRK from consolidating its position in power.

While ASEAN was able to keep the crisis on the international agenda, and set that agenda so that Vietnam's overthrow of the Pol Pot regime was not the key focus, ASEAN was not able to terminate the conflict. The crisis was finally ended because of the actions of the superpowers, thus highlighting that while ASEAN members were able to influence the actions of extra-regional powers in supporting their position, they were not able to maintain their central role once those powers sought to terminate the conflict. ASEAN's control of extra-regional powers is limited, and this remains true in the present climate.

Through regional resilience the ASEAN members have provided security for one another, and as a common security approach it partly explains why the security dilemma has been mitigated. However, regional resilience does not in itself indicate that ASEAN is a security regime, even though it embraces the norm of non-intervention in each other's internal affairs. For ASEAN to be a security regime the norms of behaviour that constrain the members' actions must be peculiar to ASEAN. Since non-intervention in the internal affairs of other states is enshrined in the UN Charter it is a principle that ASEAN members are obliged to respect with or without ASEAN. This is also true for other ASEAN norms detailed in the 1967 Bangkok Declaration and the TAC. To determine if ASEAN is a security regime, it is necessary to reveal norms of behaviour which govern the way the members interact with one another, but not how they interact with non-ASEAN members. These additional norms of behaviour when combined with regional resilience are collectively known as the 'ASEAN way'. Acharya distinguishes between the principles enshrined in the Bangkok Declaration and these additional norms peculiar to ASEAN, by referring to the former as codes of conduct governing the states interactions and the latter as 'the *process* through which such interactions are carried out' (emphasis in original).[72] It is this process which provides evidence of an ASEAN security regime.

There are at least three guiding principles that influence ASEAN interactions and they have arisen over the last thirty years of the association's existence. They combine an informal, discreet style of dialogue that values consensus decision-making and the avoidance of adversarial bargaining strategies. Often explained as distinct from the ASEAN practice of *musyawarah*, it is possible to see these various principles emanating from it. *Musyawarah* is of Arabic origin and means making decisions via discussion and consultation. The three guiding principles are: first, that decision-making is achieved through consensus; second, that if a compromise cannot be found then the issue is adjourned; and third, members are prepared to defer their own interests to the interests of the association.

The consensus norm, known as *mufakat*, is associated with village politics in Indonesia and to a lesser extent in Malaysia and the Philippines. The discussion begins at an informal level where differences can be aired and a compromise is sought. Once a general consensus is reached on the issue this acts as the starting point for discussions, with a unanimous agreement the sought-after outcome. In ASEAN, the informal stage is manifest in the close personal relationships that have developed among the statesmen. Hoang Anh Tuan quotes former Foreign Secretary of the Philippines, Carlos Romulo, saying, 'I can pick up the telephone now and talk directly to Adam Malik or Rajaratnam [former Indonesian and Singapore foreign ministers respectively]. We often find that private talks over breakfast prove more important than formal meetings.'[73] The informal stage is important because members can raise objections knowing that should a decision be taken in spite of their concerns – which could only occur because the member dropped its objection – it will not need to explain its policy reversal.

The process of *musyawarah* thus allows ASEAN members to 'save face' because none will be shamed by the decision reached. This informal bargaining occurs long before ASEAN meets with the members contacting one another about proposals and ascertaining the degree of support they are likely to garner. After some manipulation, if the proposal is acceptable to the other members then it will be placed on the ASEAN agenda, otherwise it is likely to be dropped. This does not mean that consensus equates to unanimity. If one member disagrees with a proposal but finds itself in a minority, and the issue itself will not have negative repercussions when implemented, then although it does not support the issue it will not prevent others from proceeding; a consensus is said to have been reached via the 'Minus X' principle. Lee Kuan Yew says:

> So long as members who are not yet ready to participate are not damaged by non-participation, nor excluded from future participation, the power of veto need not be exercised ... when four agree and one does not object, this can still be considered a consensus, and the four should proceed with a new regional scheme.[74]

In addition to 'saving face', consensus also maintains good relations by producing a united ASEAN position on an issue and thus the members' interests are seen to be complementary and supportive of one another. Indeed, the informal approach encourages the attitude that the negotiations are conducted among friends not opponents.

The second norm is closely related with the consensus approach. If it is not possible for the members to reach a compromise the issue is adjourned in order to prevent it from undermining the states' relationship and ASEAN as a whole. An example of ASEAN members adjourning discussions because no compromise can be reached is the Malaysia-Philippine dispute over the state of Sabah. In the aftermath of the Corregidor Affair diplomatic relations were curtailed, but when they were resumed in December 1969 'both countries ... agreed to avoid bringing up the topic in discussion and dialogues, citing the interests of ASEAN'.[75] This adjournment of issues is colloquially described as 'sweeping controversial issues under the carpet', and when they are discussed these discussions take place outside the ASEAN framework. The meeting in January 1993 between the states' respective leaders was one such meeting that helped to improve their relations. Sometimes adjourning the issue results in an outcome achieved at a later date. The decision to place security on the agenda of the ASEAN Foreign Minister's Meeting, and to create the ARF, is an example of a sensitive issue that eventually gained acceptance by the ASEAN membership. Caballero-Anthony, who refers to adjournment as 'agreeing to disagree', writes 'the importance of adopting such a mechanism yet again emphasises ASEAN's basic approach that until members can actually get comfortable with each other and elements of distrust can be reduced, if not eliminated, to build confidence and trust, the slow, incremental, low-risk, flexible style is still the effective way forward'.[76]

The third norm is extremely important since the willingness of member-states to defer their own national interests to the interests of the association indicates a willingness to suffer short-term losses for long-term gains. This is a critical element in the operation of a security regime since it highlights that states perceive that other members of the regime will restrain from taking advantage of its short-term loss. In other words, statesmen have confidence in the regime constraining the others' actions so the suspicion they have about the others is mitigated. This willingness to defer state interests to the interests of ASEAN had been a feature of Indonesia's actions during the Suharto era. Arnfinn Jørgensen-Dahl writes that with the arrival of the New Order regime, '[r]eliance on more conventional diplomatic methods and mores, eschewal of abrasive behaviour, and consciousness of the need to accommodate the interests of its regional partners came in the years that followed to characterise much of Indonesia's involvement in Southeast Asian affairs'.[77]

This willingness to defer its own interests to that of the association as a whole was most marked during the Vietnamese occupation of Cambodia.[78] Thailand, which traditionally sought to balance Vietnamese influence in Indochina and had after the Vietnamese action become the 'front-line' state, steered ASEAN towards a confrontational stance with Vietnam. This ASEAN approach was not in the Indonesian interest because Jakarta viewed Vietnam as a buffer against Chinese influence in Southeast Asia. In addition, it was feared that a confrontational stance would increase Vietnamese reliance on the USSR thus increasing Soviet influence in the region. Initially, Indonesia sought a compromise solution allowing Hanoi to retain a de facto domination of Cambodia. However, the response to this Indonesian initiative from its ASEAN partners was not supportive and indeed proved highly divisive. In a speech on 16 August 1980, Suharto, 'concerned with this disruptive effect within ASEAN', was more critical of Hanoi than he had been in the previous year and emphasised Indonesia's support for the Thai position.[79]

Throughout the Vietnamese occupation, Indonesia attempted a number of diplomatic solutions, as would befit a major regional actor. However, whenever these approaches were deemed not to be in ASEAN, and specifically, Thai interests, Jakarta halted their progress. While Vietnamese intransigence was often cited as a reason for Indonesia's actions faltering, the need to maintain ASEAN unity and support Thailand was the major factor because ASEAN was seen to be the best vehicle through which Indonesia could influence international affairs. Therefore, throughout the occupation, Jakarta was prepared to subordinate its concerns regarding the long-term threat posed by China to Thailand's desire to balance Vietnam's Soviet-sponsored communist expansion. The Sabah case also highlights the willingness of ASEAN members to exercise restraint in their relationships. The Philippines did not, for example, take advantage of the racial riots in Kuala Lumpur in 1969 to pursue its claim.

The implementation therefore of a common security approach to achieving stability and security in ASEAN, and the emergence of various principles governing members' interactions, explains why during the arms accumulation the security dilemma's operation was moderated. The 'ASEAN way' also explains why it has not been escaped. Through quiet, private negotiation rather than public dispute-settlement procedures, such as ASEAN's High Council (which has not been convened), ASEAN has managed conflicting interests among members rather than resolving them. The issues that cause their uncertainty of one another are bypassed, hence Lee Kuan Yew's assertion that the problems afflicting the Singapore–Malaysia relationship are those that existed in the past, and Malaysia's concern over the Estrada administration's establishment of a task force to review the Sabah issue. While issues that cause the uncertainty remain, so will the security dilemma. Therefore, while publicly ASEAN exhibits the type of amity which implies the ASEAN security complex resembles a type of security community, behind this public facade exists enough enmity to raise doubts about such a description.

The ASEAN security complex does not resemble a security community. Tim Huxley is clear on this point as he asserts, '[s]uch a degree of optimism is almost certainly misplaced, as at least one ASEAN member (Singapore) bases its defence strategy primarily on the deterrence of one or more ASEAN neighbours (Malaysia and Indonesia)'.[80] Acharya concurs by noting that '[w]hile ASEAN has come a long way to reducing tensions between its members, it has not yet reached the stage of a "security community"'.[81] Thus while the 'ASEAN way' has made war very unlikely among ASEAN members, the possibility cannot be ruled out. In its thirty years of existence ASEAN has come to more closely resemble a security regime, and this explains why the members were able to avoid a severe security dilemma despite the accumulation of power projection weapons. However, in the late 1990s with an expanding membership and the arrival of new security issues, such as environmental degradation and economic collapse, the ability of the 'ASEAN way' to maintain cordial relations is under threat. The final section of this chapter examines these challenges to the 'ASEAN way'.

D. The 'ASEAN way': under threat?

The late 1990s has seen the confluence of ASEAN expansion and the collapse of the 'tiger economies'. The summer of 1997 was a turning point for ASEAN, with the postponement of Cambodia's admittance to the association and the financial crisis in Thailand sparking off the Asian economic crisis. The expansion of its membership and the economic crisis have raised doubts within ASEAN about the key principles and processes associated with the 'ASEAN way'. The norms of behaviour that have maintained cordial relations within Southeast Asia are therefore being questioned, which raises doubts about ASEAN's future as a security regime and this could have implications for the security dilemma.

One of the issues which has begun to undermine the 'ASEAN way', especially the notion of *musyawarah*, is the expansion of ASEAN to include all ten states of Southeast Asia, since more members will make consensus decision-making harder to achieve. The difficulty in reaching a consensus was very much a concern prior to Vietnam's entry in 1995, because it was feared that Hanoi would continue to conduct its foreign policy in a manner that entailed gaining at others' expense – a style which requires posturing and aggressive bargaining born out of the state's war-torn historical experience. Consequently, Vietnam might have great difficulty adjusting to the ASEAN style and thus diluting the 'ASEAN way'.[82] Hoang Anh Tuan even notes that the Vietnamese conceive of compromise, the essence of the 'ASEAN way', as having a different meaning to that ascribed to by ASEAN.[83] The concerns of the ASEAN membership were revealed by the Malaysian Deputy Foreign Minister, Datuk Abdullah Ahmad Badawi, in late 1995, when he said, 'some parties had expressed doubt whether ASEAN can maintain its tradition of consensus-based decision making'.[84]

It has already been noted that ASEAN's consensus-decision making approach does not mean unanimity has to be found, but on major issues where all members' national interests are at stake, such consensus is required and this is going to be much harder to achieve among ten states than six. Hence, in the summer of 1997 when ASEAN admitted Burma (Myanmar) and Laos, concerns regarding consensus-decision making were raised again. Singapore's Foreign Minister, S. Jayakumar, raised the question that 'since the new members have their own work styles and national priorities...can we be sure that the ASEAN members will not be pulled in different directions by different powers?'[85] While echoing these sentiments Malaysia's Foreign Minister, Abdullah Ahmed Badawi, reiterated the 'Minus X' principle that consensus did not equal unanimity and that increasingly ASEAN would have to resort to this principle.[86] However, N. Ganesan is right to warn, regardless of the 'Minus X' principle, that 'an enlarged membership will yield lower levels of convergence on policy matters'.[87]

Initially, Vietnam allayed most of these concerns as it prepared to learn the 'ASEAN way' from the interactions of the ASEAN six. This was given tangible evidence by ASEAN's decision to postpone Cambodia's admission to the association in 1997. While Hanoi would have preferred Cambodia to have been admitted, it nevertheless accepted the wishes of the majority and concurred with ASEAN's decision. Given that Vietnam had much to gain from being an ASEAN member, it was unlikely, at least initially, that Vietnam would upset the decision-making process in ASEAN. The occupation of Cambodia in the 1980s and the embargo on trade, aid and investment that were imposed on Vietnam had weakened the economy. In December 1986 at the Sixth National Party Congress, the policy of *doi moi* or renovation was announced.

This policy sought to arrest the decline in the economy by replacing the central planning apparatus with a market-oriented approach. Vietnam's response to its economic problems mirrored that of Gorbachev's USSR. Hanoi realised that *doi moi* could not be achieved without the termination of the Cambodian conflict and an improvement in international relations. In May 1988, Politburo Resolution 13 was announced which highlighted a 'multi-directional foreign policy', the Vietnamese equivalent to Gorbachev's new political thinking, and in June 1991 the Seventh National Party Congress added the objective of being 'friends with all countries'. The 1990s thus witnessed

Vietnam's entry into the mainstream of international political affairs as it cast off the image of international pariah. Relations were normalised with China in November 1991 and the United States in 1995, official assistance from Japan was restored in November 1992 and membership of ASEAN attained in 1995. In 1989 Vietnam had diplomatic relations with only 23 non-communist states, by the end of 1996 this had risen to 163 states.[88]

By joining ASEAN, Vietnam sought to deepen this strategy of renovating the economy by creating peaceful and stable external relations. Membership of ASEAN achieved this by, first, strengthening Vietnam's security against external threats. Hoang Anh Tuan writes, 'ASEAN membership would enhance Vietnam's diplomatic standing and integrate Vietnam's security with the security of the whole of Southeast Asia, thus creating an external environment favourable for economic development'.[89] Second, the suspicion that marked Vietnam's relations with the ASEAN states would be lessened as these issues became subject to 'resolution' via the 'ASEAN way'. Third, relations with Washington would improve, notably the ending of the US-imposed trade and aid embargo; and in areas such as human rights and democratisation, Vietnam's membership of ASEAN would help deflect criticism.

These political changes have resulted in economic changes with Vietnam joining the Asia-Pacific Economic Co-operation (APEC) forum in 1998 and participating in the discussions leading to the establishment of an ASEAN Free Trade Area (AFTA). As the political environment has improved so has Vietnam's economy. Foreign Direct Investment (FDI) in Vietnam has risen from US$250 million in 1989 to more than US$18 billion in 1996.[90] Although Vietnam's economy showed signs of slowing in 1997 as a result of the economic problems affecting the region, it still grew by 7–8 per cent and inflation remained for the second year running in single-digit figures.[91]

Vietnam had therefore much to gain from being a cooperative partner within ASEAN, and to this effect Hanoi established in December 1995 the National ASEAN Committee headed by the Deputy Prime Minister. Vietnam also issued a directive that all ministries should establish a sub-committee to promote relations with ASEAN member counterparts. Vietnam's determination to be seen as a cooperative partner was rewarded when it was chosen to host the December ASEAN summit in 1998. Despite these encouraging signs, the concerns of the original ASEAN members about Vietnam's willingness to operate in accordance with the 'ASEAN way', appear to have been well-founded. The statement from Pham Cao Phong that, 'Hanoi is not so certain whether it accepts the rules of the game, that is, accepts all the written and unwritten norms of the relationship among ASEAN countries without any exceptions', indicates that difficult times lie ahead.[92]

Coupled with Pham Cao Phong's assertion, was the statement from Vietnamese diplomats at the December 1997 ASEAN summit – 'we are nine very different countries. It is natural that with expansion, groupings within the group will form ... [V]iews cannot be forced on anybody'. This suggests that the 'ASEAN way' will have to evolve to accommodate ASEANs expanding membership.[93] At the ASEAN summit in Hanoi the concerns voiced about Vietnam's willingness to operate within the 'ASEAN way' were given substantial credibility. Prior to the December summit, Vietnam had made it clear that it wanted Cambodia to be admitted as ASEAN's tenth member. However, it was evident that this proposal did not find favour among other members.

What transpired has raised doubts about ASEAN's decision-making process. Vietnam lobbied hard for Cambodia's admission and gained the support of Indonesia, Malaysia, Burma and Laos, but not Thailand, Singapore and the Philippines. On the eve of the summit, Vietnamese officials announced that Cambodia had been admitted, only for Thai officials to deny that this had been agreed. The following day Cambodia was 'welcomed' as ASEAN's tenth member in the opening speeches of both Indonesia's President, B.J. Habibie and Thailand's Prime Minister, Chuan Leekpai. Cambodia's formal admission was sealed in April 1999. The negotiations which led to the breaking of the impasse, according to Michael Vatikiotis, were conducted by Vietnam in an uncompromising fashion that reminded delegates of Hanoi's negotiating stance during its occupation of Cambodia – 'the experience has left a bad aftertaste'.[94]

In addition to an expanding membership raising doubts about the continuing feasibility of reaching consensus among ten states, the admittance of Burma and the decision to postpone Cambodia's entry in 1997, also raises questions about other aspects of the 'ASEAN way'. In particular, the cardinal principle of non-intervention appears under threat from new additions to ASEAN's vocabulary; constructive engagement, constructive intervention, constructive involvement, flexible engagement.[95]

In early July 1997, Cambodia's Second Prime Minister, Hun Sen, staged a coup d'état and his forces routed those of the First Prime Minister, Prince Norodom Ranariddh. Hun Sen had accused Ranariddh of fraternising with the outlawed Khmer Rouge and importing weapons for the purpose of destabilising the country. Ranariddh denied the allegations and directed the same accusations at Hun Sen. Ranariddh's

FUNCINPEC (Front Uni National pour un Canbodge Indépendant, Neutre, Pacifique et Coopératif) forces fled to the jungles bordering Thailand where the party split into at least three factions. Disillusioned by Ranariddh's leadership, Toan Chay and Foreign Minister, Ung Huot, remained in the coalition government and, on 6 August, Ung Huot became the First Prime Minister. Ranariddh fled the country into political exile, but returned in May 1998 to contest the national election.[96]

For ASEAN the outbreak of violence coincided with the association's expansion to incorporate all ten Southeast Asian states. Although Malaysia and Vietnam were prepared to admit Cambodia, the other members considered the situation too volatile and preferred instead to postpone Cambodia's entry until after elections had been held. ASEAN responded to the crisis by sending a delegation consisting of the foreign ministers from Indonesia, Thailand and the Philippines to meet Hun Sen, Ranariddh and King Norodom Sihanouk who was convalescing in China.

For Jayakumar the involvement of ASEAN was essential since '[a]ny unconstitutional change of government is cause for concern. Where force is used for an unconstitutional purpose, it is behaviour that ASEAN cannot ignore or condone'.[97] In addition to offering their good offices for dialogue, ASEAN also offered to assist in the running of the election. While it can be argued that ASEAN's role in the 1991 Paris peace accord makes Cambodia a special case for ASEAN, some analysts detect a willingness among some of the members to set precedents for future interventions. For example, the statement from Anwar Ibrahim, that 'it is now appropriate for ASEAN to seriously consider the idea of constructive interventions'[98] – which includes the strengthening of civil society and the rule of law; normally the preserve of the sovereign regime – led Jusuf Wanandi to suggest ASEAN should adopt a policy of constructive involvement and that 'the principle of non-intervention will have to reviewed'.[99] Anwar Ibrahim's assertion that ASEAN should become more proactive and reconsider the way it approaches interstate problems carries particular significance because he was the acting Prime Minister of Malaysia at the time.

It would, however, be erroneous to suggest that all ASEAN members share these sentiments. Vietnam in particular registered its concerns about ASEAN's involvement in Cambodia. Foreign Minister, Nguyen Manh Cam, informed his ASEAN counterparts that 'Vietnam regards these as Cambodian internal affairs which can be solved only by the Cambodian people. Vietnam's consistent policy is to respect strictly Cambodia's independence and sovereignty and not to interfere into its internal affairs'.[100] In order to placate such views, leading politicians, including Anwar Ibrahim, reiterated the importance of non-interference, although Hun Sen's warning to ASEAN not to interfere in Cambodia revealed the interpretation Phnom Penh placed on ASEAN's actions.[101]

ASEAN has not therefore publicly abandoned the principle of non-intervention, but there exists a growing interest in the notion of involvement, or intervention, in the affairs of other members. There were, for example, talks on such issues as human rights, governance and civil societies at the July 1999 ASEAN summit in Singapore.[102] This interest in altering the non-interference principle appears to be a response to at least three factors. First, the lower levels of economic and social development within the new members compared to the ASEAN six. Second, pressure from the international community, and in particular the United States and the European Union. And finally, the appreciation that economic interdependence is a double-edged sword which ensures that economic downturns in one state are likely to have a regional, if not global affect.

The failure of Cambodia to benefit from the region's economic success in the early to mid-1990s was perceived by some ASEAN members as partly their fault for not aiding the country's development. Hence, Anwar Ibrahim's comment that '[o]ur non-involvement in the reconstruction of Cambodia actually contributed to the deterioration and final collapse of national reconciliation. We should have nursed the baby, at least through its teething period. That's why we need to consider the idea of constructive intervention'.[103] In particular, there was a concern before the economic crisis erupted that ASEAN could become divided between the older, richer members, and the newer, poorer ones. This difference could be exacerbated when ASEAN establishes AFTA, because this could increase the gap between rich and poor, thereby leading to dissatisfaction among the poorer members and a rise in intra-ASEAN tension. Thus, constructive involvement includes the participation of ASEAN in the new members' national development programmes.

It is the prospect of Burma also suffering the same political upheavals as Cambodia which has led ASEAN to engage constructively the State Peace and Development Council (SPDC) in Rangoon.[104] Although in the case of Burma ASEAN is also under pressure from the West to improve Burma's human rights record. In this respect, ASEAN was tasked with reforming Burma at the 4th ASEAN Regional Forum (ARF) meeting held in Kuala Lumpur. The United States and the European Union were prepared to let ASEAN take the leading role in bringing about change in Burma, but in so doing there was the clear expectation that ASEAN would intervene in domestic Burmese politics. US Secretary of State, Madeleine Albright, stated: 'Burma's future and ASEAN's future are now joined. And now, more than ever, Burma's problems need an ASEAN solution.'[105]

ASEAN's constructive engagement approach has resulted in its unsuccessful attempt to persuade the Rangoon regime to hold talks with Aung San Suu Kyi, the leader of the opposition party (National League for Democracy) which won a landslide victory in the 1990 election but which has never been allowed to administer the country. In other words, ASEAN is taking a clear and unequivocal stance in the political affairs of a member state. Burma had joined ASEAN in the expectation that the association would provide Rangoon with a shield to deflect Western criticism about their human rights record. However, the economic crisis has made good relations between ASEAN and Western states imperative, leading Mahathir to inform his hosts when he visited Burma in March 1998 that 'you have to understand that Europe is very important to us'.[106] Far from providing a shield for Burma, the intransigence of the SPDC has, according to Bertil Lintner, 'forced ASEAN to rethink its traditional policy of noninterference in the internal affairs of its member states. Thailand and some other ASEAN members are concerned that Burma's stigma is tainting the whole group at a crucial time when sound relations with the EU are of utmost importance.'[107]

The entry of new members has forced ASEAN to re-examine the principle of non-intervention, although given the different views of the membership it is unlikely to be publicly abandoned. While in 1997 the issue of constructive involvement/intervention was only focused on new members, developments in late 1997 and early 1998 suggest that non-intervention among the older members is also coming under review. In an editorial, Singapore's *Business Times* noted that '[r]apid economic growth in the region has spawned a chain-link of economic interdependence such that ASEAN members ignore developments across their borders at their own peril'.[108] The economic crisis has shown that interdependence in the region is a double-edged sword; what may aid growth may also exacerbate a collapse. The region's interdependence is thus causing a rethink about non-interference.

The talk of constructive intervention begun by Anwar Ibrahim in 1997 has been taken up by the Thai Foreign Minister, Surin Pitsuwan. Surin has argued that domestic affairs can have adverse effects on neighbouring states and that 'the affected countries should be able to express their opinions and concerns in an open, frank and constructive manner', in particular the commitment to non-intervention, 'cannot and should not be absolute. It must be subjected to reality tests and accordingly it must be flexible'.[109] Surin has championed the notion of flexible engagement, although only Domingo Siazon, the Philippine Foreign Minister, has supported the idea. At the ASEAN meeting in Manila in July 1998 the response from the ASEAN membership was negative with flexible engagement replaced by 'enhanced interaction'.

At the end of the 1990s ASEAN is at crossroads. The speed with which the financial crisis spread across the region infecting each member could yet prove to be a salutary lesson. Even though intra-ASEAN trade maybe low the crisis has shown that their economies are nevertheless vulnerable to developments in neighbouring states. Indonesia's foreign minister, Ali Alatas, stated:

> We have now come to realize because of the crisis how interdependent we are, how interconnected our problems are. Now we see that it cannot remain Thailand only having a problem, it inevitably would infect us. So our problems are interconnected, our interdependence towards one another has grown, and we realize in times of crisis we must be able to show the world that we are able to cooperate even more closely with each other.[110]

The Hanoi summit revealed a continuing commitment to AFTA as the ASEAN members agreed to implement the project a year earlier than originally intended. ASEAN members are also trying to set up a surveillance process to monitor macroeconomic trends. The expectation is that this will act as an early warning system so that if trouble looms the countries will not be caught again by surprise. There are discussions about reducing the volatility of currency exchange rates, even the prospect of a common currency has been aired. While these are long-term solutions, they nevertheless indicate a realisation that the region's problems require the ASEAN members to work in concert.[111]

The problem for ASEAN is how to reconcile the need for greater joint action while also maintaining each members' sovereignty, and it is this issue which has become manifest in the debate over non-interference. Thus while former ASEAN secretary-general, Tan Sri Ajit Singh, warned that removing the principle of 'non-interference in members' internal affairs would be detrimental to the regional grouping', he nevertheless noted that because of economic developments, 'borders between countries have become very blurred'.[112] The move towards greater joint action will inevitably result in greater involvement in each other's internal affairs.

The worrying trend for ASEAN stability is that members are commenting on political and social issues within other members' domestic affairs. Both the former Indonesian President, B.J. Habibie and Philippine President, Joseph Estrada, commented on the detention of Anwar Ibrahim in September 1998.[113] They both met Anwar's daughter, Nurual Izzah, who has led protests against Mahathir, and stated their support for Anwar – Estrada telling her to tell her father 'not to waver, because he is fighting for a cause, the cause of the Malaysian people'.[114] Such outside interference in Malaysia's political/judicial process is a clear infringement of the non-interference principle. Habibie also drew protests from Singapore in early 1999 when he accused the island state of racism by not promoting or appointing Malay officers within the SAF.[115] While at the end of the 1990s ASEAN might take the road to greater interaction, it is just as possible that ASEAN will turn down the road to divergence and disunity.

It is too soon to determine what effect these changes on the 'ASEAN way' will have on the intensity of the security dilemma. Before the economic crisis began the 'ASEAN way' appeared to be adapting to meet the challenge of an expanding membership, which could have enabled the Southeast Asian security complex to continue moderating the operation of the security dilemma. However, the political consequences of the economic crisis have begun to cause a fundamental rethink among some of the members about the norms of behaviour which underpin the 'ASEAN way'. Should this create groupings within ASEAN and produce competitive behaviour, then suspicions and anxieties could rise intensifying the security dilemma.

It is this fear that led a senior ASEAN official to state that the Thai proposal for flexible engagement was rejected because ASEAN was established to 'manage relationships among countries which would be otherwise at each others' throats … This is the worst time to drop non-intervention as the principle'.[116] However, such a pessimistic outcome need not arise from re-interpreting the principles underpinning the 'ASEAN way'. The key for maintaining cordial relations, and thereby mitigating the security dilemma, lies in the acceptance of security being achieved with, as opposed to against, neighbours; that is, as long as the notion of common security is adhered to, reforming the 'ASEAN way' can have a positive outcome. Whereas non-interference underpinning regional resilience provided ASEAN with security in the past, the challenge set by first Anwar and now Surin, is that present security threats – economic collapse, environmental concerns, refugees – cut across state boundaries and require transparency and openness by members to provide common security for the region.

It is difficult to be optimistic that such an outcome will occur. Groupings within ASEAN are forming between those regimes promoting transparency, such as Thailand and the Philippines, and the authoritarian regimes of Vietnam and Burma. The confluence of enlargement and economic collapse breeding political change, have started to undermine the 'ASEAN way' and raise the level of uncertainty. The weakening of ASEAN as a security regime – the *Far Eastern Economic Review* describes the changes as creating 'dark clouds over Asean's reputation as a zone of peace, stability and progress' – removes those norms of behaviour that moderated the security dilemma's operation.[117]

Conclusion

This chapter has sought to accomplish two goals. First, to determine if the security dilemma is applicable to post-Cold War relations among the ASEAN members, and whether it helps to understand the procurement of power-projection forces before the economic crisis curtailed their acquisition in early 1998. Second, to examine the role of the 'ASEAN way' as a mitigator of the security dilemma and whether this process is itself undergoing change.

It has been argued that although ASEAN members can be classified as 'weak' states, this does not mean they are immune to the effects of the security dilemma; concern with neighbours' intentions has remained among the ASEAN states from the time of *Konfrontasi* and the Corregidor Affair in the 1960s through to the Malaysian cancellation of the FPDA exercises in 1998.[118] Indeed, the post-Cold War environment appeared to provide fertile soil for the seeds of the security dilemma to grow.

Uncertainty has abounded with the declining presence of the superpowers and the prospect of numerous territorial disputes left unresolved from the Cold War coming to the fore. The existence of these disputed territories, and thus the existence at one level of a real incompatibility, was not however found to negate the dynamics of the security dilemma. Instead, it was argued that the perception existed among the ASEAN members that their neighbours were status quo powers. However, the continuing claims on disputed territories has meant that a careful watch on neighbours' intentions was needed in case a change of ambition was noted.

Although the procurements of power-projection forces in the early to mid-1990s were not solely for this reason (indeed the main determinant was the region's economic growth) nevertheless, some of the acquisitions did appear to be intended as counters to weapons procured by other ASEAN states. It is thus argued that a security dilemma was in operation in Southeast Asia, although its intensity varied among the states, with the strongest operating between Malaysia and Singapore. The key finding though was that despite such propitious conditions the security dilemma's operation was only slight, and even in the Singapore-Malaysia relationship its intensity has varied over time and has never been sufficiently strong to make the outbreak of war on the Malaysian peninsula likely.

The second goal of the chapter was to explain why ASEAN has proven resilient to resisting the tragedy of the security dilemma. The case is posited that ASEAN members have pursued a security approach that has at its core the realisation that regional security can only be achieved with their neighbours, as opposed to against their neighbours. Thus, regional resilience is a type of common security approach, although quite different in its implementation from that advocated by the Palme Commission. The principle of non-interference in each others' domestic affairs was an important norm of behaviour that generated confidence in the member states that their neighbours would not take advantage of their internal problems (communist insurgency, ethnic secession).

However, this principle along with others, codified in the 1967 Bangkok Declaration, does not make ASEAN a security regime since these norms are not peculiar to the association. The key to ASEAN's regime formation is the process through which ASEAN members interact. The practice of *musyawarah* has fostered a discreet style of bargaining that has created an atmosphere of dialogue among friends, rather than opponents, and this has helped to reduce suspicions. Members have also been willing to support the interests of the association even when it has not been in their own national interest. This willingness to defer their own national interest to the interest of the association indicates a confidence that others will not take advantage of the situation. The greatest proponent of this was Indonesia during Vietnam's occupation of Cambodia.

ASEAN members therefore have had a number of norms of behaviour which have regulated their interactions so that suspicions and concerns about one another's ambitions have been reduced. Thus, in the uncertain environment of the post-Cold War era, despite the accumulation of new power-projection weapons the members were able to mitigate the worse effects of the security dilemma. The expansion of the membership to include all ten Southeast Asian states, and the economic crisis, have, however, drawn doubt as to the continuing validity of these norms. The talk of constructive intervention and flexible engagement indicate that among some of the ASEAN members there exists a desire to re-interpret the principle of non-interference. Initially the concern lay with new members, but as the economic crisis has affected all the states so the question of discussing difficulties in older members has been raised. Thailand is the torchbearer for this new approach and has been supported by the Philippines, though other members remain to be convinced.

It is too soon to know what effect this will have on ASEAN and consequently the operation of the region's security dilemma. The fear is that if members begin to comment on and criticise each others' domestic policies, the areas of contention that they have studiously avoided raising in the past could rise to the surface causing a general worsening of their relationships. In such circumstances the security dilemma would become more severe and there are worrying signs that this is the case in the Singapore–Malaysia relationship. However, the changes sought by Surin are not calculated to change the fundamental ASEAN approach to security. He seeks to strengthen regional security by emphasising that the security threats faced by the ASEAN members require joint action, which in turn can only be achieved by openness and transparency. The fundamental approach of security with, as opposed to against, each other is not to be changed, but rather altered to face the transnational nature of the economic threats the members face. Re-interpreting the 'ASEAN way' does not therefore mean that the security dilemma will operate more severely. Indeed, if carried out well, it could help ameliorate the security dilemma even further. However, the signs are not promising, and even Siazon – one of ASEAN's 'movers and shakers' – does not believe ASEAN leaders are ready yet to tackle the challenge of interdependence.[119]

Part III
State-induced Security Dilemma

5
ASEAN, the China Threat and the South China Sea Dispute

As they seek to enhance China's military capabilities ... the Chinese have so far shown little willingness to consider the possibility that their self-help efforts to enhance China's security may exacerbate the sense of insecurity of other states in East Asia. They claim that declarations of China's benign intentions and opposition to hegemony are sufficient to assuage other states' concerns about China's intentions. Only a small minority of Chinese analysts and officials accepts the mutual security notion that one's own security is assured only when other states also feel secure. Rather, most still seem to believe that China is more secure if other states are weaker and thus less secure.[1]

China would appear to be an ideal state to fall victim to the security dilemma. A history which teaches that China suffered 'humiliation' at the hands of foreigners, is deserving of a top seat in world diplomacy, and reflects the imperatives of domestic concerns in its foreign relations, indicates a state which will be suspicious of others' actions, yet will not consider its own actions to be threatening (its international role requires it to acquire an enhanced military capability), and will be largely immune to unwinding the spiral of insecurity by responding to others' actions (domestic matters come first). Weixing Hu and Avery Goldstein have already noted the applicability of the security dilemma to China. Hu writes that although, 'Beijing has repeatedly denied that it has any interest in filling [a] power vacuum ... its military modernization is naturally perceived as a security threat in the region ... This perception problem contributes to the "security dilemma" in Asian-Pacific security.'[2] Goldstein concurs by writing, 'at the end of the century China's policies and the reaction to them are intensifying rather than mitigating the security dilemma'.[3] It is this suggestion that China is inducing a security dilemma that is particularly interesting and the focus for this chapter.

Seeking to determine the relevance of the state-induced security dilemma to the China–ASEAN relationship entails trying to understand the ambitions of China in Southeast Asia, the response to those ambitions amongst the ASEAN membership and some of the determining factors behind China's foreign policy. All three areas are contentious, and therefore while the objective of this chapter will be to provide a plausible interpretation, the conclusion will not be definitive. This is critically important since the operation of the security dilemma requires the participation of status quo powers, and while evidence will be provided that China fits such a description, it is not a label that is readily attached by regional specialists. David Shambaugh is quite emphatic when he states, 'China today is a dissatisfied and non-status quo power which seeks to change the existing international order and norms of inter-state relations.'[4] Indeed the argument will be made that while it is entirely understandable why ASEAN's approach to China maintains a combination of engagement and containment – a statement which in itself is contentious – this approach is partly responsible for the security dilemma's operation.[5] The conclusions will therefore be at best disputable, but at worst, because of the economic crisis, anachronistic.

Like the rest of the region, China has also been affected by the economic crisis, although not at the time of writing to the same degree as South Korea or Japan. The consequences for China could be very severe, despite the confident talk of China's economy becoming the second largest in the twenty-first century, there are many economic, political and social obstacles to be overcome before such an achievement can be realised.[6] It is possible that the economic crisis could exacerbate tensions within China leading not to a confident, assertive power, but rather a state in crisis much like the former Soviet Union coping with secessionist demands and calls for political reform. When economic collapse can remove the enduring Suharto regime in Indonesia, no political system can be considered sacrosanct, including the Chinese Communist Party (CCP). However, while such outcomes are possible, at the time of writing they have not occurred, and while China's economy is not growing at the rate it was before the summer of 1997, it is nevertheless still growing. Therefore this chapter begins with a large assumption: China will continue to emerge as a key player in East Asian affairs, and will remain the primary external security issue for the members of ASEAN.

The literature on how states should relate to China in the post-Cold War era tends to focus on the question of whether it is best to engage or contain China. Both are not without their problems, with engagement criticised for excusing China's breaches of good behaviour (exporting missile technology, human rights abuses) and containment raising the prospect of another Cold War between the United States and a communist state. In 1995, the former US Assistant Secretary of Defense, Joseph Nye, warned against containment when he stated that 'if you treat China as an enemy, China will become an enemy'.[7]

Using the security dilemma to examine the ASEAN–China relationship, reveals an awareness within the regimes of ASEAN, as well as Beijing, of the paradoxical or self-defeating nature of containment, and the need to prevent this through engagement. It also reveals the distrust and lingering suspicion about Chinese intentions among the ASEAN members, which makes an element of containment perceived as an equally necessary tool in the ASEAN–China relationship. This combination of containment and engagement is epitomised by the membership of the ASEAN Regional Forum (ARF). A forum for dialogue on security matters, the ARF membership includes China, and indeed the ARF would be meaningless without Beijing's participation, while also including the US and more recently India to balance China.

In order to determine the security dilemma's relevance a number of questions need to be addressed. First, in order for China to induce a security dilemma between itself and ASEAN, it is necessary to determine whether China is becoming a hegemonic power. Does Beijing conceive of Southeast Asia to be in its sphere of influence and therefore a region in which it defines the status quo? Second, is China pursuing a policy that is generating fear and suspicion among ASEAN members about China's intentions? Third, if this is the case, has ASEAN responded and has this response generated concern in China? Such response need not be limited to the military realm. Before addressing these questions though a quick résumé of the characteristics of a state-induced security dilemma, explained in Chapter 1, is necessary.

The label state-induced is synonymous with the deliberate security dilemma introduced to the literature by Nicholas Wheeler and Ken Booth in 1992, and it captures the essence of a security dilemma identified by Jack Snyder operating amongst the European Powers prior to the outbreak of the First World War.[8] The essence of Snyder's security dilemma, a state-induced version, is that one of the actors defines its security as requiring the insecurity of others. In the traditional system-induced version such a requirement is not in evidence, both feel insecure as a consequence of the other's actions but neither defines its security as requiring the other to feel insecure. Snyder argues that because this requirement of insecurity exists it makes mitigating or even escaping the security dilemma much harder. Even if one actor is sensitive to the security dilemma, it is unlikely to accept a position of vulnerability simply because the other defines its security as requiring their insecurity. It is this problem that leads Snyder to assert, '[i]f threats could not resolve the security dilemma, neither could concessions', because, '[a]ppeasing the security fears of one's neighbour would have entailed accepting one's own insecurity'.[9] Escape lies in making the adversary's requirement that others are insecure 'more benign by…changing those circumstances – or the adversary's assessment of them – and not by the use of threats or concessions'.[10] That is, escape is only possible if this requirement that others feel insecure is altered.

In Chapter 1 it was suggested that for Snyder's definition of a security dilemma to be accurate it was necessary for the adversary to be a status quo power. This is because when the adversary seeks more than just its own security and begins to harbour revisionist ambitions, the defensive actions undertaken by the other are not paradoxical and are not making the situation worse; it is an example of Robert Jervis's deterrence model, not his spiral model. It is suggested, therefore, that the type of adversary which could instigate a state-induced security dilemma is one seeking a position of hegemony. In view of the importance of illusory incompatibility in discussing the relevance of the security dilemma, it is prudent to recall that a hegemonic state is not seeking to control neighbours through territorial conquest. As Robert Keohane asserts, 'the key distinction between hegemony and imperialism is that a hegemon, unlike an empire, does not dominate societies through a cumbersome political superstructure, but rather supervises the relationships between politically independent societies'.[11]

Thus a hegemonic power is considered to be a state that not only is the most powerful in the region, and is perceived by others as such, but also determines the norms of behaviour that dictate the interactions amongst the states. For China to be considered a rising hegemon in Southeast Asia, therefore, the ASEAN states need to acknowledge its primary role in their evolving relationship. Referring to China embarking upon a policy of hegemony in Southeast Asia does not mean that China is seeking to expand its border southwards, or that Beijing wishes to annex its smaller southern neighbours. It does, however, mean that China conceives of its security requiring its elevation to the position of regional hegemon, and in so doing placing its southern neighbours in a position of subordination that carries with it a degree of insecurity.

A. State-induced security dilemma: is China emerging as a hegemonic power?

The first difficulty with assigning China the title of hegemon is the public denials from Beijing that China is seeking such a status. Chinese Foreign Minister Qian Qichen in 1993 explicitly stated, 'China does not seek hegemony now, nor will it do so in the future, even when it is economically developed'.[12] The Chinese Defence Minister, Chi Haotian, repeated these assurances almost word for word when he visited Canberra in February 1998, and China's ambassador to the Philippines, Fu Ying, was categorical in her statement of May 1999 when she said, 'one thing is certain: China will never be a "hegemon" in the region'.[13] In view of these statements, what evidence can be found to suggest that China is embarking upon a path which will lead to its hegemony of Southeast Asia?

While in itself not disproving these Chinese assertions, it is pertinent to note that what the Chinese mean by hegemony is not the same as the Western definition. According to Chang Ya-chün 'hegemony is inevitably accompanied by such deeds as "power politics", "interference into the internal affairs of other countries", "seeking one's own sphere of influence", "possession of overseas military bases", and "annexation of the territory of other countries"... Peking considers that it has done none of the above-mentioned things; hence, it insists that it has no intention of seeking hegemony.'[14] Such a definition though better describes imperialism than hegemony, and thus while Beijing's public denials of hegemony might be useful in showing that it is not pursuing an imperialist policy, they do not negate the possibility of it assuming hegemony in Southeast Asia.

The case for China assuming hegemony over Southeast Asia is based upon: systemic theories of great powers controlling their external environment and maintaining their great power status; the history of China's relationship with Southeast Asia; China's claims in the South China Sea. Systemic theory emphasises the affect the international system has on the behaviour of states, rather than looking at the role of individual leaders and the peculiarities of separate states. The intention is not to suggest that it is possible to understand Chinese behaviour just through systemic theory, and indeed the influences on Chinese foreign policy are examined later in the chapter. The argument is that given China's growing economic, military and political strength, China will be able to greatly influence, and thereby exercise control over, its immediate geographical area.

1   China's economic potential: political influence and military capability

Since the late 1970s economic statistics show that China's economy is growing at a phenomenal rate, although in keeping with other Asian economies the financial crisis of the late 1990s has had a detrimental affect on this growth. The official target of 8 per cent growth in 1998, for example, was not met and in 1999 this has been lowered to 7 per cent. Nevertheless, China's economy has strengthened markedly. During the 1980s China's GDP doubled and by the mid-1990s it was doubling again and became the third highest in the world. China's trade volume had massively increased from $38.2 billion to more than $250 billion, while its trade surplus led to huge foreign exchange reserves; from $15 billion in the late 1980s to nearer $150 billion by mid-1997.[15] Before the economic crisis began, talk was of when China would surpass Japan's economy and even the United States.[16]

China's economic growth and its future potential has enabled China to have a direct bearing on the stability of the ASEAN economies. For example, China's decision not to devalue its currency at the height of the economic crisis in 1998 is widely regarded as responsible for heading off a further round of damaging currency devaluations in Southeast Asia. This decision, in conjunction with a contribution of $1 billion to the International Monetary Fund's rescue package for Thailand, created the impression of a responsible economic giant in the decision-making circles within ASEAN. China's economy therefore provides Beijing considerable influence in the region. China's economic growth has also enabled Beijing to increase its military budget each year since the late 1980s.[17] The 1998 defence budget announced in March signalled the largest increase for ten years. While it is notoriously difficult to determine exactly China's military expenditure, due to the high degree of secrecy and the different sources of revenue, the official figure of $8.3 billion in 1996–97 is widely regarded as too low to maintain the People's Liberation Army (PLA).[18] Western estimates vary widely but according to David Shambaugh 'a consensus is emerging... that total Chinese defence spending is in the range of $28–$36 billion, or four to five times the official figure'.[19]

China's economic growth, political influence, and military capabilities, are creating the impression that China will emerge in the first half of the twenty-first century as the dominant regional power. Denny Roy states that if 'the opportunity arises to establish a dominant role in the region, China can be expected to seize it', and asserts that like Britain in the nineteenth century and the Soviet Union, Nazi Germany and the USA in the twentieth century, '[t]here is no convincing reason to think China as a great power will depart from this pattern'.[20]

2 China's interaction with Southeast Asia: a return to the tributary system?

In seeking to determine hegemonic tendencies from Beijing it is help-ful to recall the historical relationship China enjoyed with its southern neighbours. Prior to the arrival of European influence, the Chinese assumed suzerainty over Southeast Asia. Leszeck Buszynski writes that 'kingdoms of Southeast Asia, whether Angkor, Majapahit or Burma, developed trade relations with China which the Chinese then defined in the context of their tributary system … China conferred titles and recognition upon its "vassals" in Southeast Asia and protected them against the predatory actions of neighbours'.[21] To what extent China provided protection is debatable and indeed rather misleading. The issue is not that Chinese military forces were deployed in Southeast Asia, but rather that China exerted influence (diplomatic and cultural) because of its position of primacy. In Southeast Asia the tribute system was concerned with trade and the transmitting of Confucian culture. It can be best understood in hegemonic terms by the language used. Mark Mancall captures the primary position of China when he quotes the following from Mala, a Chinese diplomat in 1676:

> First, 'every ambassador who comes to us here in China must frame his speech as if he came "up" from a humble and inferior place to an exalted one, or throne'. Second, the court officials reporting the arrival of an ambassador to the emperor state that the ambassador has come 'from a lower place to Your most exalted Throne, to strike his forehead on the ground', that is, to perform the Kow-tow cere-mony. Third, all gifts are called tribute in official documents. Fourth, the emperor's gifts to other rulers are not called gifts, but are clearly called gratuities in return for tribute or service. These conditions must be accepted by all ambassadors and other envoys 'without reserve'.[22]

While such language highlights China's supremacy, it would be wrong to infer that if such subordination was unacceptable China would punish the offender. If the tribute system was unacceptable to others they would be considered to exist outside the civilised world and to be 'barbarians'. Thus, when in 1382 Japan rejected China's position of hegemony, China broke off relations.[23] As Mancall states, the tribute system 'existed not because Confucianism dictated its existence but because it provided mechanisms for dealing with the universe on the basis of prior, detailed observation'.[24] In this sense, China's hegemony was benign, no one was forced to accept it. Wang Gungwu perfectly captures how the tributary system affirmed China's hegemony in Southeast Asia, and the relationship between it and its southern neighbours, when he writes:

> The system was never used for territorial expansion, only for extending influence and affirming China's interpretation of its central place in the universe. The system provided one of the ways of reminding China's neighbours of its view of its own centrality. In essence, the system was used to stabilise the status quo.[25]

This position of primacy can be seen in more modern times and is manifest in the expectation of Chinese officials that China is recognised by the international community as a great power. Roy refers to this when he writes that after 'centuries of viewing their country as the cultural, political and economic centre of the world, the Chinese seem to have difficulty dealing with other states as equals'.[26] The Chinese assumption that it has the right to be treated as a great power, means that requiring smaller neighbours to accept its primary position might not be a conscious policy for Beijing. If the perception exists in China that it is the dominant actor and its rise indicates a return of the natural order, evidence of it requiring its southern neighbours to acknowledge its primacy is unlikely to be found in Chinese statements. Instead, it is necessary to examine China's actions to determine hegemonic tendencies.

During the Cold War the benign aspect of China's primary position was not in evidence, and instead it was manifest in the Chinese language of 'teaching lessons' when Beijing resorted to the use of force against neighbouring states to show its displeasure with their actions. China's hegemonic tendencies can also be seen in more subtle variations of interference. For example, while China claims that it operates in accordance with the Five Principles of Peaceful Coexistence,[27] which amount to respect for state independence from outside influence, it is pertinent to recall that during the Cold War, China sought to undermine the regimes in Southeast Asia by sponsoring the activities of the Communist Party of Thailand (CPT), Malaysia (CPM), Burma (BCP) and Indonesia (PKI). This involvement in the affairs of its southern neighbours can also be witnessed in the role it played in first, the containment of the Cambodian crisis – by supporting the Khmer Rouge and Thailand with military assistance – and second, the termination of the crisis by pressurising the Khmer Rouge to accept the United Nations peace plan in 1989–90. Thus, China's actions indicate a state which has involved itself in the affairs of its neighbours. Has this continued in the post-Cold War era?

During the 1990s China's relations with the states of Southeast Asia have improved. Having halted its support for the communist insurgencies during the 1970s, China encouraged the CPM to agree to a cease-fire in 1989 as it moved from party-to-party relations to state-to-state relations. Diplomatic relations were restored with Indonesia and established with Singapore and Brunei in 1990. The Law on Citizenship, passed in 1989, relinquished China's authority over the overseas Chinese living in the region and forced them to take citizenship in their place of residence.[28] China has participated in the South China Sea workshops held annually in Indonesia and was an original member of the ASEAN Regional Forum (ARF).[29] In 1995 China even published its defence White Paper in the interests of transparency. It may not have revealed very much but was no less forthcoming than equivalent publications in Singapore, Thailand and Indonesia. Are these the actions of a state assuming regional hegemony?

The key is the extent to which China is determining the norms of behaviour being adopted and the pace of their implementation in the region. It is already evident in ASEAN that Southeast Asian security is dependent upon the actions and intentions of extra-regional powers. During the Cold War the official ASEAN position denied this with the Zone of Peace, Freedom and Neutrality (ZOPFAN) declaration, but in the post-Cold War era the ARF has codified Japan, China and the United States as the key players in the region. Hence, the following statement from the May 1993 meeting of ASEAN Senior Officials and Post-Ministerial Dialogue partners in Singapore: 'The continuing presence of the United States, as well as stable relationships among the United States, Japan, and China and other states of the region would contribute to regional stability'.[30]

While the United States and Japan are the most influential extra-regional powers in Southeast Asia, China's influence is growing. Indeed, Jusuf Wanandi writes, for 'the ARF initiative to succeed, all the great powers, especially China, must participate. China's participation is most critical because it is the emerging great power, previously isolated in the area, and still has to prove its willingness to become a responsible regional power'.[31] Beijing's growing importance was given tangible evidence when in December 1997 China, along with Japan and South Korea, attended a summit meeting with ASEAN members and this was repeated at the sixth ASEAN summit held in Hanoi in December 1998.

In the Indonesian-sponsored workshops – Workshops on Managing Potential Conflicts in the South China Sea – and the ARF, China is setting the pace of implementation and progress being reached. The workshops, which have been held annually since 1989, began with an ambitious agenda that included discussing political and strategic questions. However, with Beijing interpreting these workshops as unofficial, they were not prepared to enter into discussions concerning security confidence building measures (CBMs), such as limits on troop deployments in the Spratlys. The participation of Taiwan in these workshops perhaps also explains Beijing reluctance to give the discussions governmental status, and it most certainly explains why China will not discuss military issues.[32] The workshops have instead focused on technical issues, such as assessing fishing, mineral and hydrocarbon resources. However, even in these issues China has been reluctant to implement agreements.[33] Instead Beijing appears to view these discussions as equivalent to the ARF's track-two level discussions. This reluctance to give the workshops official status also explains why China refused to sign the 1992 ASEAN Manila Declaration, although Beijing agreed to negotiate a code of conduct based upon this declaration with the other claimants. The key for ASEAN is that the declaration calls for a repudiation of the use of force.

In the ARF, China has also been instrumental in the forum's progress. It did not set the agenda for the ARF, although Foreign Minister Qian Qichen's comments in 1995 were remarkably similar; but since its inauguration China has affected its progress.[34] First convened in July 1994 in Bangkok, the ARF meets annually in the capital cities of the ASEAN members.[35] In 1995 ASEAN set the agenda for the ARF with its Concept Paper, which proposed that the ARF provide security and stability in the region as it evolves through a three stage process. The first stage is the promotion of CBMs, the second is the development of preventive diplomacy mechanisms and the final stage is the development of conflict resolution mechanisms, subsequently renamed 'elaboration of approaches to conflicts' in deference to Chinese wishes.[36]

In keeping with the ASEAN principles of consultation and consensus decision-making the Concept Paper noted that 'the ARF process shall move at a pace comfortable to all participants'. Since China wants the process to move at a slower pace than other members – Chinese officials often make reference to 'incremental' progress or development – it gives China de facto control over the discussion and implementation of each stage.[37] The evolution from stage to stage is accomplished via a two-track process. Track I involves government officials and is concerned with CBMs, while Track II involves discussions by strategic studies institutes and other non-governmental organisations to explore possible activities at the current and subsequent stage of the ARF process, currently confidence-building and preventive diplomacy.[38] Track I has subsequently been subdivided into two with the Inter-Sessional Support Group (ISG), which is concerned with security perceptions and defence policy papers, and Inter-Sessional Meetings (ISM) which deal with cooperative activities such as peacekeeping, search and rescue coordination and disaster relief.

According to Leifer the difference in name between the two groups was to accommodate Chinese concerns that CBM discussions might give the impression of continuous institutionalised activity. The same reason is given for the term 'inter', which implies it meets on an ad hoc basis.[39] These groups are co-chaired with one of the chairs drawn from the ASEAN members. In the 1996–1997 year China and the Philippines co-chaired the ISG, with the meeting in Beijing in March 1997 marking the first time that China had hosted an official multilateral conference on security issues. The ISG was not very productive, and Rosemary Foot suggests that the reason lay with the Chinese participants who felt it was necessary to be deliberately intransigent on home soil in the presence of PLA officials.[40]

The point is not therefore that China is seeking to subjugate ASEAN through conquest, but rather that China has in the past held a position of benign hegemony in Southeast Asia and its actions indicate that it is resuming that position. This is supported by David Shambaugh when he asserts:

> Beijing … seeks to redress the Asian regional subsystem balance of power. History does not suggest that China seeks to conquer or absorb other countries in the region (except Taiwan and claimed territories in the East and South China Seas), but rather to place itself at the top of a new hierarchical pyramid of power in the region – a kind of new 'tribute system' whereby patronage and protection is

dispensed to other countries in return for their recognition of China's superiority and sensitivities. International relations scholars recognize this as a classic benevolent hegemonic system.[41]

3   South China Sea: China's intentions in the Spratlys

The third reason why China appears to be assuming the position of regional hegemon is its claims in the South China Sea. China claims sovereignty over much of the South China Sea and has refused to compromise, with reference to its claims variously described as either irrefutable or indisputable, 'despite the hegemonic implications of this position'.[42] The Chinese claim is based on historic grounds with the act of discovery said to have taken place during the Han Dynasty in the second century and administrative duties functioning at the beginning of the Tang Dynasty in the eighth century. Beijing, throughout the 1990s, has sought to bolster its claim with its 1992 Law on the Territorial Waters and their Contiguous Areas and, subsequently at the 1995 ASEAN Annual Meeting in Brunei, Chinese Foreign Minister Qian Qichen agreed to defend China's sovereignty claims in accordance with the 1982 UN Convention on the Law of the Sea (UNCLOS).[43]

In addition to the Chinese claim, ASEAN states also lay claim to parts of the South China Sea. Vietnam claims considerable areas of the South China Sea on historic grounds, while for the Philippines geographical proximity is used to justify its smaller claim. The Malaysian claim is based on a number of reefs falling within its continental shelf, while the claim from Brunei is based on its Exclusive Economic Zone (EEZ), which became active with the ratification of the 1982 International Law of the Sea on 16 November 1994.

All participants, with the exception of Brunei, have sought to strengthen their claims by stationing troops on some of the reefs.[44] In addition, Indonesia has also expressed concern that China has claimed part of its Natuna gas field. China's actions throughout the late 1980s and 1990s have provided tangible evidence of its irredentist ambitions. In addition to seizing a number of reefs and building structures on them, including an airfield on Woody Island in the Paracels, the Chinese have also granted concessions for energy corporations to survey and drill for oil. In view of these actions, how can the security dilemma, which is predicated on illusory incompatibility, be applicable to China's irredentist ambitions in the South China Sea?

It was noted in Chapter 4 that despite the overlapping territorial claims amongst the ASEAN members, and thus the existence at one level of analysis of a real incompatibility, the security dilemma was still applicable. The reason lay with none of the ASEAN members actively seeking to change the status quo, but because of the quiescent claim it was possible that the accumulation of weapons could be misinterpreted as a move to realise a revisionist ambition. Thus, despite none of the ASEAN members seeking to change the status quo, the conflicting territorial claims could heighten their misperception of each others' arms procurements leading to a rise in tension over an illusory incompatibility. For a security dilemma to be applicable to China–ASEAN relations, the ambitions of the Chinese are thus a critical issue.

During the 1990s the Chinese have been erecting 'sovereignty posts' within the Spratly Islands group, and when viewed in conjunction with the activities of the other claimants this indicates that rather than seeking to alter the status quo, China is engaged in a policy of 'catch up' to ensure its claim is not weakened by the earlier actions of the other claimants. The occupation of islands was begun by the Philippines in the early 1970s, and by 1974 Manila had stationed troops on five islands. During the 1980s this was increased by another four islands and in 1996 the Philippines occupied nine islands with 595 troops. Vietnam began occupying islands after reunification in 1975 and continued in the 1980s, taking their number to over twenty. By 1996 Vietnam occupied 25 islands with 600 troops. Malaysia began its occupation in the 1980s when it occupied three islands and by 1996 had deployed 70 troops.[45]

These claimants have also sought to bolster their sovereignty claims by developing tourism on the islands, sending scientists to the disputed area, building fishing ports and lighthouses.[46] In view of the oil and gas resources, a favoured way of asserting sovereignty is to award oil/gas concessions and begin drilling. According to the Chinese, by 1992 of the thousand oil/gas drills in the South China Sea, '121 (7 belonging to the Philippines, 90 to Malaysia, 17 to Indonesia, and 7 to Vietnam) are within China's traditional sea border'.[47] In comparison, the Chinese did not begin their island occupation until 1987 and by 1996 had occupied only eight islands and deployed 260 troops.[48]

China's actions attract more coverage than those of the ASEAN claimants, thus creating the impression that only China is engaged in construction work in the South China Sea. When, for example, China's completion of structures on Mischief Reef in early 1999 received widespread media coverage, little attention was given to the Philippines decision to upgrade facilities on Pag-Asa island or the Vietnamese structures on Lizzie Weber Reef.[49] China's occupation of islands in the

South China Sea did result in a violent clash with Vietnam in 1988, and details of this are provided below, though for now it is important to appreciate that China's occupation of islands is in keeping with actions undertaken by all claimants, and not necessarily an indication of hostile intent in Beijing.

Indeed, China's policy towards the Spratlys indicates a willingness to accept the present situation and exploit the natural resources in the area. Although Beijing has no intention of relinquishing its sovereignty claim, Chinese leaders throughout the 1990s have proposed bilateral joint development of these resources.[50] Since many of the disputed areas involve intra-ASEAN rivalries as well as China's claim, such bilateral proposals could cause divisions within ASEAN if accepted by one of the association's members.[51] ASEAN unity has remained so far and Beijing has not gained bilateral support for its joint development proposals.

The legacy of China's history, its irredentist ambitions in the South China Sea and the growth in its economic and military power indicate that China is emerging in Southeast Asia as the regional hegemon. None of this however indicates that China is a revisionist, expansionist, or malign power seeking to subjugate the states of Southeast Asia. But it does suggest that despite official protestations to the contrary, regional hegemony is the position China is adopting. Roy asserts, 'perhaps the strongest reason to consider China the most likely contender for regional hegemony in the near future is that intentions usually follow capabilities. By early next century, China will probably possess unprecedented capabilities, including both the largest population and the largest economy in the world'.[52] Ross Munro captures perfectly the evolving relationship when he writes:

> What we may be witnessing are the early stages of a reversion ... to the more 'natural' state of affairs that prevailed centuries ago. At their full flowering, China's ruling dynasties reigned over a tributary states system under which neighbours, largely independent and unoccupied by Chinese troops, sent 'tribute' to Beijing to acknowledge Chinese hegemony.[53]

Has the emergence of China as a great power initiated a security dilemma between ASEAN and China? It is now necessary to look more closely at China's military activities and the ASEAN response, especially in view of Roy's warning that 'China's recent military build-up, including the acquisition of long-range power-projection systems, does not by itself prove hegemonic designs, but it is consistent with such plans.'[54]

B. China–ASEAN security dilemma?

1 China's military strategy

The security dilemma operates at its highest pitch when states adopt an offensive military strategy to provide their security.[55] The capability to attack neighbouring states naturally leads decision-makers in these states to view with some trepidation the first state's ambitions. This is especially likely if the adoption of an offensive strategy has replaced a previously defensive approach to achieving security. Does this change indicate a revisionist ambition or merely the belief that the previous military strategy was becoming moribund? Such an alteration in defence strategy has in fact occurred in China.

In the aftermath of the civil war on mainland China, the military strategy adopted by the communists was a classic non-offensive defence approach to achieving security. In the event of an attack, Chinese forces – the People's Liberation Army (PLA) – would withdraw into the Chinese heartland where, with the assistance of the Chinese population, the enemy would be subjected to repeated attacks. With the supply lines of the enemy stretched the invading force would be compelled to withdraw. The strategy was known as 'people's war' and reflected the belief in Beijing that China's inferior military capabilities could be compensated for by mobilising the nation and gaining superiority in numbers.

By the mid-1970s this strategy was changing to reflect improvements in China's military capabilities and became known as 'people's war under modern conditions'. Still a non-offensive defence doctrine, it was now envisaged that in the event of a land attack the PLA would seek to defeat the enemy near the border. This not only reflected a higher degree of confidence in the PLA's ability to match the opponent, but also reflected the government's realisation that once the enemy had been lured into the heartland of China much of China's industrial and transportation networks would be under the enemy's control.

In the early 1980s the military strategy was once again under review. In the US, the hawkish Reagan administration caused the USSR to focus on Europe and consequently led in Beijing to the perception that the prospect of an *early* war with the Soviet Union had been reduced.

This was therefore an opportunity for China to modernise its forces. This led to a reorganisation of the PLA's field armies into group armies where infantry, armour and other ground units were to be combined. The move towards a more professional army led to a reduction in manpower – approximately 25 per cent of the PLA's manpower was cut by 1987 – and critically for the security dilemma an alteration to the non-offensive defence principles which had been evident in the 'people's war under modern conditions'.

The key difference for the new strategy was that the nature of the threat was seen to have changed. The prospect of major war was viewed as receding, but the possibility of more localised and limited conflicts on China's periphery was perceived to be on the rise. This led to the adoption of three principles that have an impact on the security dilemma. First, the need to project force to defend China's strategic frontier – which includes, amongst other areas, the Indian Ocean, the Malacca Straits and the South China Sea – since this clearly entails an offensive approach to achieve security.[56] Second, the need to strike first and gain the initiative early; this increases fear and suspicion, since the opportunity to negotiate is reduced. Third, the desire to force a quick solution, since this also highlights the imperative of speedy military action. These principles also reveal the fundamental change occurring in Chinese military strategy – no longer was security to be achieved through a prolonged, attritional approach to war.

In 1988 the Chinese conducted four military exercises, three of which were in the north revealing that the USSR was still the main focus of attention. The fourth exercise, however, concerned Chinese territory in the South China Sea and it entailed a combined naval, air and army exercise around the island of Hainan. The ability to project force from continental China had become a necessary element in China's military strategy and it reflected the move from a 'continental' strategy to one concerned with the 'periphery'. The ability to protect Chinese territory that lies away from the mainland has resulted in the new concept of 'all in-depth strike' which entails the use of tactical missiles to neutralise enemy artillery and the rapid deployment of troops behind enemy lines.

These rapid response, or 'fist' units, use the most advanced equipment available to the PLA and are trained in combined arms operations.[57] They are known as 'pockets of excellence' within the three armed services and were an integral part of the 1988 exercises. This offensive approach is complemented by the principle of 'gaining the initiative by striking first'. Fearing that in modern warfare the initiative could not be reclaimed once lost at the outset of battle, the PLA now seeks to gain the initiative first:

> This … requires us to identify an enemy attempt at the initial stage of its aggression, or at the time of restoring lost territories or protecting natural and economic resources, catching strategic initiative swiftly through offensive operation, striking first, suppressing the enemy provocation in possibly the shortest time, setting back the enemy's aggressive attempt, and winning the war.[58]

The appreciation in Beijing that limited wars are as much political as military in nature has led to the belief that once started it is necessary to force a quick resolution. This will provide China with the diplomatic advantage in political negotiations. This is quite a change from the attritional and prolonged campaigns envisaged in 'people's war'. The ability of the United States to paralyse Iraqi C^3I (command, control, communications and intelligence) facilities using sophisticated technology in 1991 confirmed to the Chinese that in modern warfare the victor needed to strike quickly and decisively at the outset of battle. Once the initiative had been gained it was possible through combined arms operations to break through strong defensive positions. Now referred to as 'limited war under high technology conditions', China's military strategy has undergone major changes under the communist leadership. It has brought about changes in military force structure, training and arms deployment.

The change of military strategy, however, is only the first element in initiating a security dilemma. It is only likely to operate when the Chinese procure the types of sophisticated equipment necessary to make this new strategy operational. Although the Chinese have begun this process, it must be noted that they are still some way from acquiring the capabilities to mount a serious threat to ASEAN security. Indeed, according to David Shambaugh, China 'will lack the airlift and sealift capability vital for power projection and rapid deployment for probably two decades or more'.[59] The acquisition of power projection forces means the acquisition of naval vessels and aircraft, in particular the type of naval capabilities to turn China's coastal defence force into a blue water fleet and the acquisition of fighter support that has mid-air refuelling capabilities.

For the naval programme, the Chinese are procuring two new classes of surface combatants, the *Luhu*-class (type 052) guided missile destroyer, and the *Jiangwei*-class (type 055) guided missile frigate, both carrying surface-to-air (SAM) and ship-to-ship missiles (SSM). In addition, China has bought two Sovremenny class destroyers from Russia, which are to be delivered in 1999, and a further two have been ordered for delivery in 2000. These warships will be equipped with Kamov Ka-28 helicopters, providing a 'substantial boost to its anti-submarine warfare (ASW) capabilities' and the SS-22 SSM.[60] China has also modernised its submarine fleet by purchasing four Russian *kilo*-class submarines and is developing its own *Song*-class type 039 submarine. Support vessels providing replenishment-at-sea have also been improved, as have amphibious landing vessels.[61]

The key to a blue water fleet though is an aircraft carrier and in March 1993, Vice Admiral Zhang Yuanhai, admitted that research had begun for a carrier although construction had not yet begun. It is also known that Chinese pilots have been conducting take-off-and-landing tests on a simulated carrier deck since April 1987. According to You Ji, 'the question no longer seems to be whether China wants to possess a carrier but when China feels its economy is strong enough for such an endeavour'.[62] These improvements to the PLAN (People's Liberation Army Navy) are, however, of a limited magnitude and the bulk of its capability is outdated equipment. China is not expected to have a blue water fleet until 2025 at the earliest and possibly not until 2050.

The modernisation of China's air force – a combination of the PLAN Air Force (PLANAF) and People's Liberation Army Air Force (PLAAF) – like the PLAN, leads to concerns regarding its potential as opposed to actual capabilities. There is a clear desire by Beijing to acquire the air support the PLAN needs to become a blue water fleet. China has procured Su-27s from Russia, which are the only Chinese combat aircraft capable of conducting air operations over the Spratly islands, and China has gained the licence to build these aircraft.[63] However, the Chinese pilots are not yet proficient in open water, all-weather, mid-air refuelling and night navigational skills. Nevertheless, China's modernisation programme is a clear attempt to enhance China's ability to project power in the South China Sea, or, as Paul Godwin states, 'the SU-27 is a clear indicator of Beijing's intent'.[64]

2　ASEAN's military build-up: a China threat?

The reasons for the arms build-up among the ASEAN members in the early to mid-1990s were numerous and these were noted in Chapter 4. How far though does the Chinese threat explain these acquisitions? And, indeed, do ASEAN members perceive a threat?

The level of concern regarding China is dependent upon Chinese actions, with it rising quite notably in 1995/96 after the Mischief Reef incident, and again in late 1998, and the 1996 military exercises in the Taiwan Strait. The level of concern also varies amongst the ASEAN states depending upon their claims in the South China Sea, and especially the Spratly Islands. Thus, concern in Thailand and Singapore, who do not lay claim to any of the reefs in the Spratly Islands, is less than other ASEAN states. Although because a rise in tension could effect freedom of navigation for the important shipping lanes in the South China Sea, they are not immune to Chinese actions.[65]

The greatest level of concern emanates from Hanoi with Manila and Jakarta close behind. The seizure of islands in the Paracels by China in 1974 and the military clash over Johnson Reef that led to the sinking of three Vietnamese ships and the loss of 77 sailors in 1988, make the Vietnam–China relationship the most tense. In the 1990s, the overlapping claims have led both states to award concessions to oil companies in areas of dispute; the Chinese to Crestone Energy Corporation in 1992 and Vietnam to the Mobil Corporation in 1994.

Both sides have denounced these actions as illegal, with Vietnam stressing that the Crestone concession in the 'Tu Chinch coral reef' lies in Vietnam's EEZ, while the Chinese claim that the Mobil concession in the Blue Dragon Oil field is illegal because this sea area belongs to the adjacent waters of the Nansha (Spratly) Islands. In July 1994 China deployed two warships to blockade a Vietnam rig to prevent the delivery of food and water.[66] In the Gulf of Tonkin Vietnam has accused China of violating its territorial waters, and in 1994 seized two Chinese vessels, claiming that during this incident Chinese boats opened fire. A further incident in March 1997 concerned China's 'Kan Tan Oil Platform No. 3', which the Vietnamese accused of conducting exploratory oil drilling 55 nautical miles from Vietnam's base line. After heated exchanges in which both states claimed the area in which the Kan Tan oil rig was operating, the rig withdrew on 1 April.[67]

Since independence, China has been the main external concern for Indonesia. President Suharto accused the Chinese of aiding the Indonesian Communist Party (PKI) in its failed coup attempt in September 1965, and during the 1980 Cambodian conflict Indonesia viewed with concern the growing influence of Beijing, especially over Thailand. Only in 1990 were diplomatic relations restored after a period of twenty-three years. In 1994, Indonesia questioned China over the significance of a demarcation line on Chinese maps that indicated the Natuna gas field fell within China's territorial claim. Despite meetings in 1995, including at presidential level at the November Asia-Pacific Economic Cooperation (APEC) summit, the situation remains unresolved. The Chinese have called for bilateral discussions on the overlapping sea boundaries, while the Indonesian position is that there is no overlap. As Allen Whiting notes, 'until the line in question disappears from [China's] maps or a more detailed delineation of Chinese claims is presented in print, uncertainty over intentions will remain'.[68]

In September 1995 former Foreign Minister Ruslan Abdulgani warned of China's expansionist tendency southwards and in September the following year Indonesia conducted military exercises around Natuna for the first time in five years. In December 1995 Indonesia broke with its traditional non-aligned status and concluded a defence agreement with Australia. While domestic factors can partly explain the agreement, the need to directly involve Australia, and indirectly the United States, in the security of Indonesia indicates that Jakarta remains wary of Chinese intentions.

For the Philippines, the incident over Mischief Reef in 1995 – where China has built structures which resemble guard posts – revealed that China would challenge an ASEAN state in the South China Sea, and so end the hope that China's assertive behaviour would be restricted to Vietnam.[69] In October 1995 then President Ramos warned that 'how China exercises its political and military clout must concern us all'; and in 1996, Manila joined Hanoi in responding to China's extension of its territorial waters by declaring it a 'black shadow over regional stability'.[70] In late 1998 Mischief Reef again became an issue of controversy when the Philippines discovered that the Chinese had expanded the structures on the reef. These structures in combination with others on different reefs, including a communication post and heli-pad at Fiery Cross, indicate a creeping Chinese military presence.[71]

Philippine President, Joseph Estrada, and Jiang Zemin met during the APEC summit in Kuala Lumpur in November to discuss the Chinese action. The Chinese refused to accept the Philippine proposals for removing the structures, but the Philippines agreed to examine the Chinese proposal for joint use and the Chinese agreed not to further expand the structures.[72] According to the Philippines' Defence Secretary, Orlando Mercado, the Chinese are building an airstrip on Mischief Reef, which he claims, 'will be the farthest projection of China's power, and a dagger at our underbelly'.[73] With the reef only 300 kilometers from Palawan, the immediate effect of the Chinese action was to set in motion a delayed modernisation programme for the Armed Forces of the Philippines (AFP), and for Estrada to reiterate the importance of the US military presence in the region.[74] The implications of this incident for escaping the security dilemma will be examined later.

In Kuala Lumpur, the official line towards China is that it is not a threat in the short and medium term but rather a long term problem with one defence analyst writing, 'Malaysia has always considered modern Communist China to be the region's greatest long-term threat.'[75] In Singapore, Prime Minister Goh Chok Tong warned in 1995 '[i]n Asia, China's rising power and arms build-up has stirred anxiety. It is important to bring into the open this underlying sense of discomfort, even insecurity, about the political and military ambitions of China.'[76] In Bangkok, concern is more directed towards China's military presence in Burma, than with the South China Sea. China has not only been Rangoon's main supplier of military equipment, but it has also constructed military facilities in the Andaman Sea which could pave the way for a Chinese military presence in the Indian Ocean. Improvements to the transport network in Upper Burma are also thought to reflect security as well as commercial concerns. According to Donald Seekins, 'Burma's neighbours, who have grown increasingly concerned about the Chinese presence, have reason to consider it an expansion of China's aspirations to Great Power status.'[77]

Apprehension amongst the ASEAN states about Chinese intentions in the region seem to be in evidence, although the degree of concern varies amongst them. Chang Pao-Min asserts, 'the ASEAN countries... have for decades seen China as *the* source of threat to the security and stability of Southeast Asia' (emphasis in original). He goes on to say, 'distrust of China... has deep historical, cultural, as well as ideological roots that cannot be easily removed, particularly for Malaysia and Indonesia'.[78] Denny Roy is equally emphatic, 'Asians are concerned about China's recent military upgrading programme. They clearly are'.[79]

The extent to which Chinese intentions explain the ASEAN arms build-up is, however, contentious. According to Whiting, writing before the economic crisis hit the region, 'none of the recent increases in arms is attributed to the China factor'.[80] David Shambaugh though asserts, 'the PLA's desired rapid deployment and blue water naval capabilities are a cause for deep concern among Southeast Asian militaries, which at present do not have the capacity to blunt a Chinese thrust southward. To enhance their readiness, ASEAN militaries – notably Malaysia and Indonesia – have embarked on force modernization programmes of their own, particularly attempting to enhance their naval and air capabilities.'[81] Shambaugh is supported by Carlyle Thayer when he writes, '[i]n 1992, reacting to Chinese assertiveness in the South China Sea, Vietnam's military budget was increased for the first time in five years'.[82] Derek da Cunha also notes that it was the 1995 Mischief Reef incident which led to 'renewed Malaysian interest in acquiring diesel electric submarines'.[83] Ball is probably right to note that the build-up was the result of many factors, of which concern with China was just one. What does not appear to be in doubt is that there is, to varying degrees amongst the ASEAN members, concern regarding Chinese intentions in Southeast Asia.

To argue that the accumulation of weapons amongst the ASEAN members was partly the result of China's military modernisation programme, is not in itself evidence of a security dilemma. The security dilemma operates when both parties take defensive actions to deter perceived offensive actions from the other, and in so doing make matters worse by appearing to confirm their malign intent. Whatever the reasons behind China's modernisation of its military capabilities, they are unlikely to include concern within Beijing that military developments in ASEAN constitute a threat to Chinese security. Although Beijing may have reasoned that the accumulation of armaments by ASEAN members made it necessary for the PLA to procure more weapons in order to achieve military dominance in the South China Sea.

However, while the accumulation of arms by the ASEAN states may have had a minor paradoxical effect of increasing China's military programme, and thereby their accumulation did paradoxically make matters worse for ASEAN by strengthening the desire in China for sophisticated weapons, the more pertinent response from ASEAN lies in the diplomatic arena. Therefore, in order to highlight the paradoxical nature of the policies being pursued it is necessary to examine the diplomatic response ASEAN has embarked upon because of its perception of threat from China. In other words, the ASEAN response to the 'China threat' which is more likely to explain the external reasons why China believes it needs to improve its military capabilities, lies in the diplomatic arena.

3   A mitigated security dilemma

It was noted earlier that debates on interacting with China coalesce around the containment or engagement approach to managing China. Those who interpret Chinese actions as malign naturally believe it is necessary to contain, while those who put a benign interpretation on

Chinese behaviour favour engagement. A popular stand is the one that favours engagement because China needs good relations in order to continue to enjoy economic growth, and thus by tying China to the world economy it reduces the likelihood of Beijing using force in its foreign relations because of the detrimental effect this will have on its economy. China will 'learn' therefore by benefiting from international cooperation to work within the norms of international behaviour.

As David Shambaugh writes, engagement 'is a process and vehicle to the ultimate goal of integrating China into the existing rule-based, institutionalized, and normative international system. Engagement is the means, integration the end'.[84] However, because China has a propensity to use force and maintains its irredentist claims in the South China Sea, there is a lingering suspicion that China might just be biding its time until its military capabilities enable it to take what it wants regardless of neighbouring sensibilities; whether this be the Spratlys, Senkaku/Diaoyu Islands or even Taiwan. Therefore, while engaging China is a good policy, it also pays to contain just in case. For the members of ASEAN containment comes in the guise of external powers capable of balancing China, in particular the US. Hence, Michael Yahuda's conclusion that the 'challenge ... for those in Southeast Asia ... who argue in favour of dealing with China through engagement and interdependence is to combine these with American power'.[85] The 1990s has thus witnessed a combination of containment and engagement by the ASEAN members.

The emergence of China as a rising power naturally raises the question of its relations with the current great powers of East Asia, in particular the United States. After the Sino–US rapprochement in the 1970s the Chinese welcomed the US presence as a means of balancing the Soviet Union and preventing Soviet hegemony in the region. With the collapse of the Soviet Union, however, the US balancing role is no longer required. Indeed, Chinese relations with Moscow have improved immeasurably, and on 10 November 1997 Russian President Boris Yeltsin and Chinese President Jiang Zemin signed an agreement ending the two countries' protracted dispute over the demarcation of their border over some 4,300 kilometres. In the 1990s Chinese concerns have centred on Washington and in particular the spread of democratic ideals that could undermine CCP rule.[86] China wants to maintain good relations with the US for economic reasons, but it no longer favours a US military presence in the region.

At the ARF summit in 1995, Qian Qichen 'indicated that Beijing no longer considers the US military presence in East Asia a force for peace and stability'.[87] The reinvigoration of the US–Japan defence agreement in June 1997 elicited a hostile response from China, while the goodwill exhibited in 1998 during US President Clinton's visit to Beijing has not indicated a sea change in Sino–US relations.[88] By the end of the 1990s, relations had soured over US plans to deploy a Theatre Missile Defence system for East Asia and leaks from the Cox report, a congressional document, accusing China of illegally procuring US military technology to improve the reliability of its missiles.[89] Since the continuation of an American military presence is not conducive to China's emergence as a regional hegemon, this provides ASEAN with the opportunity to hinder China's regional aspirations through diplomatic channels by encouraging the maintenance of a US military presence.

The general disquiet felt in Southeast Asia about China's intentions helps to explain the attempts by various ASEAN members to maintain a United States military presence in the region. In the aftermath of the Subic Bay closure in the Philippines in December 1992, the United States was able to conclude a Memorandum of Understanding with Singapore allowing permanent basing of more than 100 US service personnel and the establishment of a US Navy's logistics headquarters for the Western Pacific. With Malaysia, the United States increased the number of military exercises conducted and its warships were given access to the facilities at Malaysia's Lumut naval base. Even with Indonesia, the most independent of the ASEAN states, the United States began joint military exercises in 1990.[90]

Specific Chinese actions have also led to closer ties with the United States. During the Kan Tan oil rig incident, for example, the Vietnamese began discussions with the US on a possible military relationship. The clearest example though of how Chinese actions have led to calls for an unequivocal US commitment to the region came after the Chinese expansion of structures on Mischief Reef were discovered in late 1998. In October, the Estrada administration agreed to the resumption of joint military exercises with the United States for this first time since 1991, with Estrada using China's actions to pressure the Philippine Senate to ratify a Visiting Forces Agreement (VFA) with the United States.[91] China's actions also led Philippine Foreign Minister, Domingo Siazon, to claim that the US would come to the aid of the Philippines if China attacked the country over the dispute in the South China Sea, and he warned of a proliferation of nuclear states in East Asia if the US wavered in its defence commitments.[92] The general disquiet over China's actions in the Spratly islands has also led Singapore and Australia to reaffirm the importance of a US presence in the region.[93]

China's military build-up and its actions in the South China Sea have therefore had the paradoxical affect of being partly responsible for the continuing deployment of US military forces in East Asia.[94] This deployment in turn raises for Chinese military planners the prospect of potential conflict with the United States as China tries to resolve its sovereignty claims in the South China Sea and Taiwan. It is therefore not surprising that the PLA models its modernisation with regard to the potential for clashes with the US, although such an outcome is neither sought after, nor considered likely in Beijing. China's military build-up is therefore partly influenced by the presence of American forces in the region. These forces are in turn encouraged to remain in the region by other states, including the members of ASEAN, because of China's military build-up. The security dilemma is thus in operation as China's military modernisation, paradoxically, makes its pursuit of regional hegemony more difficult because it generates fear in neighbouring powers that its ambitions are malign and they respond by balancing China with the US.

This containment approach in turn makes matters worse by confirming Chinese suspicions that the international environment is anti-China. Avery Goldstein writes, 'Beijing considers the exaggeration of its capabilities and misinterpretations of its motives a smoke screen for ... a US-sponsored strategy of containment aimed at China that includes military assistance to regional actors and the cultivation of regional anti-China alliances. In short, this is a situation in which malign mutual perceptions seem to be feeding worst-case (or at least "bad case") planning that results in spiralling conflict.'[95] The security dilemma's severity is, however, mitigated and thus even during times of tension, such as the Mischief Reef incidents or China's military exercise off the coast of Taiwan in 1996, the level of concern remains muted. Allen Whiting notes that despite such events, there 'is no anticipation' within the decision-making circles of ASEAN members, 'of an expansionist China seeking to take over any country by attack, subversion, or economic domination'.[96] Before examining how ASEAN's engagement approach has achieved this, there remains one final element in the containment strategy that requires elucidation.

There exists in Southeast Asia the perception that the United States presence in the region is declining, and prudence dictates that should this occur ASEAN does not want to find itself alone in the shadow of its large northern neighbour. The Indonesia-Australia defence agreement, and India's entry into the ARF in 1996 can be seen as ASEAN providing substitute balancers vis-à-vis China in the event of a United

States withdrawal. The introduction of India is particularly interesting given the delicate nature of Sino–Indian relations. The border dispute between these states, China's military assistance to Pakistan and the growing Chinese presence in Burma have all caused the relationship to deteriorate.[97] In 1998 India accused China of building a heli-pad in Indian territory,[98] of assisting Pakistan in the development of its Ghauri missile (range of 1,500 kilometres and a payload of 700 kilograms, making it Pakistan's biggest and longest-range missile),[99] and most spectacularly, India carried out a series of nuclear explosions soon after Defence Minister George Fernandes described China as India's number one long term threat.[100] If the United States military presence is to decline in the future ASEAN might find in India a replacement, although one that has a more fractious relationship with Beijing than even Washington.

The security dilemma operates at its highest pitch when a state's uncertainty about its neighbour's intentions is such that any actions are viewed with deep suspicion and responded to on the basis of a worst-case scenario. Procedures that help to alleviate the uncertainty are thus important since they begin to unravel the spiral of insecurity that can develop as each takes measures to protect itself from a perceived threat. In the aftermath of the Cold War, ASEAN has sought to play the leading role in establishing such procedures for the Asia-Pacific region with the establishment of the ARF and the Indonesian-sponsored workshops for the South China Sea dispute. In addition to the ARF, ASEAN and China also engage in dialogue through five other fora.[101] These endeavours, combined with similar endeavours in other fields (most notably economic with APEC), constitute ASEAN's engagement of China.

At present this engagement in the security field has been concerned with building trust amongst the ARF members through CBMs, such as notification and observer participation at military exercises, and transparency, such as the publication of defence policy statements and registering of weapons transfers with the UN Register of Conventional Arms (UNRCA).[102] Given the voluntary nature of these exercises the tangible results have been limited, but this misses the essence of these multilateral endeavours. They are a process by which the ARF members' concerns about each other are expected to lessen as they become more confident about each other's intentions. This is captured in the three stage and twin-track process of the ARF; and at the 1997–1998 ISG, CBMs were also sub-divided into those that could be implemented in the near term (first basket) and those that would require more discussion (basket two). This sub-division was endorsed at the fifth ARF summit in July 1998.

If the tangible results of the ARF are limited, what success can be attributed to the ARF process in engaging China, that is teaching or socialising China in the norms of international behaviour? The successes can be found in first, the willingness of China to engage in CBM discussions, and second, in Beijing agreeing to put the South China Sea dispute on the ARF's agenda. While the CBM discussions have led to the Chinese publication of defence white papers, defence policy statements and submissions to the UNRCA, it is the acceptance by Chinese officials that defence transparency is a laudable goal which is critical. The PLA hosted more than 150 military delegations from 67 countries in 1997, while dispatching over 100 of its own delegates to 70 countries.[103]

In 1997, Chinese naval vessels also visited for the first time Malaysia and the Philippines, and for the third time Thailand. China also agreed to host a Basket 1 CBM in November 1998. The debate within China has moved away from whether it is in China's interest to be transparent, to how transparent it should be to generate confidence in others about its benign intentions; and as Rosemary Foot states, it is 'doubtful that such a debate would have taken place at all within Chinese official circles in the absence of the ARF'.[104] In April 1997, the South China Sea dispute was formally placed on the ARF's agenda. China's agreement not to settle the issue with force, and that it should instead be resolved on the basis of UNCLOS are important steps in reducing the ASEAN members suspicions of Chinese intentions. The engagement process, by reducing uncertainty, therefore helps to ameliorate the security dilemma's operation. Beijing's awareness that it can reduce regional fears of the 'China threat' is also a positive sign that the security dilemma can be mitigated, since it indicates an appreciation in China of ASEAN sensibilities.[105]

This engagement of Beijing helps to ease ASEAN members' uncertainty concerning China's intent, and is thus important in ameliorating the security dilemma. The security dilemma does, however, operate, and consequently there are times when the severity of its operation rises and the levels of suspicion and tension which this produces are manifest in a series of actions designed to counter those taken by the other. The Philippine response to the Chinese activities on Mischief Reef in late 1998 – which included upgrading its military facilities on Pag-Asa island and seeking to rally support for its position both bilaterally with the US, and multilaterally through the United

Nations, APEC and the Asia-Europe Meeting (ASEM) – is evidence of how China's actions have the paradoxical affect of increasing US involvement and hindering its goal of solving the South China Sea dispute bilaterally.[106] To prevent these rises in tension, it is necessary to escape the security dilemma, but, because the security dilemma is state-induced the issue of escape requires further explanation. The final section of this chapter is concerned with the added difficulty a state-induced security dilemma creates for overcoming the suspicion and fear ASEAN members have of Chinese intentions in Southeast Asia.

C. Escaping a state-induced security dilemma

The rise of China as a hegemon in Southeast Asia raises the prospect that the security dilemma operating between China and ASEAN is state-induced. That is, although China is seeking a position of hegemony, and thus requires ASEAN to defer to Beijing's interests, this means that China wants to consolidate the status quo, not overthrow it. It is a security dilemma because China's military build-up and its growing regional authority are not indications that Beijing is a revisionist power, and thus any threat perceived in the capitals of ASEAN members is based on an illusory incompatibility. It is state-induced because China's goal of hegemony requires ASEAN members to accept a position of subordination. Of course this benign interpretation of Chinese intent requires a leap of faith within the military circles of ASEAN members, and because circumstances can change, which may produce a threatening China in the future, ASEAN suspicions are, therefore, understandable. Nevertheless, the analysis of China's actions in Southeast Asia suggest that, despite public comments to the contrary, China is seeking a position of hegemony in the region.

This Chinese objective makes mitigating and ultimately escaping the security dilemma more difficult than is the case with a system-induced security dilemma. The difference between this state-induced security dilemma, and the traditional system-induced version, is that in the latter there is no requirement that either party forfeits a goal.[107] Whereas in the state-induced version, Snyder's definition that one party requires others to be insecure – interpreted here to mean hegemony – means that escape requires the forfeiting by one, or possibly both parties, of an objective. For China this would entail forgoing hegemony, while for ASEAN states it would mean forfeiting their primary role in determining the norms of behaviour governing security considerations in Southeast Asia, especially over the territorial disputes in the South

China Sea, and whether it should be resolved on a multilateral or bilateral basis. It is this requirement that something has to be forfeited – accepting one's own insecurity – which leads Snyder to claim that escape or mitigation is extremely difficult and cannot be achieved by concessions alone.

The choices available to ASEAN are (1) make China give up its sovereignty claims in the Spratlys (in Snyder's words 'change the circumstances'), or (2) ASEAN convinces Beijing that sovereignty should not be an issue, in much the same way as it has done for intra-ASEAN territorial disputes (in Snyder's words 'change the adversary's assessment of the circumstances'). The first option is not realistic for ASEAN since China has shown no sign that it is prepared to negotiate on the issue of sovereignty. The second option though is more promising and holds out the prospect that although ASEAN members might have to accept Chinese hegemony, they can still influence the norms of behaviour that come to govern the security environment through a combination of pressure and compromise with Beijing.

The use of pressurising tactics to mitigate a security dilemma is the antithesis of the usual approach, which teaches that resolve towards the other will only exacerbate the suspicion they have and make matters worse.[108] In this case though concessions and pressure are required because mitigation entails altering the hegemon's approach to achieving security (Thomas Christensen notes how pressurising China has helped to ameliorate the security dilemma in Chinese–Japanese/US relations).[109] It was suggested earlier that the security dilemma's operation is lessened because of the cooperative measures embarked upon by China and ASEAN. In particular the dialogue and agreements reached in the South China Sea workshops and the ARF. It is evident that China has no intention of relinquishing its sovereignty claims in the South China Sea, and therefore embarking upon measures that seek this outcome would be unlikely to garner success. Therefore, rather than trying to change Beijing's objectives, success is more likely if the pressurising and cooperative ventures influence Beijing's ambitions in the region short of the sovereignty issue. Although not necessarily instigated by ASEAN, although no doubt encouraged by ASEAN practice, Beijing's willingness to defer the issue of sovereignty over conflicting territorial claims in the Spratlys in order to exploit the natural resources is an encouraging sign. Indeed, China's need for a peaceful and cooperative external environment in order to maintain its economic growth should provide much scope for the ASEAN members to influence Beijing.

China's economic growth since the 1970s has been achieved by engaging with the world economy. The lessons to be drawn from the experience of Albania and North Korea is that autarky and prosperity are not mutually compatible. The result of this engagement is that from being ranked thirty-second in world trade with a share of world trade at 0.8 per cent in 1978, by the mid-1990s China was eleventh with a share of 2.9 per cent of world trade. Between 1978–1982 foreign direct investment (FDI) was about $1 million, by 1991 it had risen to $4 million, and by 1993 it had increased ten-fold, with as much as 85 per cent coming from overseas Chinese.[110] For most of the 1990s, China received more FDI than any other country and was ranked second to the US in 1995.[111] Towards the end of the 1990s FDI slowed as investors discovered that despite the potential of the Chinese market, obstacles existed which were making profits hard to come by.[112]

China's changing exports reflect the country's move towards development, with manufactured products representing 86 per cent of China's exports in 1995. This compares favourably to the high percentage (54%) of exports in the 1970s which were primary products (minerals and agriculture).[113] According to the Ministry of Trade, nearly half the Chinese economy is 'related to the international market'.[114] Consequently, China sought readmission to the General Agreement on Tariffs and Trade (GATT) in 1986 – this is still ongoing with GATT's successor, the World Trade Organisation (WTO) – and China joined APEC in 1991. China's engagement in the world economy, and perhaps more importantly the need for China to remain engaged in order to continue to prosper, has led to the prospect of China becoming constrained in its foreign policy as a consequence of its need for a peaceful external environment.

This is precisely the point Michael Leifer makes when he writes, 'the Spratly Islands has highlighted the problem of interdependence for China in its dealings with the states of Southeast Asia. It turns on how Beijing seeks to reconcile conflicting priorities of irredentist goals and good regional relations. In the case of the Spratly Islands, an untrammelled pursuit of irredentist ambition could run counter to the promotion of economic interests'. This leads Leifer to conclude, 'China's policy of economic reform would seem a hostage to its fortunes as a rising power.'[115]

Thus, although ASEAN finds itself with the difficult task of managing relations with a state that seeks hegemony, it is aided by that state's need for good regional relations. ASEAN can therefore pursue a combination of pressurising as well as engaging China in order not to alter its goals in the South China Sea, but rather its means of achieving its goals. Prior to the economic crisis, ASEAN acted with unity and resolve in its dealings with China when it considered Chinese actions to be unacceptable. The first consultative meeting between senior officials of ASEAN and China in 1995, held after the 1995 Mischief Reef incident, has been characterised by one participant as 'hectic, direct, and quite unsettling to the Chinese'.[116] Likewise in 1997 the exploratory drilling for gas by the Chinese Kan Tan Oil Platform came to an abrupt halt when Vietnam gained the support of its ASEAN colleagues over the incident.[117]

Chinese actions were thus susceptible to change via ASEAN pressure. So long as ASEAN did not seek to deny China its role of regional hegemon, then the security dilemma could be escaped, not just through pressurising tactics, but also through cooperation over issues which were mutually beneficial – but left the vexed issue of sovereignty over the Spratlys off the agenda. Thus, ASEAN has sought to gain a commitment from Beijing that force will not be used to settle the Spratlys dispute – at the Kuala Lumpur summit held on 15–16 December 1997 to commemorate ASEAN's 30th anniversary China and ASEAN pledged 'to resolve their disputes in the South China Sea through friendly consultations' – rather than the more contentious question of resolving sovereignty claims.[118] Likewise, according to Ramses Amer the prospects of a declaration on navigational rights in the sea-lanes of the Asia-Pacific are good because 'it is something that can be declared without prejudicing territorial claims' and 'will not have any bearing on the exploration of natural resources in undisputed EEZ areas, or disputed ones'.[119]

By trying to change the hegemon's understanding of the circumstances, rather than changing the circumstances – that is working within the parameter that China's sovereignty claim is not negotiable – ASEAN's approach holds out the prospect of escaping a state-induced security dilemma. The security dilemma is escaped as China and ASEAN cooperate over issues in the South China Sea for their mutual benefit, while the issue of sovereignty – although left unresolved – loses much of its relevance to their evolving relationship, in much the same way as the Philippines claim to Sabah has but a peripheral effect on Malaysia–Philippine relations. This appears to suggest that the prospect of escape is good. However, the discovery of Chinese construction work at Mischief Reef in November 1998 revealed that escape is still some way from being realised.

The Chinese claim that the construction work on Mischief Reef, which was completed in early 1999, was carried out to repair the shelters they had established there in 1995 for their fishermen. A closer inspection, however, revealed that China was expanding the structure and appeared to be adapting the Reef for military use. The Philippines claim the new concrete structures appeared to be garrisons with provisions for a heli-pad, gun embankments and berths for ships. The presence of Chinese warships around the Reef violated the code of conduct Beijing had signed with Manila after the 1995 Mischief Reef incident.[120] This code of conduct included such provisions as no upgrading or expanding of facilities by either side, and that each was to inform the other of all naval movements around the disputed islands.

The establishment of a new military facility in the Spratly Islands clearly places doubts over the professed Chinese desire not to use force to resolve the dispute, while the presence of Chinese warships damages the credibility of China's willingness to adhere to CBMs. Indeed the incident in late 1998 is one of many involving Chinese breaches of the code established with the Philippines. In January 1996 there was a minor skirmish involving Chinese and Philippine warships and between March and May of the same year the facilities on Mischief Reef were upgraded. In April 1997, tensions rose over the presence of Chinese warships near Mischief Reef, the establishment of structures on another reef, and the interception by the Philippine Navy of two Chinese vessels near Scarborough Shoal. In view of these incidents what are the prospects of escaping the China–ASEAN state-induced security dilemma?

The key is determining the extent to which two factors (economic and territorial claims) are affecting the evolution of Chinese policy towards the South China Sea dispute. If China's foreign policy is more influenced by economic considerations, this gives ASEAN members leverage over China; if, however, territorial claims take precedence, then outside influence is unlikely to greatly influence Chinese actions. According to Erica Strecker Downs and Phillip Saunders, '[w]hen forced to choose', over the conflicting claims between China and Japan to the Diaoyu Islands, 'Chinese leaders pursued economic development at the expense of nationalist goals'.[121] However, Mel Gurtov and Byong-Moo Hwang note that one of the reasons why China acted so provocatively towards Taiwan during the presidential elections in March 1996, was because 'the PLA wanted to send home the message to China's internationalists that *sacred national interests should never be sacrificed to economic interdependence*' (emphasis in original).[122] A brief examination of China's foreign policy towards regaining 'lost territory' will therefore reveal who within China is directing Chinese foreign policy, and consequently how close the ASEAN states are to escaping the Chinese state-induced security dilemma.

Before determining whether China is likely to be sensitive to the security dilemma it necessary to raise the question of which China? In post-Mao China, central political authority has become decentralised with certain regions having a great deal of autonomy in their dealings with foreign governments. This is especially the case with economic relations and scholarly/cultural exchanges; and this decentralisation has led David Goodman to assert that 'the nation-state may be a less appropriate comparative device for understanding China's develop-ment...than the notion of a continental system of great extent and diversity in which each province is regarded as a single, though not completely autarchic, social, political and economic system'.[123] However, Shambaugh notes that 'the management of foreign and national security policy is still monopolized by central authorities in Beijing; there is no such thing as a Xinjiang or Shandong foreign pol-icy'.[124] Thus, in discussing China's foreign policy towards its 'lost terri-tories', it is possible to refer to the decision-making apparatus in Beijing as representing China. Likewise, although within the PLA there are many factions, it is possible to refer to the PLA as a cohesive organ-isation in its dealings with the political leadership.[125]

The decision by the CCP to initiate a series of highly provocative military exercises during the Taiwan presidential election in March 1996 may provide an insight into Beijing's approach to acquiring other 'lost territory'. A caveat though must be added that for Beijing, Taiwan represents a different proposition to that of the Spratlys. China's sover-eignty over Taiwan is almost universally acknowledged and China has the military capability to at least impose a partial blockade of the island; neither circumstance is true for the Spratly Islands.[126] These dif-ferences mean that China is less likely to resort to force in the South China Sea than over Taiwan, which is encouraging for escaping the security dilemma. Although differences exist between these cases, the principle of reclaiming lost territory remains the same, and thus insights might be revealed.

Since 1979 China has followed Deng Xiaoping's policy of peaceful methods supported by military pressure in its dealings with Taiwan. With the need to reduce international tensions so that China's economy could develop, Beijing has pursued a non-confrontational approach towards Taipei as well as with other neighbouring states. You Ji writes: 'Deng's peaceful inducement was a sophisticated policy based on a realisation that a more belligerent policy would only further alienate the Taiwanese'.[127] This peaceful inducement encouraged Taiwanese investment in China (now worth more than US$25 billion), which in turn increased contacts between the two and 'ameliorated historical animosity'.[128]

By the early 1990s tension across the Taiwan Straits was considerably lower, and in 1995 Jiang Zemin called for equal bilateral consultations, including a summit, and spoke of Chinese not fighting Chinese.[129] With greater economic and cultural exchange Beijing reasoned that over time the status quo would sway in their favour.[130] However, when Taiwan's President, Lee Teng-hui, visited the US in June 1995 and raised Taiwan's international profile, this was perceived in Beijing as the beginning of a process leading towards independence. The granting of a visa by the United States for Lee's visit undermined the credibility of Foreign Minister Qian Qichen, who had told the Politburo that US Secretary of State Warren Christopher had assured him a visa would not be granted. According to Shambaugh, Qian and Jiang Zemin 'were both forced to make self-criticisms to the Central Military Commission'.[131] Lee's visit was certainly not considered part of the peaceful inducement plan, and indeed it was thought the time was right for military pressure. The 'carrot' approach favoured by the Foreign Ministry was replaced by the 'stick' approach advocated by the PLA.

The 'stick' approach was not intended to retake Taiwan by force but rather to avert a war with Taipei. The logic runs like this: (1) China would have to wage war against Taiwan if the latter declared independence, so (2) military threats would reduce the likelihood of a declaration of independence, and so (3) military threats would make a war less likely.[132] If it is possible to extrapolate from China's actions towards Taiwan its likely actions in the South China Sea, the implication supports the notion that China will seek the return of the Spratly Islands through cooperation and its military build-up is providing Beijing with the ability to apply pressure if the other claimants resist China's overtures. In other words, as long as the issue of sovereignty is not pursued the use of force by China is unlikely. However, while the use of force is deemed a possibility, escape is not possible; thus, a declining military influence over the direction of Chinese foreign policy would be a promising development.

The use of military pressure in 1996, however, revealed the growth of influence the PLA had achieved in the direction of China's foreign policy. This influence was manifest with an increased military presence in both the Central Military Commission (CMC) and at the 14th National

Party Congress. In 1992, three CMC members – Liu Huaqing, Zhang Zhen and Chi Haotian – wrote a protest letter to the CCP Central Commission regarding French and US arms sales to Taiwan. In 1993, a draft petition was signed by eight generals demanding an apology from the United States when the US Navy stopped and boarded a Chinese freighter (the *Yinhe*) on suspicion of carrying ingredients for chemical weapons to Iran. In 1994, during the 8th National People's Congress the PLA delegation was critical of the Foreign Ministry's policy towards the United States and Japan, and Qian Qichen's resignation is also thought to have been sought.

Ellis Joffe notes six factors that explain the rise in the PLA's influence. First, the lack of personal authority that Jiang Zemin held within the PLA compared to Mao and Deng, who both had revolutionary records of achievements and commanded long-standing loyalties from the military. Consequently, Jiang was less able to resist the influence of the PLA in the CMC, especially when that body contained Liu Huaqing and Zhang Zhen who 'far outstrip[ped] Jiang in seniority and personal prestige in the PLA'.[133] Second, in addition to having the CMC as a vehicle of influence, the PLA since 1986 has also participated in the CCP Foreign Affairs Leading Small Group (FALSG). The participation of Liu Huaqing and expected participation of Zhang Zhen in the Politburo Standing Committee provided the PLA with direct access to foreign policy decision-making.[134]

Third, the military see it as their responsibility to harness Chinese nationalism, and thus they have sought to increase their influence over the direction of China's policy towards regaining 'lost territory'. Fourth, keeping Taiwan on the agenda and at a high level of tension has ensured the PLA continues to receive a large military budget. Fifth, the change in military strategy from territorial defence to forward projection provides the PLA with good reason to influence the direction of a foreign policy that could see the PLA deploying forces outside China. Finally, the extra-budgetary earnings of the PLA ensures that the PLA has an interest in influencing the state of China's relations with other countries. Joffe writes: the 'directors of [PLA] companies may intervene in China's foreign relations for the benefit of their operations'.[135]

Given this growing influence of the PLA, the prospects of escaping the security dilemma do not appear good since it implies that China will use the 'stick' more often than the 'carrot' in dealings with other states. It would though be erroneous to suggest that the PLA is directing Chinese foreign policy, for as Mel Gurtov and Byong-Moo Hwang note, '[t]he party very definitely still commands the gun in China, and barring a dramatic change in the East Asian strategic picture, Jiang Zemin and the rest of the post-Deng party leaders are highly unlikely to let a belligerent nationalism disrupt their priority of peace and development'.[136]

Since Deng's death, Jiang has begun to consolidate his position in power. In October 1995, Jiang appointed Chi Haotian and Zhang Wannian to the CMC and at the 15th Party Congress in September 1997 made them members of the Politburo Standing Committee while removing Liu Huaqing and Zhang Zhen.[137] Vice-President Hu Jintao has become only the second civilian (Jiang is the other) to be made a member of the CMC.[138] Jiang also revived the post of CMC Secretary-General and appointed a loyal supporter – Fu Quanyou.[139] Jiang has also strengthened his position in foreign affairs by replacing Premier Li Peng with Zhu Rongji in March 1998. Michael Swaine writes, 'if Jiang Zemin is able to consolidate power and appoint a close associate as Premier and hence as the principle leader of the foreign policy sub-arena, his contacts with the PLA might serve to insulate foreign policy more successfully from direct military influence'.[140] According to David Bachman, the restraint China has shown towards Japan and the US over the Diaoyu Islands and Taiwan might reflect Jiang's growing control over the direction of China's foreign policy.[141] There are signs, albeit tentative, that Jiang is moving in this direction and this bodes well for escaping the security dilemma.

The Chinese expansion on Mischief Reef in late 1998, and Chinese construction work at another reef in the Spratly chain in March 1999, however, act as a timely warning that the PLA still retains much influence.[142] Ultimately, China's need, and preference for, a peaceful and stable region to support its development programme is the key to escaping the security dilemma. However, while China continues to build structures which have a military potential, the security dilemma will continue to operate since such action only exacerbates the suspicion ASEAN members have of China's intentions and further encourages them to seek US assistance. Escaping a state-induced security dilemma is dependent upon the ambitions of one of the actors being subject to influence. In this instance, it is dependent upon the ASEAN members altering how China resolves the South China Sea dispute.

With China accepting UNCLOS as the basis for a resolution ASEAN states' engagement appeared to be working. However, China has always preferred to resolve the dispute bilaterally rather than multilaterally, which is the preference of the ASEAN states, and this remains a contentious issue. ASEAN has achieved some success in this regard.

China's membership of the South China Sea workshops and the ARF, the agreement to put the South China Sea dispute on the ARF's agenda and China's active participation in the ARF by co-hosting an ISG meeting, are all positive signs that China is prepared to discuss security issues, and specifically the Spratlys dispute, in a multilateral forum.

However, the latest Mischief Reef incident has revealed that the ASEAN states' ability to pressurise China into accepting a resolution via a multilateral framework is not strong. The ASEAN response at the Hanoi summit to China's actions over Mischief Reef was not encouraging. Estrada had hoped to muster ASEAN support against the Chinese and although Thailand, Malaysia and Singapore did express concern to Beijing, the final communique only contained a veiled reference to the South China Sea. ASEAN Secretary-General Rodolfo Severino explained, '[w]e have bigger problems to deal with, particularly the economy'.[143]

The Chinese decision to renege on an offer made by Jiang to Estrada at the APEC meeting in November 1998 to make the facilities at Mischief Reef available to Filipino fishermen, is also indicative of a lack of influence.[144] Although in March 1999 ASEAN members did rally behind Manila when the Philippines forced the South China Sea issue on to the ASEM agenda in the face of Chinese objections, the Philippines were then disappointed by the lack of support they received from their ASEAN colleagues in the meeting.[145]

The most recent Mischief Reef incident raises doubts about the ASEAN states' ability in the aftermath of the economic crisis and its attendant political consequences, to pressurise China into accepting multilateral negotiations as the basis for a resolution. While ASEAN members are unable to influence China's ambitions in the South China Sea, the security dilemma will continue to operate to the detriment of ASEAN members, and because Beijing's actions encourage the image of a malign China, to the detriment of China itself.

Conclusion

This chapter has sought not only to expound upon the notion of a state-induced security dilemma, and its possible escape, but also to reveal what this type of security dilemma means for the debate on containing and/or engaging China.

The examination of the region through the security dilemma reveals that by pursuing a combination of both containment and engagement the states of ASEAN are exacerbating and mitigating the security dilemma at the same time. The logic for this perverse conclusion runs as follows: (1) China's economic/military growth raises concerns within ASEAN about Chinese intentions; (2) ASEAN members respond militarily and diplomatically with new arms procurements and by officially recognising the US and others as critical elements in East Asian stability via the ARF; (3) the continuing presence of the US acts as a restraint on China's emergence as the regional hegemon, thereby generating the desire to acquire the military capability to deter US interference in the region; (4) the growth in China's military capability in conjunction with its uncompromising attitude towards the Spratly Islands heightens ASEAN's fears of the 'China threat'.

The security dilemma operates, as both China and the members of ASEAN act in ways which make each other feel less secure. However, this containment approach is complemented by ASEAN engaging China, thus leading to the security dilemma's operation being mitigated. By cooperating with China through the ARF/South China Sea workshops, as well as in other fields such as APEC, ASEAN and China are able through dialogue, CBMs and transparency to remove much of the uncertainty each has about the other's intentions. In the case of ASEAN, this uncertainty focuses on Chinese intentions in the South China Sea, while for China the uncertainty is concerned not simply with the claims of ASEAN members in the Spratlys, but also with whether the ARF was going to be used to deny China a regional role and become a forum in which the other members 'gang up' against Beijing. Through engagement these concerns have been reduced and consequently the security dilemma operation is lessened.

However, because the security dilemma in operation is a state-induced version, the prospect of the dilemma remaining mitigated, or even escaped, is more complicated than in a system-induced version. The key for Jack Snyder's security dilemma, interpreted here as an example of Wheeler and Booth's deliberate security dilemma and labelled a state-induced security dilemma, is that the adversary's need for others to be insecure for its own security makes mitigating/escaping the dilemma much more difficult. As with a system-induced security dilemma, Snyder notes that resolve would not unwind the spiral of insecurity, since this would simply be interpreted by the adversary as preventing it from gaining a position of dominance. However, unlike the system-induced security dilemma, concessions would not work either, because the adversary would have no interest in reciprocating them – the concessions would merely strengthen the adversary's position vis-à-vis the other states. Hence, Snyder concludes that neither threats nor concessions could mitigate/escape the security dilemma; instead the adversary's 'intentions [could only] be made more benign by another state ... changing those circumstances – or the adversary's assessment of them'.[146]

The application of the security dilemma to the relationship between the members of ASEAN and China reveals that it is by exercising a combination of pressure and giving concessions that the other parties could alter the adversary's assessment of their goals. The difference between Snyder's conclusion and the one presented here occurs because of the interpretation placed on the adversary. It was argued in Chapter 1, and repeated at the beginning of this chapter, that in order for the adversary to fall victim to a security dilemma the adversary would have to be a status quo power. Using Keohane's definition of hegemony, it was argued that such an adversary could be a hegemon seeking to control its environment (assume a position of dominance) and thus interested in strengthening rather than undermining the status quo.

It has been argued that China is the region's emerging hegemon, but because China requires stable relations with its neighbours for its economic growth, this provides the ASEAN states with leverage in their dealings with Beijing. ASEAN members have been able to use this leverage to apply pressure on China, hence ASEAN's resolve in its dealings with Beijing over the Mischief Reef incident in 1995 and the Kan Tan oil platform in 1997. Likewise, via concessions (in this instance reaching agreements that limit state freedom), such as providing notice of military exercises and producing details of military equipment and other confidence building/military transparency measures, China could also be persuaded to reciprocate. The main reciprocation ASEAN states seek from China is an agreement not to use force and to resolve the South China Sea dispute in a multilateral forum. Although they have so far not been able to gain a Chinese agreement to either of these, they have been able to make some progress in the ARF and the South China Sea workshops. Resolve, in conjunction with concessions, holds out the possibility that how China seeks to strengthen its sovereignty claims in the South China Sea is open to alteration by outside influence.

The Chinese construction of military facilities on Mischief Reef in late 1998, and the Philippine response, are, however, tangible signs that the security dilemma continues to operate in the region. The Chinese decision to renege on an offer to make the facilities available for joint use and unilaterally to announce a two-month fishing ban in part of the Spratlys, having just agreed to exercise self-restraint, clearly places a question over the ability of ASEAN members to influence China's pursuit of its sovereignty claims in the South China Sea.[147] Consequently, the security dilemma remains in operation, and although it may operate in a mitigated form some of the time, its continued operation means that it will occasionally flare up. Despite these incidents, China's agreement to a bilateral meeting with the Philippines in March 1999 has indicated that Beijing stills sees importance in using dialogue to defuse regional tensions, and indeed Beijing was quick to clarify that the unilateral fishing ban was only applicable to Chinese fishermen.[148] Ultimately, China needs good regional relations for its continuing economic growth, and if Jiang Zemin and Zhu Rongji consolidate their leadership and continue along the path of economic reform, ASEAN members, by working within the parameter that Chinese sovereignty is non-negotiable, could yet gain Chinese cooperation to resolve the Spratlys dispute and thereby reduce their concern about the 'China threat'.

Throughout the 1990s ASEAN and China have not surprisingly initiated a security dilemma as suspicions about intentions have marked their evolving post-Cold War relationship. Through engagement, however, the security dilemma's operation has been mitigated, although because it has not been escaped it occasionally flares up. By working within the parameters of Chinese hegemony, the possibility of escape exists. However, for this to occur, not only do the states of Southeast Asia need to adjust their behaviour to create a stable post-Cold War relationship, but so too must China.

6
Conclusion: Application and Mitigation

The nature of the international system is of course such that states are constantly faced with dilemmas of one sort or another, and some can no doubt be avoided. There is, however, at least one which no states can wholly escape. This is the contradiction between the need for, and the pursuit of, friendship with at least some states, and the ultimate necessity, for reasons of national interest and survival, to be on guard against all states; to retain, as it were, a residual scepticism about intentions, even of those whose friendships are being sought, which is grounded on the general belief that all states will seek to protect their own interests first, and in so doing will, or may, sacrifice those of others.[1]

At the beginning of the 1950s when introducing the security dilemma, Herbert Butterfield and John Herz noted that because humans need to cooperate they cannot avoid the threat they pose to one another by living in isolation. Butterfield called it the 'absolute predicament' or 'irreducible dilemma' that lay at the heart of all human conflict.[2] Herz referred to it as man's inhumanity to man and called it a primary fact in human social life.[3] This need for interaction, coupled with the knowledge that the other might intend harm, creates uncertainty in statesmen's minds about the other's intentions. It is this uncertainty which Nicholas Wheeler and Ken Booth see as the defining feature of the security dilemma, hence their assertion that a 'security dilemma exists when the military preparations of one state create an unresolvable uncertainty in the mind of another as to whether those preparations are for "defensive" purposes only (to enhance its security in an uncertain world) or whether they are for offensive purposes (to change the status quo to its advantage)'.[4]

173

The quotation that opened this final chapter, by Arnfinn Jørgensen-Dahl, not only highlights this uncertainty, and in so doing implies that the security dilemma is omnipresent, but it also captures the fatalist view that such a dilemma is inescapable. In this study, the application of the security dilemma in its three guises to Southeast Asia has sought to determine, first, whether the security dilemma is as relevant as the literature suggests to relations between actors within states, and between states, and second, why it is that where the security dilemma is relevant, its operation is largely mitigated. Is it therefore omnipresent and inescapable? The answer provides a better understanding of the security dilemma, and reveals the security dynamics at work in the region. Determining if the security dilemma is omnipresent entails analysing the disputes in the region, while the question of escape requires an examination of the region's dispute settlement procedures.

The division of the book into three sections reflects the application of the security dilemma in its three guises to Southeast Asia, and while this chapter will provide a summary of the key points raised in the sections, it will do so by addressing the book's two objectives. Is the security dilemma as relevant to the actors' interactions as the literature suggests, and can it be mitigated/escaped? These two goals reveal a crucial point of difference that exists within the security dilemma literature. Those that argue the security dilemma is omnipresent and cannot be escaped, see the uncertainty that causes statesmen to be suspicious of one another as an inherent feature of the international system. Unless a world government is established which can negate the self-help feature of the international system, statesmen will remain bedevilled by the security dilemma. However, an alternative view, and one shared by the author, is that while the self-help international system is a necessary condition for the security dilemma's operation, whether it actually operates or not is dependent upon the interaction of the states. Therefore the operation of the security dilemma – whether it exists, and if it does, can it be escaped – is subject to change because it is dependent upon statesmen's actions. In the introductory chapter, Alexander Wendt's contribution to the debate was noted as significant because of his argument that states do not begin their relationship in a security dilemma; it is something that statesmen construct through their interactions.[5]

The twin objectives in this study reflect the author's concern with a growing trend in the security literature of the 1990s to apply the security dilemma to new referent objects (ethnic groups) by tying it to offence–defence theory. The actual application is in itself an exciting departure and, it is argued, can usefully complement the literature on Third World security which focuses on security issues within the state. The author's concern is not, therefore, expounding the application of the security dilemma to new referent objects of security; rather, it is the linking of the security dilemma to offence-defence theory. These are considered synonymous by Charles Glaser and Chaim Kaufmann who write, '[o]ffense-defense theory (or security dilemma theory)'.[6]

This linking of the two has led to parts of the literature determining the security dilemma's operation almost exclusively by the 'offensiveness' of military strategies. Thus, Chaim Kaufmann's argument that the 'severity of ethnic security dilemmas is greatest when demography is most intermixed, weakest when community settlements are most separate' is based on the assumption that the 'more mixed the opposing groups, the stronger the offense in relation to the defense; the more separate they are, the stronger the defense in relation to offense'.[7] Simply separating the two groups, however, does not reduce their uncertainty of each other's intentions, and therefore does not affect the severity of the security dilemma. This almost exclusive concentration on the offensiveness of military capabilities also corrupts the security dilemma by applying it to ethnic tension regardless of whether the incompatibility is illusory or real. It also, by concentrating on restructuring military capabilities along defensive lines, has a tendency to ignore methods of mitigating the security dilemma which focus on improving relations by revealing the misperception of threat on each side.

In the first section, the application of the security dilemma to ethnic conflict is examined, and here it was revealed that when referring to the security dilemma by concentrating solely on the offence-defence balance its value as a tool of enquiry is corrupted. In tracing the evolution of the security dilemma in Chapter 1, the linking of offence-defence to the security dilemma by Barry Posen and Stuart Kaufman was highlighted. Here, it was noted that the applicability of the security dilemma was determined by a rise of insecurity amongst the belligerents as a consequence of their actions. However, whether this rise of insecurity reflected an accurate assessment of the other's intentions, or a misperception of those intentions, was not considered necessary in determining the relevance of the security dilemma. A spiralling process of insecurity that was being driven by the actions each were taking, was considered sufficient evidence for the security dilemma to be applied.

This though is inaccurate since no attempt is made to determine what is causing the spiralling process of insecurity. Is it a real incompatibility between the belligerents, thus making it an example of Robert Jervis's deterrence model, or is the incompatibility illusory and the insecurity generated by a mistaken interpretation of the other's actions? In the latter case it would be an example of Jervis's spiral model and would indicate the existence of a security dilemma. The need to distinguish the cause is critically important for the application of the security dilemma, as Jervis warns, the 'existence of a spiral process does not prove the applicability of the spiral model, for increasing tension, hostility, and violence can be a reflection of the underlying conflict, not a cause of it'.[8] If one of the belligerents intended to harm the other, then in Butterfield's terms this belligerent would be a great criminal out to do deliberate harm. Indeed, by concentrating on offence-defence the literature on the security dilemma and ethnic conflict tends to miss the 'tragic' essence of the security dilemma.[9]

Therefore, in order for the security dilemma to operate it is necessary for the perception of threat from the other to be based on an illusory incompatibility. Hence, Herz's argument that it could not be a security dilemma which caused World War II, but rather it was the political ambitions of Hitler, since the Nazi regime's goal of *lebensraum* (or living space) clearly indicated a real incompatibility existed between Nazi Germany and its Eastern neighbours. It is because at the heart of the security dilemma lies an illusory incompatibility, that spiral prescriptions such as transparency, confidence-building and other means of reassuring one another about each other's benign ambitions, help to mitigate and ultimately escape the security dilemma. Concentrating solely on offence-defence thus not only leads to the security dilemma being applied incorrectly, but it also ignores the value that methods of reducing uncertainty can bring to mitigating the dilemma.

The application of the security dilemma to ethnic tension receives examination in Chapters 2 and 3. Since the examples of ethnic tension within Southeast Asia exist within sovereign states, it was necessary in Chapter 2 to examine how a security dilemma could operate in such a system. This chapter, therefore, focused on issues raised in the Third World security literature because this is concerned with security problems within a state.

It is argued that because Third World states are weak, in the sense that the regime relies upon coercion to enforce rules and thus lacks legitimacy in the eyes of the population, the security dilemma can still operate despite the existence of a sovereign regime. The states 'weakness' can lead the regime to be seen by the populace less as the provider of their security and more as the cause of their insecurity.

With no guarantor for their security they must provide for themselves, hence they exist in a self-help system. Chapter 2 noted that when a regime seeks to expand its influence throughout the state as it seeks to nation-build and state-make this can have the effect of alienating the people. Rather than welcoming the notion of belonging to a nation, these peripheral communities might seek to distance themselves from the central regime. The regime may therefore find itself competing with an alternative movement that is commanding the people's loyalty. In view of the regime's lack of legitimacy amongst the population, it might resort to violence to remove this alternative movement. However, this act may have the paradoxical effect of further alienating the peripheral community and possibly generating calls for secession. Far from state-making and nation-building, the regime's actions have had the opposite effect.

In Southeast Asia, a prime example of a regime's attempt to nation-build and state-make that alienated the populace and ultimately created demands for autonomy and even secession is Indonesia. In addition to the case of East Timor, independence is sought by activists from Irian Jaya while similar demands can be heard in Aceh province of Sumatra. The use of oppressive measures during Suharto's reign to create a sense of soldarity amongst a diverse population – both in terms of identity and geography – was confirmed as a failure by the demands presented to Suharto's successor, B.J. Habibie, by The Alliance of the Indigenous People of the Archipelago. Formed at the first indigenous conference held in Indonesia in March 1999, this alliance of ethnic groups accused the central government of acting as a colonial power and demanded, amongst other things, the return of political sovereignty to the indigenous people. Warnings were given that if these demands were not met by Jakarta they would spawn separatist movements.[10]

While it is argued that the state's sovereign status does not prevent the operation of the security dilemma, whether it actually does operate or not is dependent upon the ambitions and actions of the regime and the ethnic communities. It was noted in Chapter 2 that Brian Job is dismissive of the security dilemma's value in understanding internal security problems, and instead views the dynamics of internal security through his insecurity dilemma. The analysis suggests that while the insecurity dilemma is more flexible than the security dilemma, because it is more concerned with paradoxical actions than with illusory incompatibility, Job's reasons for dismissing the security dilemma relate more to the differences between First and Third World security concerns than the security dilemma itself. The security dilemma may therefore operate, but to understand its operation in ethnic tension it is necessary to focus on ethnic identity as the security issue. Thus, a determination of whether or not the incompatibility between ethnic groups is real is achieved by focusing on whether the maintenance of an ethnic identity is under threat. This leads the discussion away from a military bias to examine those factors which reproduce identity from one generation to the next. Therefore, the maintenance of schools which teach through the medium of an ethnic group's language becomes an issue for the security dilemma. The empirical examination of ethnic tensions within Southeast Asia and the applicability of the security dilemma was the focus for Chapter 3.

In Chapter 3 the ethnic tensions within Burma, Malaysia, Thailand and Indonesia were examined from the perspective of ethnocratic regimes, self-determination and migration. Focusing on the tragic essence of the security dilemma – the rise in tension and possible violence between groups that sought only to protect their identity – it was possible to determine how applicable the security dilemma was in each case. It was found that in most cases the security dilemma was not applicable, and that the rise in tension reflected a real threat to an ethnic groups' identity or the inviolability of the state's borders. However, in the case of the Isan in Thailand and the tensions between the Malay and non-Malay communities in Malaysia, it was argued that the dynamics of the security dilemma could be seen in operation.

In the Isan's case the Thai regime's suspicion of Isan complicity in the activities of the Communist Party of Thailand, led the government to take action which had the paradoxical effect of heightening Isan demands for autonomy. In Malaysia, the Malay concern that, unlike the Chinese, they were not enjoying the benefits of Malaysian economic growth in the 1960s, coupled with fears that their political party – the United Malays National Organisation (UMNO) – was not safeguarding their special status, led to a rise of tension directed towards the Chinese community. In the aftermath of race riots, UMNO responded to Malay demands by pursuing positive discrimination with more vigour, most notably through the New Economic Policy. The Chinese grievance at being treated as second class citizens in Malaysia intensified and in the 1970s the discrimination in higher education was especially resented. The sensitivity with which issues of culture, race and religion need to be dealt with in Malaysia is testimony, even though it is less so today than in the past, to the lingering distrust and suspicion of the Malay and Chinese communities. In the Isan and the Malaysian cases it was noted that the dilemma had been subject to change. In the former it had been escaped, while in the latter, since its peak in the 1960s, the dilemma's operation has become mitigated.

In Chapter 2 it was highlighted that through democratisation and respect for human rights, regimes could embark upon state-making and nation-building programmes that stood a greater chance of success than when they resorted to violence. Using democratisation and respect for human rights, in the guise of power-sharing and ethnic reconstruction, it was possible to examine the reasons for the dilemma's mitigation and escape.[11] Ethnic reconstruction can escape the security dilemma because if the ethnic communities are willing to share common values, then the affinity that exists within each separate community can be replicated between the groups, and thereby create a new identity. This does not mean that the original identities wither away, but rather that they are complemented by a new identity. In Thailand the Isan identity remains, although it no longer carries any political significance, and complements the Thai national identity. In this case such ethnic reconstruction was limited because the Isan already considered themselves closer to the Thai than the Lao. The Malaysian case is more complicated.

In Malaysia the mitigation of the security dilemma occurred because of the power-sharing arrangement between the main ethnic political parties in the coalition government. It is argued that because power-sharing enables the ethnic groups to influence or determine policy, this reduces their uncertainty concerning the policies' likely impact on their ethnicity. Despite the Malay domination of the political process through UMNO, Malaysia is a good example of power-sharing because the Malaysian Chinese Association (MCA) and the Malaysian Indian Congress (MIC) are able to exert influence in the *Barisan Nasional* (BN), and thereby limit the impact of policies which could be interpreted as threatening. However, power-sharing can do more than just mitigate, it can also create the conditions for escape. If power-sharing is successful, the elite may realise that cooperation can lead to stability which can in turn bring mutual benefits.

In the early 1990s as Malaysia enjoyed the economic prosperity its 'tiger economy' had brought, optimism was high that Malaysia was moving away from the ethnic divisions of its past. Mahathir's Vision 2020 of a developed Malaysian nation included a social goal in which the ethnic communities, while maintaining their separate identity, would consider themselves as sharing a Malaysian identity that went beyond holding the same passport. The political problems that engulfed

Mahathir's regime after the arrest of Anwar Ibrahim in late 1998 are highly significant in this regard. At the time of writing, the pressure for reform and the riots that ensued have not taken on, in contrast to the riots that engulfed Jakarta in May 1998, an ethnic dimension. Indeed, there is even the view that the political crisis has lowered racial barriers, with PAS and DAP plus a number of non-governmental organisations cooperating in opposition to Mahathir.[12] It is too soon to say the Malaysian security dilemma is escaped, but there are promising signs.[13]

The first section, in examining the application of the security dilemma to ethnic conflict, has sought to distance the analysis from offence-defence theory, and in so doing, not only provides a more accurate interpretation of the security dilemma, but also focuses on issues which can mitigate and escape the security dilemma by removing the uncertainty which lies at its core. The application is thus quite different from the utilisation of the security dilemma by other writers. By focusing on the need for the incompatibility between the actors to be illusory, the tragic essence of the security dilemma is highlighted. This reveals that the security dilemma is not always relevant to the ethnic tensions that exist in Southeast Asia, and in such cases spiral methods of mitigation are irrelevant.

Applying confidence-building measures to the tension between the Burmese regime and its ethnic minorities is unlikely to solve the tensions that exist in that country, without the regime first fundamentally rethinking its nation-building policies.[14] The security dilemma is not therefore as relevant to the dynamics that operate in ethnic conflict as the current literature suggests. In addition, where it does operate, the means of lessening its damaging effects is achieved by reducing the uncertainty the actors have of one another's intentions. Thus, power-sharing and ethnic reconstruction are noted as methods which can mitigate and escape the security dilemma, while the ideas promulgated by those that focus on offence-defence theory – that it can be achieved by separating the groups – is dismissed since this does little to remove their uncertainty of each other's intentions.

This does not mean that offence-defence considerations are irrelevant to the security dilemma, since the offensiveness of weapons can exacerbate the operation of a security dilemma between states. In Chapter 4 the focus turns to intra-ASEAN relations, and in particular to what extent was the security dilemma operating when these states engaged in the purchase of power-projection weapons, and why despite such weapon procurements was the dilemma's operation mitigated.

It is argued that the arms build-up in Southeast Asia, manifest by the acquisition of sophisticated weaponry by the ASEAN states, occurred for many different reasons. The economic wealth the ASEAN members enjoyed prior to the crisis, coupled to the availability of weapons as arms manufacturers sought new markets in the aftermath of the Cold War, certainly enabled the arms build-up to occur. These reasons though do not in themselves explain why the ASEAN states procured certain kinds of navy vessels and fighter aircraft, the like of which they had not procured before. While factors such as corruption and prestige can help to explain specific purchases, such as the Thai aircraft carrier, the key reason is the perception of a declining US presence leaving the region responsible for its own safety. The perception was that ASEAN members were being left to manage old territorial disputes frozen during the Cold War and new ones created by Exclusive Economic Zones, as well as coping with extra-regional powers such as an emerging China.

The acquisition of power-projection weapons can, because they are capable of attacking the territory of neighbouring states, generate disquiet amongst those states that their procurement indicates the adoption of a revisionist ambition. Such an interpretation is more likely to occur if the relationship between the states is beset with difficulties arising from conflicting territorial claims or other reasons which create suspicion and uncertainty about the other's intentions. Prior to the economic crisis, the degree to which the acquisitions were designed to counter those of others in the region varied. There appeared to be an action-reaction pattern to the procurement plans of Singapore and Malaysia and between Malaysia and Thailand. However, the notable finding was that despite propitious conditions for the security dilemma to operate at a high intensity, its operation was mitigated, and even in the Singapore-Malaysia relationship its intensity has not been sufficient to make the outbreak of war likely.

In his seminal article, 'Cooperation under the Security Dilemma', Robert Jervis argued that because the security dilemma's operation is exacerbated by the offensiveness of the weapons procured, it is possible to lessen its effectiveness with the procurement of discernibly defensive weapons.[15] By procuring defensive weapon systems, and more importantly deploying such systems in a manner which limits any offensive ability they may have, statesmen can lessen the fear neighbouring powers may have about being the targets for these new acquisitions. Hence, Andrew Butfoy's statement that, 'the most obvious way of re-shaping capabilities to ameliorate the security dilemma is to eschew those military postures which are the most suitable for military aggression'.[16] While the types of weapons procured do have an effect upon the intensity of the security dilemma, the operation of the security dilemma is also affected by state interaction in other areas of their relationship.

In Southeast Asia it was found that, because there existed a set of principles and norms of behaviour that regulated the interactions amongst the ASEAN members, the security dilemma's operation was muted, despite the accumulation of offensive weaponry. These principles, and the processes through which they are implemented, are collectively known as the 'ASEAN way'. They help to mitigate the security dilemma by establishing norms of behaviour that each member is expected to operate in accordance with, and thus reduce the others' uncertainty of its intent. The more predictable their actions the less suspicious others will feel. This is a notably different approach to mitigating or even escaping the security dilemma from altering force postures, and relates closely to the moderating effects on the security dilemma of security regimes, communities and common security.

It was argued in Chapter 4 that the ASEAN approach to security was a form of common security. The replacement in Indonesia of Sukarno by Suharto in 1966 ushered in a new Indonesian approach to achieving security. Rather than seeking to gain security at the expense of others, which under Sukarno was manifested in *Konfrontasi* with Malaysia, Suharto sought to achieve security for Indonesia with its neighbours. This achieving of security together was encapsulated in the pursuit of regional resilience. Regional resilience was taken from the Indonesian concept of national resilience, which in essence sought the security of the state through nation-building and state-making. By addressing the internal dangers of subversion the viability of the state would be secured and communist insurgency and ethnic separatism would be prevented from infecting neighbouring states. National resilience could therefore create regional stability (regional resilience). In turn, regional resilience would enable the regimes to concentrate on their national development, by creating a stable external environment in which each could be assured that others would not interfere in their domestic affairs. Regional resilience was codified in the 1976 Treaty of Amity and Cooperation and the 1971 Zone of Peace, Freedom and Neutrality (ZOPFAN) declaration.

The key principle of regional resilience was that each could gain security by agreeing not to interfere in another's domestic affairs, and while such a common security approach is not that proposed by the Palme Commission, it is nevertheless an acknowledgement by the

ASEAN members that because the problems of neighbours can effect them, security has to be achieved together. In this instance, the best method of preventing security problems from spreading throughout the region was not to undermine regimes by interfering in their internal affairs. The economic crisis of the late 1990s, and its subsequent political and social ramifications, has brought into doubt the continuing validity of non-interference. This principle was already subject to review prior to the economic crisis, with Anwar Ibrahim raising the prospect of constructive intervention in Cambodia.

In 1998, the Thai Foreign Minister, Surin Pitsuwan, called for flexible engagement in dealing with problems that emanated from neighbouring states. While Surin was particularly concerned with the flow of refugees into Thailand from Burma and border violations caused by the military regime in Rangoon, he was also calling upon ASEAN to adjust the principle of non-interference to cope with the challenges of interdependence and globalisation. Noting that the financial and economic crisis posed 'clear and present dangers' to ASEAN, Surin's paper (submitted to officials prior to the ASEAN summit in July 1998), stated that where domestic affairs have external dimensions, 'the affected countries should be able to express their opinions in an open, frank and constructive manner'.[17] While non-interference is coming under review, this does not mean that the notion of common security is necessarily being replaced. The challenge for ASEAN is to adjust their means of achieving mutual security in an interdependent region where non-interference in the domestic affairs of neighbours is no longer a suitable strategy for preventing the contagion of economic, social and environmental problems.

While the pursuit of common security aids security dilemma mitigation, regional resilience is not the only reason ASEAN has been able to avoid the most detrimental effects of the security dilemma. The 'ASEAN way' alludes not only to such principles as non-interference and mutual respect for territorial integrity, but also to the process through which the members interact. It is this process that gives ASEAN a sense of uniqueness and indicates that it is a security regime. The guiding principles of consensus decision-making and compromise, which emanate from the practice of *musyawarah*, have created an informal approach to dialogue which in turn encourages the perception that negotiations are conducted amongst friends not opponents. It is this habit of consultation which has helped to reduce the uncertainty statesmen have about their neighbours' intentions, and it is here that ASEAN's strength can be found.[18] However, with the expansion of

ASEAN membership, concerns were raised that some of the new members, especially Vietnam, might make consensus decision-making unworkable. Hanoi's uncompromising stance in the negotiations over Cambodia's admittance to ASEAN in December 1998 did confirm these fears, and it raised serious doubts about an ASEAN-Ten, even with the 'Minus X' principle, operating according to *musyawarah*.

It is too soon to know what the challenges to the 'ASEAN way' will mean for the operation of the security dilemma. So far the ASEAN membership has been unwilling to replace the non-interference principle, but it is clearly under threat as the public comments by the Philippine President, Joseph Estrada, about the Malaysian judicial process during the Anwar trial indicated. Ali Alatas, the Indonesian Foreign Minister, has warned that by interfering in domestic affairs 'we will return to the situation before ASEAN was born, with a lot of suspicion, a lot of tension'.[19] The deterioration during 1998 of Malaysia-Singapore relations, in which the security dilemma operates more strongly than elsewhere in the region, would indicate that Alatas is right to warn that without the 'ASEAN way' tensions will rise.

In Chapter 5 the application of the security dilemma moved away from intra-ASEAN relations to consider its applicability to the post-Cold War relationship between ASEAN and China. Michael Yahuda writes, 'China's emergence as a rising power has raised new problems for its smaller neighbours in the region as to how best to accommodate it while preserving their independence'.[20] In this chapter the attention focused on a state-induced security dilemma, and when the analysis turned to mitigation/escape it provided an insight into the containment/engagement debate concerning relations with China.

In Chapter 1 Jack Snyder's use of the security dilemma was seen to be an example of what Wheeler and Booth in the early in the 1990s categorised as a deliberate, or state-induced, security dilemma.[21] Snyder used the security dilemma to explain the deterioration of relations between two states when one requires the insecurity of the other. This interpretation can, however, raise problems for the application of the security dilemma. It is argued that the security dilemma explains the deterioration of relations between two states that do not intend one another harm, and thus the requirement of insecurity can be problematic. However, if this requirement is broadened to include states that desire neighbouring powers to accept its position of dominance, that is to acknowledge its hegemony, then the security dilemma might be relevant.

In this case, the requirement of insecurity is the hegemon's desire for others to accept a position of subordination, but because it is interested in hegemony it does not seek to change the status quo but rather consolidate it. Neighbouring states will no doubt feel insecure, since the hegemon's actions are likely to appear little different from an imperialist seeking to dominate them through conquest. It is thus likely that these neighbouring states will take actions to prevent themselves becoming vulnerable. Such an interpretation would, however, be based on a misperception of the hegemon's intentions, and attempts therefore by the neighbouring states to increase their ability to defend themselves, and consequently raise for the hegemon the prospect of it losing its position of dominance, are likely to result in a deterioration of relations between states that are ultimately only concerned with their own security; the security dilemma can therefore be applied.

In Chapter 5 China was portrayed as the state seeking hegemony and the ASEAN members as the worried neighbours. It was noted that the Chinese interpret their recent historical relations with other states from the perspective of being the victim. This victimisation along with China's past role as the region's great power has created a sense of entitlement in Beijing, which makes Chinese relations susceptible to the security dilemma. Rosemary Foot writes that this sense of entitlement 'makes it hard for the country to be sensitive either to the sense of entitlement that other countries might have, or to its bigness, or to the fears that its geopolitical dominance can evoke in its neighbours'.[22] Evidence of China as a hegemon is derived from its growing economic potential, its history with Southeast Asia and its ambitions in the South China Sea. Although China's impressive economic growth has been affected by the region's economic problems, it is nevertheless continuing to grow and finance China's military modernisation programme. With the Beijing leadership curtailing the PLA's non-budgetary earnings, a marked increase in the defence budget can be expected.

The analysis of China's history with Southeast Asia revealed that a tribute system operated in which the Chinese emperor was supreme. This tribute system though does not equate well with modern political terms expressing the relationship between sovereign states. Greg Austin writes that while 'it had been conceived and perpetuated by China to reflect its dominance or superiority, the tribute system was often seen by fully independent neighbouring states as a formalistic ritual to which they acceded out of considerations of convenience, ceremony, or commerce. The idea of legal obligation as in the case of a genuine vassal state was not always present.'[23] The tribute system is useful in that it reveals the Chinese assumption of pre-eminence in dealing with others. Hence the expectation that China will be treated as a great power and that as a consequence of its supremacy it will be able to influence, if not determine, the interaction amongst the states of Southeast Asia.

In this sense China acts as a hegemon, but the tribute system implies that this will not be forced upon the ASEAN members. The problem for the ASEAN members is that they have to have relations with China, for trade and security purposes, and this entails accepting their subordinate position. Evidence of this can be found in the operation of the ASEAN Regional Forum (ARF). In Chapter 5 it was noted how despite ASEAN being the primary driving force behind the ARF, China was able to influence greatly the processes and speed through which the ARF operates. It is the ASEAN members willingness to allow China such an influential role which reveals their subordinate position. It is argued that China's hegemony can therefore be considered benign because it is not forced upon unwilling recipients, it merely reflects the natural state of affairs.

Although China's irredentist ambitions in the South China Sea might seem to sit uneasily with the notion of China as a status quo power, it is important to remember that China's establishment of structures on the reefs and islets there is not peculiar to China, but a common practice started by the ASEAN states. It is thus argued that China's actions are not indicative of a revisionist state changing the current position, but rather one claimant amongst many ensuring that in the current status quo the strength of its claim is not weakened. Thus, while the construction of buildings by the Chinese on Mischief Reef gained widespread coverage in November 1998, less attention was given to the Philippine decision to upgrade facilities on Pag-Asa island, Vietnam's erection of structures on Lizzie Weber Reef, or Malaysia's construction of a building on Investigator Shoal.[24]

Where the Chinese have acted differently has been their utilisation of force against the other claimants. However, the only military clash was in 1988 with the Vietnamese (not an ASEAN member at the time) and there has been no repeat; the 'use of force' by China during the 1995 Mischief Reef incident is in no sense comparable. Indeed, although not signatories to the 1992 ASEAN-Manila Declaration, the Chinese have agreed to abide by it and have reiterated that they seek a diplomatic solution. Jiang Zemin stating at the APEC summit in Kuala Lumpur in November 1998, '[w]e are committed to settle whatever problem there is in the South China Sea peacefully and through diplomatic means'.[25]

It is China's emergence at the end of the twentieth century as a potential great power for the twenty-first century, coupled with its ability to influence the direction of security dialogue in the region, which raises the issue of hegemony. Hence Denny Roy's assertion that, 'China is not only the state with the greatest potential to don the mantle of hegemony, but it is also the state that, more than any other, could single-handedly determine the success or failure of a multilateral security regime through its decision to either support or sabotage the process'.[26] China's emergence as the regional hegemon raises the prospect that a security dilemma operating between China and ASEAN is state-induced. The build-up of China's military and the changing strategy of its armed forces were noted as raising concerns within ASEAN that China's ambitions were potentially threatening. All ASEAN members remain suspicious of China's long-term goal, but the degree of concern amongst the ASEAN members varies and only some of the procurement plans of ASEAN members are clearly linked to Chinese actions.[27] It was noted that for a security dilemma to operate between China and ASEAN it was also necessary for China's defence preparations to be at least partly a response to the actions of ASEAN members. It was noted, too, that it was unlikely to be the case that ASEAN members' procurement plans were raising concerns, but rather, ASEAN's diplomatic efforts in seeking to maintain a US military presence in the region was having that effect.

It is suggested, therefore, in Chapter 5 that the security dilemma operating between China and ASEAN members is driven by China's military build-up and the ASEAN members attempts to contain China, partly through military weapons, but more pertinently by balancing China's power with the presence of the US, and to a lesser degree, Australia and India. However, the security dilemma's operation is mitigated since there is little if any immediate fear of a Chinese threat. Even during the November 1998 incident over Mischief Reef, Estrada said, 'there is nothing to be apprehensive about. They (the Chinese) will never attack us'.[28] The mitigation of the security dilemma can be explained by the policy of engagement that the ASEAN states have pursued with respect to China. This engagement occurs through a variety of China-ASEAN fora, the Indonesian sponsored workshops on the South China Sea and the ARF, and the Chinese navy has visited ASEAN members as a confidence building exercise. The steady progress at the ARF with the inter-sessional meetings examining preventive diplomacy augurs well over the long term for a decrease in suspicion and increase in trust between China and the members of ASEAN, as well as other

ARF members. However, because the security dilemma is state-induced such cooperative undertakings are not likely to escape the security dilemma without China's ambitions, or at least pursuit of its ambitions, becoming subject to alteration.

Jack Snyder's argument, that because one of the belligerents requires the other's insecurity for it to feel secure, suggests that the security dilemma cannot be escaped through the pursuit of spiral prescriptions such as confidence-building measures (CBMs) since these will only confirm the feeling of insecurity felt by the other party. Escape can only be achieved by either changing the adversary's goal – that is, convincing the adversary that it no longer requires the other's insecurity for its security – or change the adversary's assessment of its goals – that is, convincing it that by altering, but not giving up, its approach to requiring the other's insecurity its security is maintained. It is suggested in Chapter 5 that escaping this type of security dilemma requires the ASEAN members to show resolve, as well as conciliation, in their dealings with China within certain parameters. In the dialogue and agreements sought over the South China Sea dispute, these parameters are manifest in the lack of discussion over sovereignty. The approach adopted by both sides is to discuss CBMs while leaving the vexed issue of sovereignty off the agenda.

If ASEAN members are unable to apply pressure on China then the cooperative ventures embarked upon would simply codify China's position without providing security for ASEAN, and would therefore not escape the security dilemma. There are though some positive signs that ASEAN members have been able to alter China's approach to resolving the South China Sea dispute, and therefore escape is possible. For example, China's preference is to resolve the South China Sea via bilateral diplomacy, and while this still remains Beijing's preference, China has become an active participant in the ARF and the Indonesian sponsored workshops, indicating that Beijing is willing to discuss the South China Sea dispute in a multilateral forum.[29] However, other events indicate that escape is still some way from being realised. The decision to expand the facilites on Mischief Reef and the presence of Chinese warships in the area, since the CBM measures Beijing agreed with Manila after the 1995 incident, plus the decision to renege on an offer of joint use of the facilities, all indicate that China is prepared to pursue its sovereignty claims in the South China Sea with little regard given to the effect they have on neighbouring powers.[30] Unsurprisingly, the security dilemma began to operate more severely in late 1998/early 1999 with the Philippines seeking bilateral military support from the US and diplomatic support from multilateral fora, including the United Nations.

Whether the security dilemma will be escaped is dependent upon China altering its approach to safeguarding its sovereignty claims in the South China Sea. The need for China to achieve stable external relations for its economic growth and the reforms being implemented in China – economic, and tentatively political and social – combined with the ASEAN tradition of shelving conflicting claims, holds out the prospect that escape is possible. If Beijing is prepared to learn to operate within the norms of international behaviour, then China's emergence as a great power in the twenty-first century is unlikely to raise fears and suspicions which so aggravated the security dilemma between Beijing and Manila in late 1998/early 1999.

Southeast Asia has proven to be an apt region in which to determine the applicability and severity of the security dilemma. In examining ethnic tensions it has shown that the security dilemma is not always relevant to understanding the dynamics at work. Likewise, in examining relations between the ASEAN members and between ASEAN and China, while the security dilemma can be seen in operation, the significant finding is that its operation is mitigated. The interactions amongst the ASEAN members – the 'ASEAN way' – contains the elements of common security and security regime theory which mitigate the dilemma's worst effects. Not only has this helped moderate the dilemma between the ASEAN members, but by extending this to engage with China in the ARF and other fora, it is also helped to mitigate the security dilemma between them. In the latter case, China's need for stable external relations is also an important contributory factor. While the security dilemma remains though, the suspicion and fear which is marked by its presence will continue to bedevil the interactions amongst the region's actors. The regional economic crisis, and its attendant political and social ramifications, have raised doubts about the continuing validity of the 'ASEAN way', and to a lesser extent economic reform in China. Although ending the non-interference principle does not equate to ending the 'ASEAN way', it will be a harbinger of change which will produce uncertainty, and uncertainty begets the security dilemma.

Notes

1 Introduction: Evolution of the Security Dilemma

1 Quoted from Amitav Acharya, 'The Association of Southeast Asian Nations: "Security Community" or "Defence Community"?', *Pacific Affairs*, 64/2 (Summer 1991), p. 176.
2 Quoted from Bertil Lintner, Shada Islam and Faith Keenan, 'Growing Pains', *Far Eastern Economic Review*, 28 January 1999, p. 26.
3 See Nicholas J. Wheeler and Ken Booth, 'The Security Dilemma' in John Baylis and N.J. Rengger (eds.), *Dilemmas of World Politics: International Issues in a Changing World* (Oxford: Clarendon Press, 1992), pp. 29–60.
4 Tim Huxley, 'Southeast Asia in the study of international relations: the rise and decline of a region', *The Pacific Review*, 9/2 (1996), p. 200.
5 Muthiah Alagappa, 'Asian Practice of Security: Key Features and Explanations', in Muthiah Alagappa (ed.), *Asian Security Practice: Material and Ideational Influences* (Stanford: Stanford University Press, 1998), p. 613.
6 Huxley, op. cit., 'Southeast Asia in the study of international relations', p. 220. For a concise analysis of Realism's relevance in the aftermath of the economic crisis see Amitav Acharya, 'Realism, Institutionalism, and the Asian Economic Crisis', *Contemporary Southeast Asia*, 21/1 (April 1999), pp. 1–29.
7 The security dilemma has been used to redirect security concerns away from its Cold War obsession with military power, to understanding the development of identity formation, as well as broadening the scope of security to encompass economic, environmental and other concerns. See Simon Dalby, 'Contesting an Essential Concept: Reading the Dilemmas in Contemporary Security Discourse', in Keith Krause and Michael C. Williams (eds.), *Critical Security Studies: Concepts and Cases* (London: The University College of London Press, 1997), pp. 12–18.
8 For reference to Xenophon see Gideon Y. Akavia, 'Defensive Defense and the Nature of Armed Conflict', *The Journal of Strategic Studies*, 14/1 (March 1991), p. 23. For Thucydides see Robert J. Lieber, *No Common Power: understanding international relations* (New York: HarperCollins, 1991), p. 6, and Robert Jervis, 'Realism, Game Theory, and Cooperation', *World Politics*, 40/3 (April 1988), p. 317.
9 John Herz, *Political Realism and Political Idealism: A Study in Theories and Realities* (Chicago: Chicago University Press, 1951).
10 Herbert Butterfield, *History and Human Relations* (London: Collins, 1951).
11 Ibid., pp. 19–20.
12 Ibid., p. 21.
13 Ibid., p. 20.
14 Herz, op. cit., *Political Realism and Political Idealism*, p. 3.
15 Ibid., pp. 3–4.
16 Ibid., p. 12.
17 Ibid., pp. 15–16.

18 John Herz, *International Politics in the Atomic Age* (New York: Columbia University Press, 1966), p. 234n5.
19 In particular Butterfield links Hobbesian fear to the revisionist states of Nazi Germany and Napoleonic France. See Herbert Butterfield, *International Conflict in the Twentieth Century* (London: Routledge and Kegan Paul., 1960), pp. 85–87.
20 Herz, op. cit., *International Politics in the Atomic Age*, p. 239.
21 Ibid., p. 241.
22 Ibid.
23 Robert Jervis, *Perception and Misperception in International Politics* (Princeton: Princeton University Press, 1976), p. 64.
24 Robert Jervis, 'Security Regimes', *International Organization*, 36/2 (Spring 1982), p. 360.
25 Jervis, op. cit., *Perception and Misperception in International Politics*, p. 68.
26 Charles L. Glaser, *Analyzing Strategic Nuclear Policy* (Princeton: Princeton University Press, 1990), p. 77.
27 Quoted from Jervis, op. cit., *Perception and Misperception in International Politics*, p. 74.
28 Ibid., p. 80.
29 Ibid., p. 75.
30 Barry Posen, 'The Security Dilemma and Ethnic Conflict', *Survival*, 35/1 (Spring 1993), p. 28.
31 Wheeler and Booth, op.cit., 'The Security Dilemma', pp. 29–60.
32 Jack Snyder, 'Perceptions of the Security Dilemma in 1914', in Robert Jervis, Richard Ned Lebow and Janice Gross Stein (eds.), *Psychology and Deterrence* (Baltimore: The Johns Hopkins University Press, 1985), p. 155.
33 Ibid., p. 153.
34 Ibid., p. 165.
35 Ibid., p. 166.
36 For an examination of this see Alan Collins, *The Security Dilemma and the End of the Cold War* (Edinburgh: Keele University Press, 1997), Ch. 2.
37 Snyder, op. cit., 'Perceptions of the Security Dilemma in 1914', pp. 154–155.
38 Bradley S. Klein, *Strategic Studies and World Order* (Cambridge: Cambridge University Press, 1994), p. 21.
39 Barry Buzan, *People, States and Fear: An Agenda for International Security Studies in the Post-Cold War Era* (Hemel Hempstead: Harvester Wheatsheaf, 2nd ed., 1991), pp. 294–295.
40 Herz, op. cit., *Political Realism and Political Idealism*, p. 200.
41 Jervis, op. cit., 'Security Regimes', p. 178.
42 The precise role anarchy performs is a disputed topic in the literature. For some, anarchy is not a cause of the security dilemma but rather a necessary condition. That is, because anarchy promotes self-help behaviour and leaves states uncertain of others' intent it creates propitious conditions for the security dilemma, but is itself not a cause. Hence Alexander Wendt's assertion that '[w]e do not *begin* our relationship ... in a security dilemma; security dilemmas are not given by anarchy or nature'. Instead, it is the interaction of states and the perceptions that statesmen gain from such contact that will determine if the security dilemma occurs. In contrast,

Robert Jervis argues, '[b]ut the heart of the security dilemma argument is that an increase in one state's security can make others less secure not because of misperception or imagined hostility, but because of the anarchic context of international relations'. Whether a cause or a necessary condition, what is clear is that its role is important. See Alexander Wendt, 'Anarchy is what states make of it: the social construction of power politics', *International Organization*, 46/2 (Spring 1992), p. 407; Jervis, op. cit., *Perception and Misperception in International Politics*, p. 76.

43   Buzan, op. cit., *People, States and Fear*, p. 177.
44   Wendt, op. cit., 'Anarchy is what states make of it', p. 395.
45   The key text in the common security literature is the report by the Commission on Disarmament and Security Issues conducted under the chairmanship of Olof Palme, *Common Security: A Programme for Disarmament* (London: Pan Books, 1982). The essence of these shared interests being new is not only captured in Gorbachev's *new* thinking but also in the Palme's Commission's recommendation for action requiring a *new* departure.
46   Charles E. Osgood, *An Alternative to War and Surrender* (Chicago: University of Illinois, 1962). Amitai Etzioni, *The Hard Way to Peace: a new strategy* (New York: Collier Books, 1962).
47   Snyder, op. cit., 'Perceptions of the Security Dilemma in 1914', p. 155.
48   Ibid.
49   Wendt, op. cit., 'Anarchy is What States make of it', p. 418.
50   Robert Jervis, 'Cooperation under the Security Dilemma', *World Politics*, 30/1 (January 1978), pp. 167–214.
51   The value of the offence/defence variable for the security dilemma has in certain instances gained such a prominent position that it has almost become synonymous with the security dilemma. This is particularly evident in Posen's article concerning ethnic conflict. While the 'offensiveness' of a force posture is an important factor in exacerbating a security dilemma there are also important cognitive factors such as enemy imaging, zero-sum thinking and ethnocentrism that play an equally vital role. Reducing the security dilemma to the offence/defence variable is highly misleading. See Posen, op. cit., 'The Security Dilemma and Ethnic Conflict', pp. 27–47.
52   Jervis, op. cit., 'Security Regimes', p. 374.
53   Jervis, op. cit., 'Cooperation under the Security Dilemma', p. 201.
54   Ibid., p. 214.
55   Snyder, op. cit., 'Perceptions of the Security Dilemma in 1914', pp. 158–160.
56   Ken Booth, 'The interregnum: world politics in transition', in Ken Booth (ed.), *New Thinking About Strategy and International Security* (London: Harper Collins, 1991), p. 20.
57   In addition to Stuart Kaufman and Barry Posen the security dilemma has been applied to ethnic conflict by David Lake/Donald Rothchild and Šumit Ganguly. See 'Ethnic Nationalism, Conflict, and War', *International Security*, 21/2 (Fall 1996). These writings are examined in Chapter 3.
58   Stuart J. Kaufman, 'An "international" theory of inter-ethnic war', *Review of International Studies*, 22/2 (April 1996), p. 151.
59   Ibid.
60   Posen, op. cit., 'The Security Dilemma and Ethnic Conflict', p. 27.
61   Ibid., p. 28.

62 Ibid., p. 37.
63 Kaufman, op. cit., 'An "international" theory of inter-ethnic war', p. 158.
64 Ibid., p. 157.
65 Ibid., p. 162.
66 Ibid., p. 170.
67 Ibid., p. 151. Kaufman's use of structure leads him to adopt two classifications (structural and perceptual) of the security dilemma. These labels were created by Jack Snyder in order to highlight two different factors that drive a security dilemma. The structural security dilemma refers to the tangible issues of offensive/defensive force postures and geographical terrain, while the perceptual security dilemma includes the intangible beliefs and convictions of statesmen. Both attributes can work independently, though more often collectively, to drive the dynamics of the security dilemma. Kaufman, however, produces an erroneous analysis of the relationship between them. He states that the 'real potency of perceptual security dilemmas, in ethnic conflict as in international conflict, is that they can create real, structural, security dilemmas' (p. 152). The implication being that a perceptual security dilemma is an imaginary or inferior version, while the structural variant is the real thing. This though is simply untrue; perceptual factors are just as important, if not more so, than structural factors. Indeed, the perception of statesmen may explain why in the mid to late 1980s the West was slow to react to the structural changes Gorbachev was initiating with his arms control proposals. Hence Snyder's conclusion that 'the addition of perceptual factors makes the security dilemma a more powerful theory of international conflict. It breathes life into the concept of "offence dominance", and it helps to explain why people underrate the feasibility of cooperation' (Jack Snyder, op. cit., 'Perceptions of the Security Dilemma in 1914', p. 164).
68 Stuart J. Kaufman, 'Spiralling to Ethnic War', *International Security*, 21/2 (Fall 1996), p. 109.
69 Ibid., p. 111.
70 Ibid., p. 112.
71 Butterfield, op. cit., *History and Human Relations,* pp. 21–22.
72 For a precise analysis of this point that comes to the same conclusion see Paul Roe, 'The Intrastate Security Dilemma: Ethnic Conflict as a "Tragedy"?', *Journal of Peace Research,* 36/2 (March 1999), pp. 187–188.
73 Glenn Snyder, 'The Security Dilemma in Alliance Politics', *World Politics,* 36/4 (July 1984), p. 461.

2 Third World Security: Security and Insecurity Dilemma

1 Ole Waever, Barry Buzan, Morten Kelstrup and Pierre Lemaitre, *Identity, Migration and the New Security Agenda in Europe* (London: Pinter Publishers, 1993). For reference to Copenhagen school see Bill McSweeney, 'Identity and security: Buzan and the Copenhagen school', *Review of International Studies*, 22/1 (January 1996), pp. 81–93.
2 Barry Buzan, 'Societal security, state security and internationalisation', in Ole Waever *et al.*, ibid., p. 46. Utilising society and identity as referent

objects for security has been criticised for assuming that they are fixed and not subject to change. It is argued that the identity of individuals, and thus the society they inhabit, evolves and changes over time. The response from Buzan and Waever is that while identity formation may be a process, why can it not, when it has become constructed, act as a referent object before the process of change takes place again? They write do we 'not imply that identities do not change, only that we should not expect everything to change all the time: certain things stay the same throughout the period relevant for an analysis'. Barry Buzan and Ole Waever, 'Slippery? contradictory? sociologically untenable? The Copenhagen school replies', *Review of International Studies*, 23/2 (April 1997), p. 243.

3　Barry Buzan, 'Societal security, state security and internationalisation', in Ole Waever *et al.*, ibid., p. 46.

4　Ibid.

5　Brian L. Job, 'The Insecurity Dilemma: National, Regime, and State Securities in the Third World', in Brian L. Job (ed.), *The Insecurity Dilemma: National Security of Third World States* (Boulder: Lynne Rienner, 1992), pp. 11–35.

6　David I. Steinberg, *The Future of Burma: Crisis and Choice in Myanmar* (London: University Press of America, 1990), p. 69.

7　Barry Buzan, *People, States and Fear: An Agenda for International Security Studies in the Post-Cold War Era* (Hemel Hempstead: Harvester Wheatsheaf, 2nd ed., 1991), pp. 96–107.

8　Mohammed Ayoob, *The Third World Security Predicament: State Making, Regional Conflict, and the International System* (Boulder: Lynne Rienner, 1995).

9　Caroline Thomas, *In Search of Security: The Third World in International Relations* (Boulder: Lynne Rienner, 1987). Whether these are security issues is contentious. Ayoob argues that only factors which threaten the state structure (territory, institutions, governing regime) should be considered security issues. Thus he argues that 'debt burdens, rain-forest decimation, or even famine do not become part of the security calculus... unless they threaten to have political outcomes that either affect the survivability of state boundaries, state institutions, or governing elites or weaken the capacity of states and regimes to act effectively in the realm of both domestic and international politics'. Ayoob, ibid., p. 9. What is and what is not a security issue and who determines this, is the focus of attention for Ole Waever and his work on 'securitization'. See Barry Buzan, Ole Waever and Jaap de Wilde, *Security: A New Framework For Analysis* (Boulder: Lynne Rienner, 1998), Ch. 2.

10　Edward E. Azar and Chung-in Moon, 'Legitimacy, Integration and Policy Capacity: The "Software" Side of Third World National Security', in Edward E. Azar and Chung-in Moon (eds.), *National Security in the Third World: The Management of Internal and External Threats* (College Park: Center for International Development and Conflict Management, University of Maryland, 1988), p. 78.

11　John Hutchinson and Anthony D. Smith (eds.), *Ethnicity* (Oxford: Oxford University Press, 1996), p. 4.

12　David Brown, *The State and Ethnic Politics in South-East Asia* (London: Routledge, 1994), p. xiii.

13 See James McKay, 'An Exploratory Synthesis of Primordial and Mobilisationist Approaches to Ethnic Phenomena', *Ethnic and Racial Studies*, 5/4 (1982) pp. 394–420. George Scott, 'A Resynthesis of the Primordial and Circumstantial Approaches to Ethnic Group Solidarity: towards an explanatory model', *Ethnic and Racial Studies*, 13/2 (1990), pp. 148–171.

14 Buzan, op. cit., 'Societal security, state security and internationalisation', p. 43.

15 W.K. Che Man, *Muslim Separatism: The Moros of Southern Philippines and the Malays of Southern Thailand* (Singapore: Oxford University Press, 1990), p. 74.

16 Although in the literature it is common to refer to the actors' intentions as either benign or malign, this can lead to unnecessary deliberations about the difficulties of determining intent. The crucial issue is whether the objectives the actors' pursue are really incompatible, or whether the incompatibility they perceive to exist is illusory. For example, a regime which embarks upon a policy of nation-building that entails the maintenance of the different ethnic groups as it seeks 'unity in diversity', but in its implementation becomes a policy of assimilation into the dominant ethnic group, is pursuing a goal which is a real threat to the maintenance of the other groups' ethnicity. The security dilemma does not operate since the regime's actions are a real threat to the group's ethnicity, despite the argument that this was not the intention of the regime.

17 Job, op. cit., 'The Insecurity Dilemma', p. 17.

18 Ibid., p. 18.

19 Ibid., pp. 27–28.

20 Ibid., p. 29.

21 Ibid.

22 Randall L. Schweller, 'Neorealism's Status-Quo Bias: What Security Dilemma?', *Security Studies*, 5/3 (Spring 1996), p. 104.

23 Buzan, op. cit., 'Societal security, state security and internationalisation', p. 43.

24 Myron Weiner, *The Global Migration Crisis: Challenges to States and to Human Rights* (New York: HarperCollins College Publishers, 1995), p. 135.

25 Ibid.

26 For a concise account of Karl Deutsch's inconsistent views of ethnicity and assimilation see Walker Connor, 'Nation-building or Nation-destroying', *World Politics*, 24/3 (April 1972), pp. 319–355.

27 Brown, op. cit., *The State and Ethnic Politics in South-East Asia*, p. 28.

28 For an account of how regime violence becomes more indiscriminate as the cycle of repression continues see T. David Mason, 'Indigenous Factors', in Barry M. Schutz and Robert O. Slater (eds.), *Revolution and Political Change in the Third World* (Boulder: Lynne Rienner, 1990), pp. 30–53.

29 The Free Papua Movement (OPM) began in 1965 after Indonesia's takeover of Irian Jaya (also known as West Irian) and despite Indonesian efforts, the OPM's activities have continued. In early 1996 the OPM gained publicity for its cause when it was responsible for holding captive 14 hostages, including a number of foreigners. For details see Nick Rufford, 'British Hostages Plead for Army to Hold Back as Deadline Nears', *The Sunday Times*, 21 January 1996.

30 Buzan, op. cit., 'Societal security, state security and internationalisation', p. 46.

31 Jonathan Rigg, *Southeast Asia a Region in Transition: A Thematic Human Geography of the ASEAN Region* (London: Unwin Hyman, 1991), p. 26.

32 John Gittings, 'Weakest Pay the Price for Recession as African-Style Poverty Hits Asia', *The Guardian*, 17 October 1998.

33 Ibid.

34 T. David Mason and Dale A. Krane, 'The Political Economy of Death Squads: Toward a Theory of the Impact of State-Sanctioned Terror', *International Studies Quarterly*, 33/2 (June 1989), p. 183.

35 Although not a challenge to the governing regime, and indeed they cooperate with it, the MENDAKI (for the Malays) and SINDA (for the Indians) in Singapore are examples of economic self-help organisations that have acquired political value. See Michael Hill and Lian Kwen Fee, *The Politics of Nation Building and Citizenship in Singapore* (London: Routledge, 1995), pp. 232–236.

36 John Sweeney, 'Arrest of Anwar Spurs Solidarity', *The Guardian*, 28 September, 1998.

37 Margot Cohen, 'Turning Point', *Far Eastern Economic Review*, 30 July 1998, p. 15. Hereafter known as *FEER*.

38 Whether the response will be along ethnic lines is contentious. According to Marxism, ethnic differences will be replaced by class divisions that will create a class consciousness. If the disadvantaged classes seek political goals along ethnic lines such ethnicity represents a 'false consciousness'. Nelson Kasfir, 'Explaining Ethnic Political Participation', in Atul Kohli (ed.), *The State and Development in the Third World* (Princeton: Princeton University Press, 1986), pp. 91–92.

39 Al-Arqam was outlawed on 26 August. For details of the movement see Michael Vatikiotis, 'Radical Chic', *FEER*, 26 May 1994, pp. 33–36.

40 Charles Tilly highlights the involvement of the military in the decision-making process as different from the European experience of state-building. While the military were involved in Europe, he argues that Third World militaries have acquired a much greater input into the political arena; an involvement that might hinder the state-building process. He writes, 'we need to be aware that the rise of military power in Third World states is not simply a natural phase of state formation, one that previous experience tells us will pass gradually as states mature'. Charles Tilly, *Coercion, Capital, and European States, AD 990–1992* (Oxford: Blackwell, 1992), p. 224.

41 Mason and Krane, op. cit., 'The Political Economy of Death Squads', p. 184.

42 John Alionby, 'Crackdown Ordered as Bloody Riots Drag Indonesia Back to the Brink', *The Observer*, 15 November 1998.

43 John Alionby, 'Barricades Burn in Malaysia Riot', *The Guardian*, 26 October 1998.

44 Michael Vatikiotis, 'The Reform Tango', *FEER*, 5 November 1998, p. 11.

45 Ibid.

46 Thomas, op. cit., *In Search of Security*, p. 13.

47 Ayoob recognises that state-making is rarely achieved through a formulated plan. Rather it occurs as a by-product of other objectives. He quotes Charles Tilly's conclusion that the European experience 'does not show us

modernising elites articulating the demands and needs of the masses, and fighting off traditional holders of power in order to meet those needs and demands. Far from it. We discover a world in which small groups of power-hungry men fought off numerous rivals and great popular resistance in pursuit of their own ends, and inadvertently promoted the formation of national states and widespread popular involvement in them'. Ayoob, op. cit., *The Third World Security Predicament*, p. 31.

48 The assumption that Third World states are engaged in state-making along European lines and are doomed to replay the tortuous and violent process of Europe's past is contentious. Ayoob, however, argues that we can understand the Third World from this perspective because first, the rhetoric of Third World governments makes it clear they want to emulate the model of the developed world, and second, in order for the people to engage in international affairs they have no choice; they must be represented by a state in order to engage in the international society of states. Ibid., p. 27.

49 Mohammed Ayoob, 'The Security Problematic of the Third World', *World Politics*, 43/2 (January 1991), p. 266.

50 Charles Tilly, 'Reflections on the History of European State-Making', in Charles Tilly (ed.), *The Formation of National States in Western Europe* (Princeton: Princeton University Press, 1975), p. 69.

51 Mohammed Ayoob, 'The Security Predicament of the Third World State: Reflections on State Making in a Comparative Perspective', in Brian L. Job (ed.), *The Insecurity Dilemma: National Security of Third World States* (Boulder: Lynne Rienner, 1992), p. 78.

52 Ayoob, op. cit., *The Third World Security Predicament*, pp. 32–33.

53 Robert L. Rothstein, 'The "Security Dilemma" and the "Poverty Trap" in the Third World', *The Jerusalem Journal of International Relations*, 8/4 (1986), p. 16.

54 The reliance on the military has the compounding effect of making the political process even more militarized. Nicole Ball writes that by 'seeking military solutions to [internal] political disputes ... governments both ensure that a substantial proportion of their budgets are allocated to the security sector and make it more likely that the armed forces will play a central role in the process of government itself'. Nicole Ball, 'Demilitarizing the Third World', in Michael T. Klare and Daniel C. Thomas, *World Security: Challenges for a New Century* (New York: St Martin's Press, 2nd ed., 1994), p. 219.

55 Ayoob claims that the United Nations willingness to admit the new states of the former Soviet Union and Yugoslavia has 'sent the message to prospective Third World separatists that the international community is no longer committed to the maintenance of existing state boundaries'. Ayoob, op. cit., *The Third World Security Predicament*, p. 174.

56 With the end of the Cold War foreign aid and trade preferences are moving away from the criterion of ideology towards respect for human rights. The United States since 1994 have tied China's Most-Favoured-Nation (MFN) trading status to its human rights record. In 1997 Newt Gingrich, the Speaker of the House of Representatives, asserted 'a Chinese-American relationship that did not include discussion of human rights was impossible'. The United States implemented sanctions against the Myanmar regime for its human rights record in May 1997. See 'Human Rights: A suitable target for foreign policy?',

The Economist, April 12–18 1997, and 'Burma is Said to Arrest Dissidents as US Sanctions Take Hold', *International Herald Tribune*, 22 May 1997.

57 Samuel Huntingdon has referred to the spread of democracy in the 1990s as the 'Third Wave' of democratisation while Larry Diamond asserts the 'stunning changes in Eastern Europe and the Soviet Union reverberated visibly throughout the Third World'. In Southeast Asia this has been notable in the Philippines, Thailand and Cambodia. Larry Diamond, 'The Globalization of Democracy', in Robert O. Slater, Barry M. Shultz and Steven R. Dorr (eds.), *Global Transformation and the Third World* (Boulder: Lynne Rienner, 1993), p. 33.

58 Ayoob, op. cit., *The Third World Security Predicament*, p. 179.

59 Ibid., p. 178.

60 Margot Cohen, 'Turning Point', *FEER*, 30 July 1998, pp. 12–18.

61 Despite positive signs in spring 1998 that political reform was being encouraged, developments in late 1998 cast doubt on this. In spring Chinese publications were openly raising the issue of democracy, but in December Li Peng stated that the leadership role of the Communist Party was sacrosanct as two Chinese dissidents were detained by the authorities. Despite this there remains cautious optimism that the reform agenda is still on track. See Matt Forney, 'Beijing Spring', *FEER*, 2 April 1998, pp. 20–22; John Gittings, 'China cracks down on pro-democracy veterans', *The Guardian*, 2 December 1998; Susan V. Lawrence, 'Beijing Chill', *FEER*, 14 January 1999, pp. 12–13.

62 The most famous of these publications being He Qinglian's *The Pitfalls of China's Modernization*. See Susan V. Lawrence, 'Agent of Change', *FEER*, 23 July 1998, pp. 10–12, and Susan V. Lawrence, 'Celebrity Critic', *FEER*, 22 October 1998, pp. 12–14.

63 For details of a Chinese civil society see Matt Forney, 'Voice of the People', *FEER*, 7 May 1998, pp. 10–12. For the Falun Gong sect see Lorien Holland, 'Breaking The Wheel', *FEER*, 5 August 1999, pp. 16–17.

64 The need to combine democratisation/human rights and state-making is noted by the former UN Secretary-General, Boutros Boutros-Ghali. He writes 'if every ethnic, religious or linguistic group claimed statehood, there would be no limit to fragmentation, and peace, security and economic wellbeing for all would become ever more difficult to achieve. One requirement for solutions to these problems lies in the commitment to human rights with a special sensitivity to those of minorities, whether ethnic, religious, social or linguistic. The sovereignty, territorial integrity and independence of States within the established international system, and the principle of self-determination for peoples, both of great value and importance, must not be permitted to work against each other in the period ahead. Respect for democratic principles at all levels of social existence is crucial: in communities, within States and within the community of States. Boutros Boutros-Ghali, *An Agenda for Peace: Preventive Diplomacy, Peacemaking and Peacekeeping* (New York: United Nations, June 1992), paragraphs 17–19.

65 Clark D. Neher and Ross Marlay, *Democracy and Development in Southeast Asia: The Winds of Change* (Colorado: Westview Press, 1995), p. 14.

66 Donald G. McCloud, *Southeast Asia: Tradition and Modernity in the Contemporary World* (Boulder: Westview Press, 1995), p. 274.

67 Renée de Nevers, 'Democratization and Ethnic Conflict', *Survival*, 35/2 (Summer 1993), p. 42.
68 Myron Weiner, *The Indian Paradox: Essays in Indian Politics* (New Delhi: Sage, 1989), p. 37.
69 Quoted from Ayoob, op. cit., *The Third World Security Predicament*, p. 180. Tentative steps towards solving Indonesia's internal security problems via autonomy began in January 1999. For details see John McBeth and Margot Cohen, 'Loosening The Bonds', *FEER*, 21 January 1999, pp. 10–13.
70 Ayoob, op. cit., *The Third World Security Predicament*, p. 181.
71 This will be examined in the next chapter. For a concise overview of democratisation and ethnic conflict see Renée de Nevers, op. cit., 'Democratization and Ethnic Conflict', pp. 31–48.
72 Robert Jervis, *Perception and Misperception in International Politics* (Princeton: Princeton University Press, 1976), p. 66.
73 Donald L. Horowitz, 'Ethnic and Nationalist Conflict', in Michael T. Klare and Daniel C. Thomas, *World Security: Challenges for a New Century* (New York: St Martin's Press, 2nd ed., 1994), p. 179.
74 Tin Maung Maung Than, 'Myanmar: Preoccupation with Regime Survival, National Unity, and Stability', in Muthiah Alagappa, *Asian Security Practice: Material and Ideational Influences* (Stanford: Stanford University Press, 1998), p. 395.
75 Mason, op. cit., 'Indigenous Factors', pp. 48–49.
76 Ayoob, op. cit., 'The Security Predicament of the Third World State', p. 72.
77 Ayoob, op. cit., *The Third World Security Predicament*, p. 178.

3 Ethnic Tensions and the Security Dilemma in Southeast Asia

1 Muthiah Alagappa, 'The Dynamic of International Security in Southeast Asia: Change and Continuity', *Australian Journal of International Affairs*, 45/1 (May 1991), p. 4.
2 In the Southern Philippine island of Mindanao the Moro National Liberation Front (MNLF) signed a peace agreement with Manila in 1996 creating for the Muslims an Autonomous Region. Another, larger armed group, the Moro Islamic Liberation Front (MILF), continue to fight for Mindanao independence. See 'Murad: MILF bent on independence', *The Philippine Star*, 3 December 1998.
3 See Syed Azhar and Roslina Mohammed, 'Security and Stability Vital', *The Malaysian Star*, 27 July 1997.
4 Mr Tang was faced with a court injunction freezing assets of £4.93 million and his wife was prevented from leaving the country. Nick Cumming-Bruce, 'Singapore to bankrupt dissident by legal action', *The Guardian*, 29 January 1997, also see *The Guardian*, 30 January 1997. In May a Singapore court ordered Mr Tang to pay £3.5 million in damages after members of the PAP brought 13 lawsuits against him claiming that 'by denying their accusations he damaged their credibility with voters' (*The Guardian*, 30 May 1997). The PAP leadership also filed 10 lawsuits against the leader of the opposition Workers' Party, J.B. Jeyaretnam, for defamation because he read

out a statement from Mr Tang at an election rally. This case caught international attention with Mr Jeyaretnam's employment of British QC, George Carman, and although Mr Jeyaretnam achieved a qualified success an appeal court found in favour of the PAP and quintupled the damages Mr Jeyaretnam would have to pay. Unable to pay these damages Mr Jeyaretnam would have to vacate his seat in parliament. This did not occur however as it was agreed that Mr Jeyaretnam could pay in five instalments and thus avoid bankruptcy proceedings and keep his seat in parliament. See Nick Cumming-Bruce, 'British QCs in Singapore Legal Battle', *The Guardian*, 19 August 1997; John Gittings, 'Singapore Court Bankrupts MP', *The Guardian*, 24 July 1998; *Far Eastern Economic Review*, 15 October 1998, p. 16. Hereafter known as *FEER*.

5　In Singapore the ruling People's Action Party (PAP) could not lose the 1997 election because opposition candidates were only contesting 36 seats, less than half of the 83 seats in parliament. Despite this, PAP's insecurity was manifest by a peculiar warning Goh Chok Tong issued in his national day speech in August 1996 – 'If Singapore falters we will have no option but to ask Malaysia to take us back. Such a merger will be on Malaysia's terms'. Many commentators saw this, as did Malaysia's prime minister, Dr Mahathir Mohamad, as nothing more than scare tactics by PAP to ensure Singaporeans voted for PAP in the election. See 'Singapore's Sheepdog Trials', *The Economist*, 14 September 1996, p. 71. Also see Ramthan Hussain, 'Victory, Before the Vote', *The Guardian*, 24 December, 1996, and for yet more PAP insecurity, Stephen Vines, 'Singapore Tries to Induce Feelgood Factor', *The Independent*, 1 January 1997. In response to legal proceedings, a favourite tactic of the PAP to stifle opposition in Singapore, Tang fled to the Malaysian state of Johor. Singapore's Senior Minister, Lee Kuan Yew, claimed this implied Tang was of dubious character since Johor was 'notorious for shootings, muggings and car-jackings'. The Malaysians demanded an apology from the Singapore government and there followed a freeze on Malaysian-Singapore relations. See 'Cooling off Ties with S'pore', *New Straits Times*, 27 March 1997.

6　The bewilderment that Goh Chok Tong's comment caused – that Singapore might need to merge with Malaysia again – apparently revealed an appalling lack of knowledge about Singapore's history among school children.

7　For details of the exhibition see Ben Dolven, 'Singapore's Psyche', *FEER*, 20 August 1998, pp. 36–37. For shared values see Chua Beng Huat, 'Racial Singaporeans: Absence after the Hyphen', in Joel S. Kahn (ed.), *Southeast Asian Identities: Culture and the Politics of Representation in Indonesia, Malaysia, Singapore, and Thailand* (Singapore: Institute of Southeast Asian Studies, 1998), pp. 39–40.

8　Michael Vatikiotis, 'No Safety Net', *FEER*, 8 October 1998, p. 11.

9　Ethnic riots in Indonesia occur throughout the archipelago with tribal groups fighting in the Outer Islands and Chinese/Muslim clashes occurring on Java. See John Aglionby, 'Indonesia riven by ethnic rioting', *The Guardian*, 4 January 1997, and '20 held for rioting in central Java', *New Straits Times*, 22 February 1995. At the other extreme, ethnic discrimination in Singapore is manifest by the formation of non-political organisations such as Perhakam. For details see 'Injustice towards S'pore Malays exposed: Tabloid', *The Straits Times*, 20 June 1997.

10 David Brown, *The State and Ethnic Politics in Southeast Asia* (London: Routledge, 1994), p. 37.
11 President Habibie is a native of South Sulawesi and has appointed Bugis and Makassar individuals to positions of responsbility in his administration. See Margot Cohen and Dan Murphy, 'Swept Away', *FEER*, 8 April 1999, pp. 26–29.
12 Brown, op. cit., *The State and Ethnic Politics in Southeast Asia*, p. 38.
13 David I. Steinberg, *The Future of Burma: Crisis and Choice in Myanmar* (London: University Press of America, 1990), p. 75.
14 Josef Silverstein, *Burmese Politics: The Dilemma of National Unity* (New Brunswick: Rutgers University Press, 1980), p. 151.
15 Steinberg notes how the leader of the Shan ethnic minority in 1970 'looked with envy on the Shan-language primary school textbooks' in the province of Yunnan in China. Steinberg, op. cit., *The Future of Burma*, p. 75.
16 Although the ethnic dimension constitutes a major proportion of the internal security problems facing the Rangoon regime, it is not alone. The student protests of 1988, which forced the military regime to introduce multiparty elections in May 1990, and the subsequent failure of the regime to recognise the overwhelming victory achieved by National League for Democracy (NLD) in that election, has resulted in the regime losing its legitmacy among the populace. The house arrest of the NLD's popular leader, Aung San Suu Kyi, and the regime's appalling human-rights violations has also brought widespread international condemnation.
17 Quoted from Silverstein, op. cit., *Burmese Politics*, p. 151.
18 David Brown writes that 'it was only in the 1950s that a sense of Shan unity began to develop, when their system of *muong* village groups under *sawbwa* leadership failed to protect their autonomy'. Independent Burma was based on a federal system of states of which the Shan state was the largest. Possibly because it had the right to secede within ten years of independence the Shan state suffered constant interference from the national regime. After the military coup in 1962 Burma continued as a quasi-federal state although in practice it became a unitary state. For more details see Silverstein, op. cit., *Burmese Politics*, pp. 214–216; Chao-Tzang Yawnghwe, 'Burma: The Depoliticization of the Political', in Muthiah Alagappa, *Political Legitimacy in Southeast Asia: The Quest for Moral Authority* (Stanford: Stanford University Press, 1995), pp. 170–192. For Brown quote, op. cit., *The State and Ethnic Politics in Southeast Asia*, p. 53.
19 Josef Silverstein, 'Fifty Years of Failure in Burma', in Michael E. Brown and Šumit Ganguly (eds.), *Government Policies and Ethnic Relations in Asia and the Pacific* (London: The MIT Press, 1997), p. 190.
20 The actual development of a Karen ethnic identity beyond the local village, according to Ananda Rajah, is an invention created by the Karen National Union (KNU). He argues that in areas where the KNU control 'means of social reproduction, namely, schools' a national consciousness has developed. However, elsewhere in Burma and Thailand, Karen 'do not … identify themselves with the separatist movement or imagine themselves to be part of that community'. Ananda Rajah, 'Ethnicity, Nationalism, and the Nation-State: The Karen in Burma and Thailand ', in Gehan Wijeyewardene (ed.), *Ethnic Groups across National Boundaries in Mainland Southeast Asia* (Singapore: Institute of Southeast Asian Studies, 1990), p. 121.

21 Clive J. Christie, *A Modern History of South East Asia: Decolonization, Nationalism and Separatism* (London: Tauris Academic Press, 1996), p. 63.
22 Quoted from Brown, op. cit., *The State and Ethnic Politics in Southeast Asia*, p. 50.
23 Josef Silverstein, 'The Federal Dilemma in Burma', in John T. McAlister, Jr., *Southeast Asia: The Politics of National Integration* (New York: Random House, 1973), p. 433.
24 *Bumiputeras* refers to Malays and other indigenous groups in Malaysia and is derived from *bumiputra* which means sons of the soil. These terms are used to distinguish between the Malays and non-Malays.
25 Milton J. Esman, *Ethnic Politics* (Ithaca: Cornell University Press, 1994), p. 65.
26 William Case, 'Comparative Malaysian Leadership: Tunku Abdul Rahman and Mahathir Mohamad', *Asian Survey*, 31/5 (May 1991), p. 467.
27 Ibid.
28 Amnesty International concluded that Mahathir's use of the ISA was unjustified since the people arrested 'did not in any way use or advocate the use of violence'. The fact that the arrested individuals included Lim Kit Siang, the leader of the opposition Democratic Action Party (DAP), and other individuals critical of the Mahathir regime adds weight to the belief that the Malaysian prime minister used the events of 1987 to further his own consolidation of power. Jean DeBernardi and Christopher Taronwski, 'Managing Multicultural Societies: The Status of Minority Groups in Singapore, Malaysia and Thailand', in Amitav Acharya and Richard Stubbs (eds.), *New Challenges for ASEAN: Emerging Policy Issues* (Vancouver: University of British Columbia Press, 1995), p. 86. Also see Suhaini Aznam, 'Mahathir Cracks Down', *FEER*, 5 November 1987, p. 14.
29 The low percentage of the Malay in the 1931 census can partly be explained by the inclusion of the Chinese living in Singapore.
30 Crawford Young, *The Politics of Cultural Pluralism* (Madison: The University of Wisconsin Press, 1976), pp. 121–125.
31 During the 1960s the UMNO leadership started a number of economic institutions such as the MARA (Council of Trust for the Indigenous), Bank Bumiputra (Indigenous Bank) and Bank Pertanian (Agricultural Bank), all designed to help Malays venture into economic activities. They tried to change the way Malays thought about their 'way of life' so that they could take advantage of the opportunities being created for them. The then Deputy Prime Minister, Tun Abdul Razak, even called upon Malays to take up the challenge of modernity. For details see Hussin Mutalib, *Islam and Ethnicity in Malay Politics* (New York: Oxford University Press, 1990), p. 48. The New Economic Policy (NEP) introduced after the 1969 race riots involved even greater state intervention in the economy as it redistributed corporate assets in favour of Malays. Such interventions included making shares available to Malays at preferential rates and obliging companies to train Malays for managerial positions.
32 For details on Chinese resentment towards the education policy see Esman, op. cit., *Ethnic Politics*, pp. 69–70.
33 See Gordon P. Means, *Malaysian Politics: The Second Generation* (Singapore: Oxford University Press, 1991), pp. 60–61.
34 Harold Crouch, 'Malaysia: Neither Authoritarian Nor Democratic', in Kevin Hewison, Richard Robison and Garry Rodan (eds.), *Southeast Asia in*

the 1990s (St Leonards: Allen & Unwin, 1993), p. 145. For more on share ownership see DeBernardi and Taronwski, op. cit., 'Managing Multicultural Societies', p. 83.

35 For details of the riots and fears of both communities see Karl von Vorys, *Democracy without Consensus: Communalism and Political Stability in Malaysia* (Princeton: Princeton University Press, 1975), pp. 308–338.

36 Case, op. cit., 'Comparative Malaysian Leadership', p. 460.

37 James Jesudason, *Ethnicity and the Economy: The State, Chinese Business, and Multinationals in Malaysia* (New York: Oxford University Press, 1989), p. 52.

38 Quoted in N.J. Funston, *Malay Politics in Malaysia: A Study of the United Malays National Organisation and Party Islam* (Kuala Lumpur: Heinemann, 1980), p. 208.

39 John Slimming, *Malaysia: Death of a Democracy* (London: John Murray, 1969), p. 18.

40 Ibid., p. 26.

41 Funston, op. cit., *Malay Politics in Malaysia*, p. 211.

42 Suhaini Aznam, 'The Language of Politics', *FEER*, 29 October, 1987, p. 21.

43 Harold Crouch, 'Malaysia: Do Elections Make a Difference?', in R.H. Taylor (ed.), *The Politics of Elections in Southeast Asia* (New York: Woodrow Wilson Center Press, 1996), p. 132.

44 Laurence K.L. Siaw, 'Malaysia in 1979: Restructuring the Economy, Realigning Political Forces', *Southeast Asia Affairs 1980* (Singapore: Institute of Southeast Asian Affairs, 1980), p. 218.

45 Donald L. Horowitz, 'Cause and Consequence in Public Theory: Ethnic Policy and System Transformation in Malaysia', *Policy Sciences*, 22/3–4 (November 1989), p. 261.

46 See Ho Wah Foon, 'Non-Muslims Upset Over Compulsory Islamic Studies', *The Straits Times*, 28 June 1997.

47 Charles F. Keyes, *Isan: Regionalism in Northeastern Thailand* (Ithaca: Data Paper 65, Cornell University Southeast Asia Program, 1967), p. 3.

48 The *Far Eastern Economic Review* adds the Indochina war to these factors: 'In the 1960s, a combination of economic and racial discrimination, plus the spillover from the Indochina war, gave birth to the northern hill tribes and northeastern Isan (Thai-Lao) minority'. *FEER*, 1 December 1978, p. 40.

49 In 1962 the official figure was 75 per cent of Northeasterners lived below the poverty line, by 1975 this had been reduced to 38 per cent. Brown, however, suggests that in 1979 this figure was between 67 per cent and 82.9 per cent. See Brown, op. cit., *The State and Ethnic Politics in Southeast Asia*, p. 179.

50 Keyes, op. cit., *Isan*, p. 39.

51 Quoted from Brown, op. cit., *The State and Ethnic Politics in Southeast Asia*, p. 183.

52 Ibid., p. 186.

53 Keyes, op. cit., *Isan*, p. 60.

54 Brown, op. cit., *The State and Ethnic Politics in Southeast Asia*, p. 183.

55 Charles F. Keyes, 'Ethnic Identity and Loyalty of Villagers in Northeastern Thailand', *Asian Survey*, 6/7 (1966), p. 369.

56 Keyes, op. cit., *Isan*, p. 60.

57 Brown, op. cit., *The State and Ethnic Politics in Southeast Asia*, p. 189.

58 Keyes, op. cit., *Isan*, p. 35.

59   Ibid., p. 53.
60   *Bangkok Post*, 15 December 1961, quoted from ibid.
61   W.K. Che Man, *Muslim Separatism: The Moros of Southern Philippines and the Malays of Southern Thailand* (Singapore: Oxford University Press, 1990), p. 17.
62   Ibid., p. 36. There are four liberation fronts representing the Patani Malays. They are the Barisan Nasional Pembebasan Patani (BNPP – National Liberation Front of Patani); Barisan Revolusi Nasional (BRN – National Revolutionary Front); Patani United Liberation Organisation (PULO – Pertubuhan Perpaduan Pembebasan Patani); and Barisan Bertsatu Mujahideen Patani (BBMP – United Fronts of Patani Fighters).
63   Christie, op. cit., *A Modern History of South East Asia*, p. 177.
64   Che Man, op. cit., *Muslim Separatism*, p. 42.
65   A World Bank Country Study, *Indonesia: The Transmigration Program in Perspective* (Washington, D.C.: World Bank, 1988), p. 91.
66   John Aglionby, 'Spice Island Turns to Stife Island', *The Observer*, 7 March 1999.
67   Myron Weiner, *The Global Migration Crisis: Challenges to States and to Human Rights* (New York: HarperCollins College Publishers, 1995), p. 135.
68   Barry Buzan, 'Societal security, state security and internationalisation', in Ole Waever, Barry Buzan, Morten Kelstrup and Pierre Lemaitre, *Identity, Migration and the New Security Agenda in Europe* (London: Pinter Publishers, 1993), p. 45.
69   The transmigration programme has largely been a failure in the other criteria as well. See Mariël Otten, 'Transmigrasi: From Poverty to Bare Subsistence', *The Ecologist*, 16 2/3, 1986, pp. 71–76.
70   Marcus Colchester, 'Banking on Disaster: International Support for Transmigration', *The Ecologist*, 16 2/3, 1986, p. 62.
71   Marcus Colchester, 'Unity and Diversity: Indonesia's Policy Towards Tribal Peoples', *The Ecologist*, 16 2/3, 1986, p. 89.
72   Ibid.
73   Catherine Caulfield, *In the Rainforest* (London: Heinemann, 1984), pp. 197–198.
74   Ibid., p. 198. The differences between the mainly Christian Irian Jayans and the transmigrant Muslims led to more than 1,000 settlers fleeing Irian Jaya after Muslims attacked a Christian church in Jakarta. Such incidents provide a vivid manifestation of the failure of transmigration to overcome the differences between the different people that make up Indonesia. See, '1,000 Settlers Flee Irian Jaya', *The Straits Times*, 3 December 1998.
75   Jonathan Rigg, *Southeast Asia a Region in Transition: A Thematic Human Geography of the ASEAN Region* (London: Unwin Hyman, 1991), p. 104.
76   Michael Vatikiotis, 'The Centre Takes All', *FEER*, 30 November 1989, p. 32; 'Indigenous Indonesians Rally in Jakarta', *The Straits Times*, 23 March 1999.
77   Dewi Fortuna Anwar, 'Indonesia: Domestic Priorities Define National Security', in Muthiah Alagappa, *Asian Security Practice: Material and Ideational Influences* (Stanford: Stanford University Press, 1998), p. 494.
78   See John Aglionby, 'Indonesia Riven by Ethnic Rioting', *The Guardian*, 4 January 1997; John Aglionby, 'Peace Pact Fails to End Indonesian Ethnic Strife', *The Guardian*, 5 March 1997; John Aglionby, 'Scores Die as Ethnic Rivalries Spark Violence in Borneo', *The Guardian*, 20 March 1999.
79   It is not only in developing countries that these problems arise. The indigenous Aborigine population in Australia is likewise suffering from cultural

anomie. For details of Aboriginal health problems see *The Sydney Morning Herald*, 3 April 1997.

80 See John Vidal, 'Forests for Life: Livelihood: The Dispossessed', *The Observer*, 29 September 1996; Grace Chin, 'Vanishing World of the Bidayuh', *The Malaysian Star*, 17 July 1997; Frances Harrison, 'Engines of Change Power Jungle State into 21st Century', *The Guardian*, 10 July 1999.

81 James F. Eder, *On the Road to Tribal Extinction: Depopulation, Deculturation, and Adaptive Well-Being Among the Batak of the Philippines* (Berkeley: University of California Press, 1987).

82 Rigg, op. cit., *Southeast Asia*, p. 76.

83 Rigg writes, '[a]lthough the transition to settled agriculture and the incorporation of tribal peoples into the modern Southeast Asian state could certainly be achieved with far greater cultural sensitivity than has so far been shown, it is difficult to ignore the fact that in most cases such a transition is inevitable and imminent'. Ibid., p. 78.

84 Chaim D. Kaufmann, 'Possible and Impossible Solutions to Ethnic Civil Wars', *International Security*, 20/4 (Spring 1996), p. 147.

85 Chaim D. Kaufmann, 'When All Else Fails: Ethnic Population Transfers and Partitions in the Twentieth Century', *International Security*, 23/2 (Fall 1998), p. 122.

86 Charles L. Glaser, 'The Security Dilemma Revisited', *World Politics*, 50/1 (October 1997), p. 171.

87 When Erica Strecker Downs and Philip Saunders write that '[e]ven though nationalist myths are primarily aimed at a domestic audience, other states may misinterpret them as a serious threat and respond in kind, giving rise to a security dilemma', they are capturing the tragic essence of the situation that the security dilemma occurs as an unintended consequence of an action. Erica Strecker Downs and Philip C. Saunders, 'Legitimacy and the Limits of Nationalism: China and the Diaoyu Islands', *International Security*, 23/3 (Winter 1998/99), p. 115.

88 Robert Jervis, 'Cooperation Under the Security Dilemma', *World Politics*, 30/1 (January 1978), pp. 167–214.

89 Barry R. Posen, 'The Security Dilemma and Ethnic Conflict', *Survival*, 35/1 (Spring 1993), pp. 27–47.

90 Kaufmann, op. cit., 'Possible and Impossible Solutions to Ethnic Civil Wars', p. 148.

91 Ibid., p. 139.

92 Ibid., p. 159.

93 David A. Lake and Donald Rothchild, 'Containing Fear: The Origins and Management of Ethnic Conflict', *International Security*, 21/2 (Fall 1996), p. 52.

94 Robert Jervis, *Perception and Misperception in International Politics* (Princeton: Princeton University Press, 1976), p. 67.

95 Kaufmann writes, '[e]ven if power-sharing can avert potential ethnic conflict or dampen mild ones, our concern here is whether it can bring peace under the conditions of intense violence and extreme ethnic mobilization that are likely to motivate intervention...The answer is no'. Kaufmann, op. cit., 'Possible and Impossible Solutions to Ethnic Civil Wars', pp. 155–156.

96 They prefer to regard the security dilemma as referring to situations where actors have incentives to resort to the use of pre-emptive force. This narrow

definition of the security dilemma, which rests entirely on the offensive/defensive weapon characteristic, is highly contentious and they acknowledge 'some readers may prefer the broader use of the term security dilemma', which 'rests on information failures and problems of credible commitments'. Lake and Rothchild, op. cit., 'Containing Fear', p. 52n26 and p. 52.

97 Ibid., pp. 51–52.

98 Ibid., p. 57.

99 The MCA claims to have been instrumental in the setting up of the Mandarin language Chinese college, known as the New Era College. See 'MCA to help raise funds for new Chinese college', *The Straits Times*, 7 July 1997.

100 Harold Crouch, 'Malaysia: Neither authoritarian nor democratic', in Kevin Hewison, Richard Robison and Garry Rodan (eds.), *Southeast Asia in the 1990s* (St Leonards: Allen & Unwin, 1993), p. 152.

101 See Crouch, op. cit., 'Malaysia: Do elections make a difference?', p. 128.

102 Crouch, op. cit., 'Malaysia: Neither authoritarian nor democratic', p. 153.

103 Ibid., p. 147.

104 William Case, 'Malaysia: Aspects and Audiences of Legitimacy', in Muthiah Alagappa (ed.), *Political Legitimacy in Southeast Asia: The Quest for Moral Authority* (Stanford: Stanford University Press, 1995), p. 87.

105 William Case has written of the ethnic bargain as the division between the Malay and Chinese of political and economic responsibilities. This bargain he asserts was manifest in the Alliance with Malays holding the dominant political posts while the financial and trade ministries were reserved for officials from the MCA. See Case, 'Comparative Malaysian Leadership', p. 459, and ibid., p. 79.

106 Renée de Nevers, 'Democratization and Ethnic Conflict', *Survival*, 35/2 (Summer 1993), p. 45.

107 For instance although Malays account for 57 per cent of the peninsula population they are the majority ethnic group in 70 per cent of the seats. For details see Crouch, op. cit., 'Malaysia: Neither Authoritarian nor Democratic', pp. 136–140.

108 In October 1995 Mahathir secured the successful adoption of an UMNO resolution barring the contest for the two top positions. See James Chin, 'Malaysia in 1996', *Asian Survey*, 37/2 (February 1997), p. 182.

109 Crouch, op. cit., 'Malaysia: Neither Authoritarian nor Democratic', p. 139.

110 James Putzel, 'Why Has Democratization Been a Weaker Impulse in Indonesia and Malaysia than in the Philippines?', in David Potter, David Goldblatt, Margaret Kiloh and Paul Lewis (eds.), *Democratization* (London: Polity Press, 1997), p. 254.

111 See the exchange between Gerald Segal and Charles Hampden-Turner in 'Asia's Infinite Game', *Prospect*, March 1997. Also see Alan Dupont, 'Is There An Asian Way?', *Survival*, 38/2 (Summer 1996), pp. 13–33.

112 Donald G. McCloud, *Southeast Asia: Tradition and Modernity in the Contemporary World* (Boulder: Westview Press, 1995), pp. 270–271.

113 Quoted from Case, op. cit., 'Malaysia: Aspects and Audiences of Legitimacy', pp. 82–83.

114 Ibid., p. 104.

115 Brown, op. cit., *The State and Ethnic Politics in Southeast Asia*, p. xviii.
116 'Like Mr Banharn last year, General Chavalit, whose party won 125 seats, owes his victory to the poorest region of Thailand, the north-east'. See 'Thailand's Familiar Aspirations', *The Economist*, 23 November 1996, p. 87.
117 Thongchai Winichakul, 'The Changing Landscape of the Past: New Histories in Thailand Since 1973', *Journal of Southeast Asian Studies*, 26/1 (March 1995), p. 115.
118 Brown, op. cit., *The State and Ethnic Politics in Southeast Asia*, p. 199.
119 Ibid., p. 203.
120 Winichakul, op. cit., 'The Changing Landscape of the Past', p. 116.
121 Malaysian Foreign Minister, Abdullah Ahmad Badawi, contends that Malaysia 'cannot go into the 21st Century with people living a separate identity except that they hold the same passport, hold the same identity card'. For Badawi the creation of a Malaysian identity is a clear objective. See Frank Ching, 'Forging Malaysia's Identity', *FEER*, 29 August 1996, p. 36.
122 T.N. Harper, 'New Malays, New Malaysians: Nationalism, Society and History', *Southeast Asian Affairs 1996* (Singapore: Institute of Southeast Asian Studies, 1996), p. 242.
123 James V. Jesudason, 'Chinese Business and Ethnic Equilibrium in Malaysia', *Development and Change*, 28/1 (1997), p. 131.
124 Ibid., p. 139.
125 K.S. Nathan, 'Malaysia: Reinventing the Nation', in Muthiah Alagappa, *Asian Security Practice: Material and Ideational Influences* (Stanford: Stanford University Press, 1998), p. 548.
126 Lake and Rothchild, op. cit., 'Containing Fear', p. 57.
127 Kaufmann, op. cit., 'Possible and Impossible Solutions to Ethnic Civil Wars', p. 159.
128 For an account of these theories see Walker Connor, 'Nation-Building or Nation-Destroying?', *World Politics*, 24/3 (April 1972), pp. 319–355.
129 See Murray Herbert, 'The Party Begins', *FEER*, 15 April 1999, p. 16.
130 Randall L. Schweller, 'Neorealism's Status-Quo Bias: What Security Dilemma?', *Security Studies*, 5/3 (Spring 1996), p. 104.

4   ASEAN's Security Dilemma

1 Hari Singh, 'Vietnam and ASEAN: The Politics of Accommodation', *Australian Journal of International Affairs*, 51/2 (July 1997), p. 226.
2 Nicola Baker and Leonard C. Sebastian, 'The Problem With Parachuting: Strategic Studies and Security in the Asia/Pacific Region', *Journal of Strategic Studies*, 18/3 (September 1995), p. 19.
3 Brian L. Job, 'The Insecurity Dilemma: National, Regime, and State Securities in the Third World', in Brian L. Job (ed.), *The Insecurity Dilemma: National Security of Third World States* (Boulder: Lynne Rienner, 1992), p. 18.
4 Peter H. Jackson, *Quasi-States: Sovereignty, International Relations, and the Third World* (Cambridge: Cambridge University Press, 1990), pp. 168–169.
5 Ibid., p. 171.
6 For details of this border clash see Ananda Rajah, 'Ethnicity, Nationalism, and the Nation-State: The Karen in Burma and Thailand', in Gehan

Wijeyewardene (ed.), *Ethnic Groups across National Boundaries in Mainland Southeast Asia* (Singapore: Institute of Southeast Asian Studies, 1990), pp. 102–110.

7 Quoted from 'Thai PM warns of military strikes against raiders crossing border', *South China Morning Post*, 26 March 1998.

8 Sukhumbhand Paribatra and Chi-Anan Samudavanija, 'Internal Dimensions of Regional Security in Southeast Asia', in Mohammed Ayoob (ed.), *Regional Security in the Third World* (London: Croom Helm, 1986), pp. 76–77.

9 ASA was formed in July 1961 and consisted of Malaya, the Philippines and Thailand. It was short-lived foundering on a territorial dispute between the Philippines and Malaya in the island of Borneo. Maphilindo, an acronym of the three states that established it – Malaya, the Philippines, Indonesia – survived for an even shorter period. Formed in Manila during 1963, it collapsed when Malaysia was formed on 16 September 1963. *Konfrontasi* lasted between 1963 and 1966 and describes the state of relations between Indonesia and Malaysia when the former challenged the latter's legitimacy.

10 Malcolm Chalmers, 'ASEAN and Confidence Building: Continuity and Change after the Cold War', *Contemporary Security Policy*, 18/1 (April 1997), p. 38.

11 In Thailand the United States created a War Reserve Stockpile of weapons which could be used if Vietnam invaded Thailand. In Malaysia joint military exercises which had been conducted secretly since 1971 were formalised in 1984 with the establishment of a Bilateral Training and Consultative Group. In addition to these arrangements the United States were linked indirectly to the region through the Five Power Defence Arrangements which contains the United Kingdom, Australia and New Zealand with whom the United States were allied through NATO and ANZUS. For details see Tim Huxley, *Insecurity in the ASEAN Region* (London: Royal United Services Institute Whitehall Paper, 1993), pp. 21–22.

12 For details see ibid., pp. 23–25.

13 Michael Leifer, *ASEAN and the Security of South-East Asia* (London: Routledge, 1990), p. 37.

14 Mely Caballero-Anthony, 'Mechanisms of Dispute Settlement: The ASEAN Experience', *Contemporary Southeast Asia*, 20/1 (April 1998), p. 57.

15 Derwin Pereira, 'Help is not just aid, says Jarkarta', *The Straits Times*, 24 February 1999. Also see Ben Dolven and John McBeth, 'Distant Neighbours', *Far Eastern Economic Review*, 9 July 1998, p. 19. Hereafter known as *FEER*.

16 The Malaysian political system discriminates against the substantial minority of Chinese citizens in the Malay's favour. This ensures that the coalition government remains dominated by the Malay. In Singapore the political system is non-racial but because the population is overwhelmingly Chinese, it is Chinese who dominate. Singapore was expelled from the Malaysian Federation for championing the cause of a political system which treated all Malaysians equally.

17 Tim Huxley, 'Singapore and Malaysia: A Precarious Balance?', *The Pacific Review*, 4/3 (1991), p. 207.

18 In the event of a Singapore incursion into Malaysia, Huxley suggests the advance would stop some 80 km in Johor which would provide Singapore with strategic depth and seize water supplies. Ibid., p. 208.

19 S. Jayasankaran, 'Under the Gun', *FEER*, 3 September 1998, p. 20.

20 Although not named, it is widely believed that the ASEAN member in question was Singapore. See Suhaini Aznam, 'Neighbourly Interest', *FEER*, 21 December 1989, pp. 20–21.

21 Statement made in an interview with the *FEER*, 24 September 1998, p. 11.

22 Quoted from Amitav Acharya, 'Realism, Institutionalism; and the Asian Economic Crisis', *Contemporary Southeast Asia*, 21/1 (April 1999), p. 11.

23 In November 1998 Malaysia said that it would resume its involvement in the FPDA in 1999, after it had discussed details with Singapore. See 'Malaysia back in FPDA exercises', *The Straits Times*, 30 November 1998.

24 Muthiah Alagappa, 'International Politics in Asia: The Historical Context', in Muthiah Alagappa (ed.), *Asian Security Practice: Material and Ideational Influences* (Stanford: Stanford University Press, 1998), p. 80.

25 Michael R.J. Vatikiotis, 'A Giant Treads Carefully: Indonesia's Foreign Policy in the 1990s', in Robert S. Ross (ed.), *East Asia in Transition: Toward a New Regional Order* (Singapore: Institute of Southeast Asian Studies, ME Sharpe, 1995), p. 220.

26 The EAEG was later renamed the East Asian Economic Caucus (EAEC), but ran into opposition from the United States, and Japan remained ambivalent. The EAEC also has to compete with APEC which (established in 1989) has become the preferred process for multilateral economic cooperation.

27 Singh, op. cit., 'Vietnam and ASEAN: The Politics of Accommodation', p. 225.

28 Leifer, op. cit., *ASEAN and the Security of South-East Asia*, p. 43.

29 For details see 'Southern Discomfort: Muslim Separatist Violence Raises Its Head Again', *FEER*, 2 September, 1993, pp. 20–21, and 'Troubled Frontier: Thai Muslim Violence Concerns Malaysia As Well', *FEER*, 16 September, 1993, p. 12. In March 1998 forty guerrillas surrendered to the Thai authorities. See *FEER*, 19 March 1998, p. 17.

30 Wilfried A. Herrmann, 'Security in Southeast Asia', in William M. Carpenter and David G. Wiencek (eds.), *Asian Security Handbook: An Assessment of Political-Security Issues in the Asia-Pacific Region* (Armonk: ME Sharpe, 1996), p. 38.

31 For details see 'Thais May Retaliate Over Killings', *New Straits Times*, 25 November 1995, and 'Thailand's Fisheries Chief Set to Challenge Malaysia', *New Straits Times*, 30 November 1995.

32 Alagappa, op. cit., 'International Politics in Asia', p. 77.

33 For details of the claim see Michael Leifer, *The Philippine Claim to Sabah* (Hull Monographs on South-East Asia, 1968).

34 The Corregidor Affair occurred in March 1968. Corregidor is the name of a military base where Filipino Muslims were being recruited to infiltrate Sabah. In response to a mutiny in the camp the recruits were killed. When this became public knowledge the Malaysians were outraged especially since this coincided with the arrest in Sabah of twenty-six armed Filipinos. To make matters worse the Philippine government in an effort to cover up its actions, which were embarrassing for foreign consumption and were alarming for Muslims in Mindanao, used the incident to revive their claims for Sabah. Sabre-rattling resulted between the two states with diplomatic staff recalled from their respective capitals and Malaysia even reported the

incident to U Thant, the UN Secretary-General. For details see Leifer, op. cit., *ASEAN and the Security of South-East Asia*, pp. 31–37.

35 'Malaysia asks RP not to revive claims over Sabah', *The Philippine Star*, 22 November 1998.

36 In addition to these lie the internal problems of secession and specific territorial disputes between ASEAN members (in particular Vietnam) and China.

37 Desmond Ball, 'Arms and Affluence: Military Acquisitions in the Asia-Pacific Region', *International Security*, 18/3 (Winter 1993/94), pp. 87–88.

38 Amitav Acharya, 'A New Regional Order in South-East Asia: ASEAN in the Post-Cold War Era', *Adelphi Paper 279* (London: International Institute for Strategic Studies, 1993), p. 33.

39 The data is from *The Military Balance 1997/98* (London: International Institute for Strategic Studies, 1997), p. 295 and p. 267.

40 Thailand reduced its order of F/A-18s by eight in March 1998 and Indonesia postponed indefinitely its order of 12 SU-30s and eight Mi-17 helicopters from Russia in January 1998. See Craig Skehan, 'US Won't Punish Thais for Welshing on Deal', *The Sydney Morning Herald*, 12 March 1998, and John Haseman, 'Indonesia Cuts Back on Spending as Crisis Bites', *Jane's Defence Weekly*, 21 January 1998.

41 See 'Defence Purchases in the Year 2000', *New Straits Times*, 22 April 1998; 'Buying of Attack Copters being Re-evaluated', *New Straits Times*, 23 April 1998; 'Navy Will Spend $600M on Frigates', *The Straits Times*, 28 April 1998.

42 'RSAF Receives Advanced F-16 Jet', *The Straits Times*, 10 April 1998; S. Jayasankaran, 'Under the Gun', *FEER*, 3 September 1998, p. 20.

43 'Philippines' $13b Force Modernisation Plan', *The Straits Times*, 28 April 1998.

44 An arms race can occur between a status quo and revisionist power in which case it would not signify the existence of a security dilemma. Thus an arms race *could* rather than *would* signify a security dilemma. For Ball's 13 factors see Ball, op.cit., 'Arms and Affluence: Military Acquisitions in the Asia-Pacific Region', pp. 81–95.

45 Ibid., p. 81.

46 J.N. Mak and B.A. Hamzah, 'The External Maritime Dimension of ASEAN Security', *Journal of Strategic Studies*, 18/3 (September 1995), p. 123.

47 See Gerald Segal, 'Managing New Arms Races in the Asia/Pacific', *The Washington Quarterly*, 15/3 (Summer 1992), pp. 83–101. Douglas M. Johnson, 'Anticipating instability in the Asia-Pacific Region', *The Washington Quarterly*, 15/3 (Summer 1992), pp. 103–112. Michael T. Klare, 'The Next Great Arms Race', *Foreign Affairs*, 72/3 (Summer 1993), pp. 136–152. Susan Willet, 'Dragon's Fire and Tiger's Claws: Arms Trade and Production in Far East Asia', *Contemporary Security Policy*, 15/2 (August 1994), pp. 112–135. The use of the term 'arms race' by Segal and Klare is indistinguishable from 'arms build-up'.

48 Chien-pin Li, 'Fear, greed, or garage sale? The analysis of military expenditure in East Asia', *The Pacific Review*, 10/2 (1997), pp. 274–288.

49 Mak and Hamzah, op. cit., 'The External Maritime Dimension of ASEAN Security', pp. 134–135.

50 Ibid., p. 134.

51 Ibid.

52 Malcolm Chalmers, *Confidence-Building in South-East Asia*, Bradford Arms Register Studies No. 6 (Trowbridge: Westview Press, 1996), p. 104.
53 Ball, op. cit., 'Arms and Affluence: Military Acquisitions in the Asia-Pacific Region', pp. 104–105.
54 Chalmers, op. cit., *Confidence-Building in South-East Asia*, p. 105.
55 Ball, op. cit., 'Arms and Affluence: Military Acquisitions in the Asia-Pacific Region', p. 105.
56 For more details see Chalmers, op. cit., *Confidence-Building in South-East Asia*, pp. 82–85.
57 Huxley, op. cit., *Insecurity in the ASEAN Region*, p. 58.
58 Ibid., p. 60.
59 For reference to a security regime see Barry Buzan, 'The Post-Cold War Asia-Pacific Security Order: Conflict or Cooperation?', in Andrew Mack and John Ravenhill (eds.), *Pacific Cooperation: Building Economic and Security Regimes in the Asia-Pacific Region* (Canberra: Allen & Unwin, 1994), p. 136. For security community references see Barry Buzan, 'The Southeast Asian Security Complex', *Contemporary Southeast Asia*, 10/1 (June 1988), p. 6 and p. 11. Noordin Sopiee also refers to ASEAN as a quasi-security community in Noordin Sopiee, 'ASEAN and Regional Security', in Mohammed Ayoob (ed.), *Regional Security in the Third World* (London: Croom Helm, 1986), p. 229.
60 Barry Buzan, *People, States and Fear: An Agenda for International Security Studies in The Post-Cold War Era* (Hemel Hempstead: Harvester Wheatsheaf, 2nd ed., 1991), p. 190. For details of homogeneous and heterogeneous complexes see Barry Buzan, Ole Waever, Jaap de Wilde, *Security: A New Framework for Analysis* (London: Lynne Rienner, 1998), pp. 15–19.
61 Barry Buzan, 'Third World Regional Security in Structural and Historical Perspective', in Brian L. Job (ed.), *The Insecurity Dilemma: National Security of Third World States* (Boulder: Lynne Rienner, 1992), p. 168.
62 For conflict formation see Raimo Väyrynen, 'Regional Conflict Formations: An Intractable Problem of International Relations', *Journal of Peace Research*, 21/4 (1984), pp. 337–359. For security community see Karl Deutsch, *Political Community and the North Atlantic Area: International Organization in the Light of Historic Experience* (Princeton: Princeton University Press, 1957).
63 Ibid., p. 5.
64 Amitav Acharya, 'The Association of Southeast Asian Nations: "Security Community" or "Defence Community"?', *Pacific Affairs*, 64/2 (Summer 1991), p. 162.
65 Leifer, op. cit., *ASEAN and the Security of South-East Asia*, p. 24.
66 The adoption of common security by ASEAN is not accepted by all commentators. Mak and Acharya with reference to ASEAN's security approach in the 1990s see it as incompatible with the 'ASEAN way'. Mak's argument centres on the 'transparency demands of common security' being at odds with the closed secretive arrangements associated with ASEAN practice, while Acharya is dismissive because of its western connotations. The argument posited here is that the core notion of common security – security is achieved with others not against others – is encapsulated in the ASEAN approach to achieving security, although the implementation of common security is different to that sought by the Palme Commission. See J.N. Mak, 'The "ASEAN way" and Transparency in South-East Asia', in Bates Gill and

J.N. Mak (eds.), *Arms, Transparency and Security in South-East Asia* SIPRI Research Report No. 13 (New York: Oxford University Press, 1997), pp. 38–48. Amitav Acharya, 'Ideas, identity, and institution-building: from the "ASEAN way" to the "Asian-Pacific way"?', *The Pacific Review*, 10/3 (1997), pp. 319–346.

67 Leifer, op. cit., *ASEAN and the Security of South-East Asia*, p. 2.

68 The Indonesian concepts of national and regional resilience are enshrined in articles 11 and 12 of the TAC. Russell H. Fifield, *National and Regional Interests in ASEAN: Competition and Co-operation in International Politics*, Occasional Paper 57 (Singapore: Institute of Southeast Asian Studies, 1979), p. 16.

69 Malcolm Chalmers, 'The Debate on a Regional Arms Register in Southeast Asia', *The Pacific Review*, 10/1 (1997), p. 105.

70 Singapore initially abstained but subsequently endorsed the incorporation of East Timor by Indonesia. See Leifer, op. cit., *ASEAN and the Security of South-East Asia*, p. 42.

71 For a succinct account of ASEAN's actions during the Cambodian crisis see Muthiah Alagappa, 'Regionalism and the Quest for Security: ASEAN and the Cambodian Conflict', *Australian Journal of International Affairs*, 47/2 (October 1993), pp. 189–209.

72 Acharya, op. cit.,'Ideas, identity, and institution-building', p. 329.

73 Hoang Anh Tuan, 'ASEAN Dispute Management: Implications for Vietnam and an Expanded ASEAN', *Contemporary Southeast Asia*, 18/1 (June 1996), p. 67.

74 Quoted from Acharya, op. cit., 'Ideas, identity, and institution-building', p. 332.

75 Kamarulzaman Askandar, 'ASEAN and Conflict Management: The Formative Years of 1967–1976', *Pacifica Review*, 6/2 (1994), p. 67.

76 Caballero-Anthony, op. cit., 'Mechanisms of Dispute Settlement: The ASEAN Experience', p. 61.

77 Arnfinn Jørgensen-Dahl, 'Indonesia as Regional Great Power', in Iver B. Eumann (ed.), *Regional Great Powers in International Politics* (London: St Martin's Press, 1992), p. 85.

78 For an account of Indonesian initiatives during the Cambodian crisis see Andrew J. MacIntyre, 'Interpreting Indonesian Foreign Policy: The Case of Kampuchea 1979–1986', *Asian Survey*, 27/5 (May 1987), pp. 515–534.

79 Ibid., p. 519.

80 Huxley, op. cit., *Insecurity in the ASEAN Region*, p. 11.

81 Amitav Acharya, 'Regional Military-Security Cooperation in the Third World: A Conceptual Analysis of the Relevance and Limitations of ASEAN (Association of Southeast Asian Nations)', *Journal of Peace Research*, 29/1 (February 1992), p. 12. This represents a change for Acharya who had previously described ASEAN as a security community. See, Acharya, op. cit., 'The Association of Southeast Asian Nations: "Security Community" or "Defence Community"?', pp. 172–173.

82 Sukhumbhand Paribatra, 'From ASEAN Six to ASEAN Ten: Issues and Prospects', *Contemporary Southeast Asia*, 16/3 (December 1994), p. 253.

83 Hoang Anh Tuan, 'ASEAN Dispute Management: Implications for Vietnam and an Expanded ASEAN', *Contemporary Southeast Asia*, 18/1 (June 1996), pp. 75–76.

84 Quoted from Allen E. Goodman, 'Vietnam and ASEAN: Who Would Have Thought It Possible?', *Asian Survey*, 36/6 (June 1996), p. 598.

85 'ASEAN "Needs to Find" New Equilibrium', *The Straits Times*, 5 August 1997.

86 'Larger ASEAN could Pose Challenge to Cohesion', *Business Times*, 22 July 1997.

87 N. Ganesan, 'Testing Neoliberal Institutionalism in Southeast Asia', *International Journal*, 50/4 (Autumn 1995), p. 803.

88 Carlyle A. Thayer, 'Vietnam and ASEAN: A First Anniversary Assessment', *Southeast Asian Affairs 1997* (Singapore: Institute of Southeast Asian Studies, 1997), p. 365.

89 Hoang Anh Tuan, 'Why Hasn't Vietnam Gained ASEAN Membership?', *Contemporary Southeast Asia*, 15/3 (December 1993), p. 283.

90 Goodman, op. cit., 'Vietnam and ASEAN: Who Would Have Thought It Possible?', p. 595.

91 Carolyn L. Gates, *Regional Outlook Southeast Asia 1998–99* (Singapore: Institute of Southeast Asian Studies, 1998), p. 61.

92 Quoted from Thayer, op. cit., 'Vietnam and ASEAN: A First Anniversary Assessment', p. 372.

93 Greg Torode, 'Open Societies Call by Thailand Exposes Divisions', *South China Morning Post*, 15 December 1997.

94 Michael Vatikiotis, 'Awkward Admission', *FEER*, 24 December 1998, p. 17.

95 Not all commentators view ASEAN's actions towards Burma or Cambodia as indicating a change in the ASEAN practice of non-intervention. John Funston argues that a 'common misconception in discussions of this issue was the belief that ASEAN's doctrine of non-intervention meant never becoming involved in the affairs of neighbours', instead he argues, 'helping neighbouring governments and countries – acting as a mutual support group – is very much the essence of ASEAN'. The key though is the response from the countries concerned, and in both Burma and Cambodia the regimes warned ASEAN against intervention. John Funston, 'ASEAN: Out of its Depth?', *Contemporary Southeast Asia*, 20/1 (April 1998), p. 27.

96 For more details see Harish Mehta, *Regional Outlook Southeast Asia 1998–99* (Singapore: Institute of Southeast Asian Studies, 1998), pp. 18–21.

97 'ASEAN can't condone use of force: Jaya', *The Straits Times*, 25 July 1997.

98 Anwar Ibrahim, 'Crisis Prevention', *Newsweek*, 21 July 1997.

99 Jusuf Wanandi, 'Key Test: How to Cope with Future Challenges', *The Straits Times*, 26 July 1997.

100 'Vietnam Opposes Interference in Cambodian Affairs', *The Straits Times*, 25 July 1997.

101 'Don't Interfere, or We Will Stay Out of ASEAN', *The Straits Times*, 12 July 1997.

102 Ben Dolven, 'Sharper Image', *FEER*, 5 August 1999, pp. 17–18.

103 'The Word is "Constructive Interventions"', *The Straits Times*, 15 July 1997.

104 In mid-November 1997 the military junta replaced the State Law and Order Restoration Council (SLORC) with the SPDC. It is a largely cosmetic change with the new name implying a more permanent presence.

105 'Most Successful ARF Meeting since Inception', *The Straits Times*, 28 July 1997.

106 Quoted from Bertil Lintner, 'Lightning Rod', *FEER*, 12 November 1998, p. 29.
107 Ibid.
108 'ASEAN Enters a New Frontier', *Business Times*, 29 July 1997.
109 Quoted from an informal paper submitted to senior officials by Thailand prior to ASEAN meeting in Manila, 23–30 July 1998. See Nayan Chanda and Shada Islam, 'In the Bunker', *FEER*, 6 August 1998, pp. 24–28.
110 Quoted from Frank Ching, 'ASEAN: Stronger After Crisis?', *FEER*, 25 February 1999, p. 37.
111 Etel Solingen has even argued that the region's problems have indicated that ASEAN is a strong organisation. He writes, '[a]ll in all, ASEAN leaders responded to the worst economic and political debacle in thirty years by conforming to the premise that internationalist strategies compel helping – not undermining – the most ravaged partners, and that any attempt to take advantage of feebler neighbours would undermine the collective'. Etel Solingen, 'ASEAN, *Quo Vadis*? Domestic Coalitions and Regional Cooperation', *Contemporary Southeast Asia*, 21/1 (April 1999), p. 49.
112 Quoted from 'Interference will Hurt Asean', *The Malaysian Star*, 24 February 1999.
113 Habibie has expressed his concern about Anwar's detention privately to Mahathir, while Estrada has been more public. At a meeting in Singapore, Estrada inferred that Anwar might not receive a fair trail by stating that he would like to see him treated with due process. He also expressed a desire to meet Anwar at the APEC meeting in Malaysia in late November, 1998. See 'Changing the Script in the Philippines', *The Economist*, 24 October 1998, pp. 91–92.
114 John Aglionby, 'Anwar's Teenage Daughter Picks Up Baton of Reform', *The Guardian*, 19 October 1998.
115 See Lim Seng Jin, 'No Place for Discrimination', *The Straits Times*, 28 February 1999.
116 Nayan Chanda and Shada Islam, 'In the Bunker', *FEER*, 6 August 1998, p. 25.
117 Berti Lintner, Shada Islam, Faith Keenan, 'Growing Pains', *FEER*, 28 January 1999, p. 26.
118 Malaysian Defence Minister Syed Hamid Albar stating that 'some of the meetings were supposed to be held in Singapore. With the current environment, we felt it was inappropriate'. A Western diplomat added, 'I don't think Malaysia would want Singapore's armed forces on their terrain right now'. See S. Jayasankaran, 'Under the Gun', *FEER*, 3 September 1998.
119 Siazon at the 1998 Manila meeting stated, 'I am not trying to convince Asean to change now. Because the time is not ripe'. See Nayan Chanda and Shada Islam, 'In the Bunker', *FEER*, 6 August 1998, pp. 24–28. For movers and shakers quote see Berti Lintner, Shada Islam, Faith Keenan, 'Growing Pains', *FEER*, 28 January 1999, p. 26.

5 ASEAN, the China Threat and the South China Sea Dispute

1 Banning N. Garrett and Bonnie S. Glaser, 'Chinese Perspectives on Nuclear Arms Control', *International Security*, 20/3 (Winter 1995/96), p. 75.

2 Weixing Hu, 'China's Security Agenda After the Cold War', *The Pacific Review*, 8/1 (1995), p. 131.

3 Avery Goldstein, 'Great Expectations: Interpreting China's Arrival', *International Security*, 22/3 (Winter 1997/98), p. 65.

4 David Shambaugh, 'Containment or Engagement of China? Calculating Beijing's Responses', *International Security*, 21/2 (Fall 1996), p. 186.

5 Shambaugh states the members of 'ASEAN ... have already made it quite clear that they have no interest in containing China'. Ibid., p. 207.

6 The challenges facing the new leadership of Jiang Zemin and Zhu Rongji are immense, and would be difficult enough to overcome without the added burden of the region's economic crisis. On the economic front China is seeking to transform its inefficient state-owned enterprises into profit making competitive firms that can survive in the global market, an especially difficult task once China joins the World Trade Organisation. Achieving an overhaul of these state enterprises while trying to avoid unemployment spiralling upwards is proving onerous. In March 1998 the official unemployment figure stood at 12 million. The old trick of banks providing loans to bail out ailing companies has been stopped with bad loans thought to encompass more than 20 per cent of the banks portfolios. With the banking system saddled with nonperforming loans banks too are being forced to reform with the inevitable outcome that some will close – on the 21 June 1998 the Hainan Development Bank became the first bank in Communist China to be closed. Rising unemployment coupled with poor welfare provision has led to social unrest with workers demonstrating in Nanchong and Mianyang. The prevalence of corruption within the system exacerbates the feeling of injustice and could lead to demands for political reform. The lesson to be learnt in Beijing from the fall of the Suharto regime in Indonesia, is that economic growth must be accompanied with political reform and the signs are that Jiang is tentatively moving in this direction. The Chinese Academy of Social Sciences has been commissioned to study how different democracies around the world operate, although it is not known what Jiang proposes to do with this information. If the transformation of China's economy and possibly its social-political makeup was not daunting enough, Beijing also faces terrorist activities in Xinjiang province from Uighurs supported by Muslim forces trained in Afghanistan. The rise of secessionist demands in China's far west could encourage Tibetan demands for independence; China could implode much like the Soviet Union. For a concise overview of the economic problems facing China see *The Economist*, 24 October 1998, p. 15 and pp. 23–28.

7 Quoted from Bruce Gilley, 'Sharper Image', *Far Eastern Economic Review*, 10 December 1998, p. 29. Hereafter known as *FEER*.

8 Nicholas Wheeler and Ken Booth in 'The Security Dilemma', in John Baylis and N.J. Rengger (eds.), *Dilemmas of World Politics: International Issues in a Changing World* (Oxford: Clarendon Press, 1992), pp. 29–60. Jack Snyder, 'Perceptions of the Security Dilemma in 1914', in Robert Jervis, Richard Ned Lebow and Janice Gross Stein (eds.), *Psychology and Deterrence* (Baltimore: The Johns Hopkins University Press, 1985), pp. 153–179.

9 Ibid., 'Perceptions of the Security Dilemma', pp. 154–155.

10 Ibid., p. 155.

11   Robert O. Keohane, *After Hegemony: Cooperation and Discord in the World Political Economy* (Princeton: Princeton University Press, 1984), p. 45.

12   Quoted from Denny Roy, 'Hegemon on the Horizon?', *International Security*, 19/1 (Summer 1994), p. 155.

13   See 'Chi Haotian Rejects China Threat Theory' and 'Chi Holds Talks with Defence Official on Military Exchanges', *BBC World Summary of News*, 19 February 1998; 'China's Gentler Face', *FEER*, 10 June 1999, p. 29.

14   Chang Ya-chün, 'Peking's Asia-Pacific Strategy in the 1990s', *Issues & Studies*, 29/1 (January 1993), pp. 95–96.

15   Figures from Avery Goldstein, op. cit., 'Great Expectations', pp. 40–41.

16   Analysts varied on when these events would happen. Some projected that Japan's economy would be surpassed in 2005 while the US could be surpassed in either 2020 or even 2010. See Mamdouh G. Salameh, 'China, Oil and the Risk of Regional Conflict', *Survival*, 37/4 (Winter 1995–96), p. 142.

17   Once inflation is taken into account the 159 per cent growth in military expenditure between 1986 and 1994 amounts to little more than an increase of 4 per cent in real terms.

18   The Chinese are extremely reluctant to publish the details of their military expenditure. Shaoguang Wang writes that until 'China published its first defence White Paper in November 1995, the annual state budget had contained only a single-line entry for defence. Even the White Paper did not reveal much about what was included in the official military budget' (p. 889). The official military budget does not account for all the expenditures incurred by the People's Liberation Army (PLA). It is generally believed that China's total defence spending includes three major components: the official published defence budget; defence-related allocations in the budgets of other Chinese government ministries; and the PLA's various sources of extra budgetary earnings. The latter involves the PLA running nearly 10,000 business including many in non-defence related industries. The better known include pharmaceutical giant 999 Enterprise, Carrie Enterprises, and China Poly Group. These extra budgetary earnings are estimated to have earned the PLA between $5–10 billion in recent years. Concern amongst the party leadership that a self-funding army might be less loyal to the government than one dependent upon central funding, is thought to be behind Jiang Zemin's order on 22 July 1998 for the PLA to withdraw from managing companies in non-defence related industries. Although analysts estimates of China's military expenditure vary above the official figure by as much as 12 times, Shaoguang Wang claims that it is only 1.54 per cent times higher. See Shaoguang Wang, 'Estimating China's Defence Expenditure: Some Evidence from Chinese Sources', *The China Quarterly*, No. 147 (September 1996), pp. 889–911. For details of the PLA's extra budgetary earnings and Jiang Zemin's order to curtail some of these earnings see Susan V. Lawrence, 'Out of Business', *FEER*, 6 August 1998, pp. 68–69.

19   David Shambaugh, 'China's Military in Transition: Politics, Professionalism, Procurement and Power Projection', in David Shambaugh and Richard H. Yang (eds.), *China's Military in Transition* (Oxford: Clarendon Press, 1997), p. 23.

20   Denny Roy, 'The "China Threat" Issue: Major Arguments', *Asian Survey*, 36/8 (August 1996), p. 762. A number of commentators also note China's

rise towards hegemony. David Shambaugh writes that China has 'aspirations to become the dominant power in the Asia-Pacific region'. Harlan Jencks asserts, the 'Chinese assume that they should be the dominant regional power' and this means, 'no Asian government should take any action contrary to Chinese interests'. Larry Wortzel detects 'almost turn-of-the-century modes of quasi-imperial competition [in Beijing] for regional hegemony'. See David Shambaugh, 'Pacific Security in the Pacific Century', *Current History*, 93/587 (December 1994), p. 425. Harlan W. Jencks, 'The PRC's Military and Security Policy in the Post-Cold War Era', *Issues and Studies*, 30/11 (November 1994), p. 103 and p. 68. Larry M. Wortzel, 'China Pursues Traditional Great-Power Status, *Orbis*, 38/2 (Spring 1994), p. 157.

21 Leszeck Buszynski, 'China and the ASEAN Region', in Stuart Harris and Gary Klintworth (eds.), *China as a Great Power: Myths, Realities and Challenges in the Asia-Pacific Region* (New York: St Martin's Press, 1995), p. 162.

22 Mark Mancall, *Russia and China: Their Diplomatic Relations to 1728* (Cambridge, Mass.: Harvard University Press, 1971), p. 108.

23 Greg Austin, *China's Ocean Frontier: International Law, Military Force and National Development* (St Leonards: Allen & Unwin, 1998), p. 358.

24 Mancall, op. cit., *Russia and China*, p. 8.

25 Wang Gungwu, 'China's Place in the Region: The Search for Allies and Friends', *The Indonesian Quarterly*, 25/4 (Fourth Quarter 1997), p. 421.

26 Denny Roy, 'The Foreign Policy of Great-Power China', *Contemporary Southeast Asia*, 19/2 (September 1997), p. 123.

27 The Five Principles are: mutual respect for sovereignty and territorial integrity; mutual non-aggression; non-interference in each other's internal affairs; equality and mutual benefit; and peaceful coexistence.

28 While this helped to alleviate fears amongst some of the regimes in Southeast Asia (mainly Malaysia, Indonesia) that their Chinese nationals were not potential fifth-columnists, it has not meant that China will ignore ethnic violence directed against the Chinese. During the riots that overthrew Suharto in Indonesia the ethnic Chinese became targets of rape, murder and arson. This led to Chinese Foreign Minister, Tang Jiaxuan, at the ASEAN Regional Forum in Manila in July 1998 insisting that the Chinese Indonesians should be provided with no less protection than any other Indonesian citizen, and the *People's Daily* criticised Jakarta for not doing enough to safeguard the Chinese. China may not be seeking to subvert the regimes of Southeast Asia anymore, but this does not mean that it will ignore violence directed against the overseas Chinese. For more on this see Michael Vatikiotis, Matt Forney and Ben Dolven, 'Compatriot Games', *FEER*, 20 August 1998, pp. 20–23. For details of the 1989 Law on Citizenship see Jusuf Wanandi, 'ASEAN's China Strategy: Towards Deeper Engagement', *Survival*, 38/3 (Autumn 1996), p. 119. The issue of dual nationality can be traced back to the Bandung Conference in April 1955, where China and Indonesia reached an agreement forcing the Chinese residing in Indonesia to accept either Chinese or Indonesian nationality. The agreeement was not actually ratified until 1960.

29 The ARF's membership now stands at 22. This includes the original members: Australia, Brunei, Canada, China, European Union (Presidency), Indonesia, Japan, Laos, Malaysia, New Zealand, PNG, Philippines, Republic

of Korea, Russia, Singapore, Thailand, USA and Vietnam. Cambodia was admitted at the second ARF in 1995, India and Burma at the third in 1996 and Mongolia at the fifth in 1998. The third ARF agreed the following criteria for future membership: commitment to key ARF goals and previous ARF decisions and statements; relevance to the peace and security of the ARF 'geographical footprint' (North East and South East Asia and Oceania); gradual expansion; and consultation and consensus by all ARF members on all future membership decisions.

30   Quoted from Michael Leifer, 'The ASEAN Regional Forum', *Adelphi Paper 302* (London: International Institute for Strategic Studies), p. 20.

31   Wanandi, op. cit., 'ASEAN's China Strategy', p. 121.

32   Taiwan was 'prevented from sponsoring the technical working group meeting on safety of navigation, shipping, and communication' because China did not agree to Taipei hosting an international conference. See, Cheng-yi Lin, 'Taiwan's South China Sea Policy', *Asian Survey*, 37/4 (April 1997), p. 329.

33   Despite a proposal on biodiversity gaining approval Beijing still refused to implement it. See Rosemary Foot, 'China in the ASEAN Regional Forum: Organizational Processes and Domestic Modes of Thought', *Asian Survey*, 38/5 (May 1998), p. 434.

34   His comments appeared on the 1 August and imply that China, if it did not have a direct impact on the agenda, was at least consulted to ensure that they were acceptable to Beijing. He said:

> The Chinese side advocates the development of regional cooperation in security matters in stages in the spirit of dealing with issues in ascending order of difficulty, and of seeking common ground while reserving differences. For some time to come, the countries concerned may hold preliminary informal discussions and consultations on the principles, content, scope and method of cooperation in security matters. Meanwhile, they should carry out specific activities of cooperation on which parties have reached a consensus or which are not highly contentious, and institute some practical and feasible confidence building measures in a practical manner.

Quoted from Michael Leifer, 'China in Southeast Asia: Interdependence and accommodation', in David S.G. Goodman and Gerald Segal (eds.), *China Rising: Nationalism and interdependence* (London: Routledge, 1997), pp. 170–171n14.

35   In 1995 the ARF met at Bandar Seri Begawan in Brunei, in 1996 at Jakarta in Indonesia, in 1997 at Kuala Lumpur in Malaysia and in 1998 at Manila in the Philippines. The sixth ARF meeting in 1999 was in Singapore. At these gatherings the members are represented by their foreign minister and one senior official. At the fourth ARF in 1997 this was extended to include defence ministers.

36   Leifer, op. cit., 'ASEAN Regional Forum', p. 42.

37   At the 1996 meeting China's foreign minister stated that the ARF would continue to play an important role provided it gave 'full consideration to the region's diversity, maintains its nature and rules of procedure and develops incrementally on the basis of shared interests and needs of its members

in the spirit of consensus'. Quoted from Foot, op. cit., 'China in ASEAN Regional Forum', p. 432.

38 In the fourth ARF summit it was agreed that the ARF process should move towards the second stage on preventive diplomacy, while still continuing with CBMs. Consideration of preventive diplomacy took place in the 1997–1998 year at the ISG, co-chaired by Australia and Brunei.

39 See Leifer, op. cit., 'ASEAN Regional Forum', p. 42.

40 Foot, op. cit., 'China in ASEAN Regional Forum', p. 437.

41 Shambaugh, op. cit., 'Containment or Engagement of China?', p. 187.

42 Michael Leifer, 'Chinese Economic Reform and Security Policy: The South China Sea Connection', *Survival*, 37/2 (Summer 1995), p. 58.

43 This probably reflects Beijing's reasoning that they have strong case in international law. Beijing rejects the assumption that any of the islands were *terra nullius* in the 1970s when the ASEAN members began to stake their claim. They also argue that while the 1982 Law of the Sea uses the continental shelf to divide sea borders, it notes that states may have territory, including islands, that are situated on the continental shelf of another state.

44 For a comparison of claims which supports China's case see Sheng Lijun, 'Beijing and the Spratlys', *Issues & Studies*, 31/7 (July 1995), pp. 20–24. For an excellent and detailed assessment of the competing claims, which concludes that China's claims are at the very least equal to any other and if the islands are treated as a single group are the strongest, see Greg Austin, op. cit., *China's Ocean Frontier*, pp. 131–161.

45 In addition to the ASEAN states, Taiwan also has claims on the Spratlys and has occupied Itu Aba since 1946 and currently has approximately 110 troops stationed on the island.

46 For more details on claims and the means by which the claimants have strengthened their claims see Mark J. Valencia, 'China and the South China Sea Disputes', *Adelphi Paper 298* (London: International Institute for Strategic Studies).

47 Sheng Lijun, op. cit., 'Beijing and the Spratlys', pp. 25–26.

48 Figures for 1996 occupations are taken from Cheng-yi Lin, op. cit., 'Taiwan's South China Sea Policy', p. 324.

49 Rigoberto Tiglao, Andrew Sherry, Nate Thayer and Michael Vatikiotis, 'Tis the Season', *FEER*, 24 December 1998, pp. 18–20; Johnna Villaviray, 'RP eyes expansion of Spratlys facilities', *The Manila Times*, 25 February 1999; 'RP queries Vietnam on Spratly structures', *Philippine Daily Inquirer*, 13 March 1999.

50 For details of academic proposals for joint development see Sheng Lijun, op. cit., 'Beijing and the Spratlys', pp. 37–43.

51 After the November 1998 incident over Mischief Reef when the Philippines agreed to examine Chinese proposals for joint use, the Vietnamese sought clarification of the proposal and reiterated the view that any cooperation must be agreed by all claimants. See Liberty Dones, 'RP Agrees to Joint Use of Chinese Structures in Mischief', *The Philippine Star*, 21 November 1998, and 'Cooperation: All Parties Should Take Part', *The Straits Times*, 1 December 1998.

52 Denny Roy, 'Assessing the Asia-Pacific "Power Vacuum"', *Survival*, 37/3 (Autumn 1995), p. 53.

53   Ross H. Munro, 'China's Waxing Spheres of Influence', *Orbis*, 38/4 (Fall 1994), p. 605.
54   Roy, op. cit., 'Assessing the Asia-Pacific "Power Vacuum"', p. 53.
55   For details of the offence/defence relationship and the security dilemma see Robert Jervis, 'Cooperation under the Security Dilemma', *World Politics*, 30/1 (January 1978), pp. 167–214.
56   David Shambaugh, 'The Insecurity of Security: the PLA's Evolving Doctrine and Threat Perceptions Towards 2000', *Journal of Northeast Asian Studies*, 13/1 (Spring 1994), p. 15.
57   By the mid-1990s these elite forces were estimated to represent 15–20 per cent of the PLA. See Goldstein, op. cit., 'Great Expectations', p. 44.
58   Quoted from Nan Li, 'The PLA's Warfighting Doctrine, Strategy and Tactics, 1985–95: A Chinese Perspective', in David Shambaugh and Richard H. Yang (eds.), *China's Military in Transition* (Oxford: Clarendon Press, 1997), p. 188.
59   David Shambaugh, 'China's Military: Real or Paper Tiger?', *The Washington Quarterly*, 19/2 (Spring 1996), p. 24.
60   For details see 'Lethal Weapon', *FEER*, 24 December 1998, p. 8; 'Russian Kamovs Set to Boost Chinese ASW', *Jane's Defence Weekly*, 4 March 1998, p.14.
61   More details on the equipment can be found in Paul H.B. Godwin, 'From Continent to Periphery: PLA Doctrine, Strategy and Capabilities Towards 2000', in David Shambaugh and Richard H. Yang (eds.), *China's Military in Transition* (Oxford: Clarendon Press, 1997), p. 211.
62   You Ji, *In Quest of High-Tech Power: The Modernisation of China's Military* (Campbell: Australian Defence Studies Centre, 1996), p. 90. According to John Downing the Chinese are expected to launch a helicopter carrier by 2000 and an aircraft carrier by 2010. See John Downing, 'China's aircraft carrier program', *Asia-Defence Reporter*, Oct.–Nov. 97, pp. 6–7. Also see *FEER*, 13 November 1997, p. 13. The purchaser of the incomplete Ukrainian aircraft carrier, *Varyag*, is thought to be acting for the Chinese. Buying the vessel will provide China with 'a modest research tool for its navy modernization programme'. See Bruce Gilley, 'Scrap Value', *FEER*, 9 April 1998, pp. 26–28; Bruce Gilley, 'Flying Start', *FEER*, 11 March 1999, p. 24.
63   Although the SU-27s can reach the Spratly islands from Woody and Hainan Islands their combat time is very limited. At best it is considered to be less than 30 minutes and with the use of after-burners this could be reduced to 5 minutes. The ability to refuel in air is a crucial step in providing the PLAN with adequate fighter cover. Even with pilot training the facilities and airfield at Woody Island is considered inadequate for sustained air-operations. The actual number of SU-27s that China has acquired is contentious. You Ji and Felix Chang suggests it could be as high as 72, while Ray Braybook puts the figure nearer 50 and claims that China's licence entitles it to build 200 Su-27s. See You Ji, ibid., p. 65. For details of the range of Chinese fighter planes see Felix K. Chang, 'Beijing's Reach in the South China Sea', *Orbis*, 40/3 (Summer 1996), pp. 353–374; Ray Braybook, 'Fighters from Russia', *Asia-Defence Reporter*, Dec. 97/Jan. 98, p. 16.
64   Godwin, op. cit., 'From Continent to Periphery', p. 216.
65   The Thai Vice-Admiral, Nitz Srisomwong, noted that the 'dispute over territorial rights to the Spratly Islands in the South China Sea is worrying the

Thai navy because it could affect the country's sea lines of communication'. Quoted from 'Thai Navy Fears Spratlys Dispute may Close Sea Lanes', *The Straits Times*, 2 July 1997.

66 Although there was some initial confusion over whether the Chinese had blockaded the rig, the evidence now suggests that the incident did indeed occur. See Esmond D. Smith Jr., 'China's Aspirations in the Spratly Islands', *Contemporary Southeast Asia*, 16/3 (December 1994), p. 275.

67 See Michael Vatikiotis, Murray Hiebert, Nigel Holloway and Matt Forney, 'Drawn to the Fray', *FEER*, 3 April 1997, pp. 14–16.

68 Allen S. Whiting, 'ASEAN eyes China: The Security Dimension', *Asian Survey*, 37/4 (April 1997), p. 306.

69 For a comprehensive account of the lead up to the incident and the immediate Philippine response see Valencia, op. cit., 'China and the South China Sea Disputes', pp. 44–48. Given that China has occupied features claimed by the Philippines since 1987 it could be argued that Mischief Reef was not the first time that China had challenged an ASEAN member. However, the Chinese did send nine navy vessels to Mischief Reef, arrest Philippine fishermen and leave troops to guard the reef. While the use of force was not equivalent to that used against Vietnam in 1988, Gerald Segal argues 'China clearly did "use force" to eject the Philippine fisherman'. See Gerald Segal, 'East Asia and the "Constrainment" of China', *International Security*, 20/4 (Spring 1996), p. 121n34.

70 In May 1996 China's National People's Congress defined the Paracel Islands as an archipelago and used this as the base line for a 200 nautical mile EEZ. See Whiting, op. cit., 'ASEAN eyes China', pp. 316–317.

71 Jose Rodel Clapano, 'Chinese have Men in Five Spratly Reefs', *The Philippine Star*, 15 November 1998.

72 'China Can Finish Spratly Structures', *The Philippine Star*, 26 November 1998.

73 Quoted from Rigoberto Tiglao, Andrew Sherry, Nate Thayer and Michael Vatikiotis, 'Tis the Season', *FEER*, 24 December 1998, p. 18. In December the incident continued to rumble on when the Philippine navy arrested 20 Chinese fishermen caught fishing within the Philippines' EEZ, they were later released after serving a 30–day jail term. See '20 Chinese Fishermen Nabbed Near Mischief', *The Philippine Star*, 1 December 1998; 'China Seeks Release of Fisherman', *The Malaysian Star*, 4 December 1998; 'AFP blamed for Mischief structures', *The Philippine Star*, 18 February 1999.

74 See 'Estrada Bats for US Presence in SEA', *The Philippine Star*, 17 November 1998; 'US Offers Aid for RP Arms Purchase', *The Philippine Star*, 22 November 1998; 'Estrada Vows to Produce Modern, Professional AFP', *The Philippine Star*, 27 November 1998.

75 J.N. Mak, 'The Chinese Navy and the South China Sea: A Malaysian Assessment', *The Pacific Review*, 4/2 (1991), p. 150.

76 Quoted from Roy, op. cit., 'The "China Threat" Issue', p. 760.

77 Donald M. Seekins, 'Burma-China relations: playing with fire', *Asian Survey*, 37/6 (June 1997), p. 534.

78 Chang Pao-Min, 'Vietnam and China: New Opportunities and New Challenges', *Contemporary Southeast Asia*, 19/2 (September 1997), p. 145.

79 Roy, op. cit., 'Hegemon on the Horizon', p. 155. In discussions with government officials in April 1998 it was made evident to the author that while

publicly China was not referred to as a threat, Beijing's intentions were uppermost in the minds of ASEAN member's militaries.

80 Whiting, op. cit., 'ASEAN Eyes China', p. 300.

81 Shambaugh, op. cit., 'Insecurity of security', pp. 12–13.

82 Carlyle A. Thayer, 'Force Modernization: The Case of the Vietnam's People's Army', *Contemporary Southeast Asia*, 19/1 (June 1997), p. 4.

83 Derek da Cunha, 'Southeast Asian Perceptions of China's Future Security Role in its "Backyard"', in Jonathan D. Pollack and Richard H. Yang (eds.), *In China's Shadow: Regional Perspectives on Chinese Foreign Policy and Military Development* (Washington, D.C.: RAND, 1998), p. 116.

84 Shambaugh, op. cit., 'Containment or Engagement of China?', p. 181.

85 Michael Yahuda, 'How Much Has China Learned About Interdependence', in David S.G. Goodman and Gerald Segal (eds.), *China Rising: Nationalism and Interdependence* (London: Routledge, 1997), p. 23.

86 The danger for Beijing is that in opening China's market and thereby benefiting from access to Western technology, China is also open to cultural and material influences from the capitalist world. These influences could undermine communist rule by spreading Western values, such as democracy and individual human rights. This danger is referred to as 'peaceful evolution' and is regarded as a conscious policy of the West.

87 Gaye Christoffersen, 'China and the Asia-Pacific', *Asian Survey*, 36/11 (November 1996), pp. 1083–1084.

88 For a clear and concise account of the impact of Clinton's Beijing visit on Chinese-US relations see Denny Roy, 'Current Sino-US Relations in Strategic Perspective', *Contemporary Southeast Asia*, 20/3 (December 1998), pp. 225–240.

89 For a concise background of why the Cox investigation began and what it might mean for US-Chinese relations see Shawn W. Crispin, 'Technical Problem', *FEER*, 25 February 1999, pp. 31–32; for claims by the CIA and FBI of Chinese spying and theft of US nuclear secrets see Ed Vulliamy, 'China steals US nuclear secrets', *The Observer*, 7 March 1999; for details of the US Theatre Missile Defence system and China's response See Jim Wolf, 'Going Ballistic', *FEER*, 18 February 1999, pp. 26–27. For a general comment on the likelihood that the relationship is set for a turbulent ride in the next couple of years see Bruce Gilley, 'Red Scare', *FEER*, 25 March 1999, pp. 22–23.

90 In May 1998 these were put on hold because of US concern that Indonesian forces would be used to suppress the reformist movement during Suharto's last few days in power. See John McBeth, 'Strategic Withdrawal', *FEER*, 20 August 1998, pp. 24–26.

91 'Estrada calls for closer ties with US', *The Straits Times*, 5 December 1998. The Visiting Forces Agreement (VFA) will enable the Philippine Armed Forces to conduct military exercises with the United States in the South China Sea. The Senate ratified the VFA on the 25 May 1999, details of the agreement are provided in 'Estrada willing to beg for VFA approval', *The Philippine Star*, 27 March 1999, and Rigoberto Tiglao, 'Growing Up', *FEER*, 3 June 1999, p. 27.

92 Nirmal Ghosh, 'Asia-Pacific Dynamics Hinges on US-Manila Defence Pact', *The Straits Times*, 22 February 1999.

93 Irene Ngoo, 'S'pore-Aussie Talks Focus on Security', *The Straits Times*, 23 February 1999.

94 In 1997, the US Defense Secretary, William Cohen, 'proposed maintaining 100,000 military personnel in Asia to preserve the balance of power'. *FEER*, 29 May 1997.

95 Goldstein, op. cit., 'Great Expectations', p. 66.

96 Whiting, op. cit., 'ASEAN Eyes China', p. 300.

97 For details of Indian concern about China's presence in the Bay of Bengal see Berti Lintner, '... But Stay on Guard', *FEER*, 16 July 1998, p. 21.

98 *FEER*, 23 April 1998, p. 11.

99 See Ahmed Rashid, 'Lethal Weapons', *FEER*, 23 April 1998, pp. 21–24.

100 See 'Unholy Act', *FEER*, 21 May 1998, pp. 18–20.

101 The ASEAN-China Senior Officials Political Consultations, ASEAN-China Joint Committee on Economic and Trade Cooperation, ASEAN-China Joint Committee in Science and Technology, ASEAN Committee in Beijing and the ASEAN-China Joint Cooperation Committee (ACJCC) established in March 1997.

102 The ARF's Inter-Sessional Support Group on Confidence Building Measures (CBMs) in the 1997–1998 session produced a set of matrices and tables detailing the implementation of CBMs by ARF members. These can be found on the internet at http://www.dfat.gov.au/arf/arfhome.html

103 'PLA review of '97 boasts strong diplomatic links', *Jane's Defence Weekly*, 14 January 1998, p. 16.

104 Foot, op. cit., 'China in the ASEAN Regional Forum', p. 430.

105 A senior analyst in the China Institute of International Studies notes, '[t]here is not one ASEAN country that does not have this fear that the US will withdraw ... they first fear that Japan will fill the vacuum and secondly that China will'. Quoted from Banning Garrett and Bonnie Glaser, 'Multilateral Security in the Asia-Pacific Region and its impact on Chinese Interests: Views from Beijing', *Contemporary Southeast Asia*, 16/1 (June 1994), p. 16. Thomas Christensen also notes Beijing's awareness that their actions cause fear among the ASEAN members and what this means for mitigating the security dilemma. See Thomas J. Christensen, 'China, the US-Japan Alliance, and the Security Dilemma in East Asia', *International Security*, 23/4 (Spring 1999), p. 69n62.

106 For details of Pag-Asa island see Johanna Villaviray, 'RP eyes expansion of Spratlys facilities', *The Manila Times*, 25 February 1999, and 'Philippines says can upgrade outpost in Spratlys', *CNN*, 3 March 1999. For US support see 'Estrada calls for closer ties with US', *The Straits Times*, 5 December 1998. For calls of UN involvement, which came in March 1999 when Estrada called upon UN Secretary General Kofi Annan to intervene, see 'Mischief structures will stay - Beijing', *The Philippine Star*, 23 March 1999. For increased US presence note the comment from retiring US Admiral Joseph Prueher that 'we have a fairly robust military presence transiting through the South China Sea frequently. We do not advertise it a lot but we're looking at making a little bigger show of our presence there than we have in the past'. See Richard Halloran, 'Reading Beijing', *FEER*, 25 February 1999, p. 28.

107 In order to mitigate a system-induced security dilemma it is necessary that the two parties convince one another of their benign intentions, and reducing or forfeiting weapon acquisitions is one method of achieving this.

However, because they are victims of a security dilemma the initial reason for the weapon acquisitions was the fear they had of the other. Therefore reducing their weapons does not constitute a forfeit of state objectives, indeed it supports the state objective of achieving security by unwinding the spiral of insecurity. In a state-induced security dilemma because one state defines its security as requiring others to occupy a position of subordination, its security requirement requires them to forfeit a degree of independence.

108 The classic work on this is Robert Jervis, *Perception and Misperception in International Politics* (Princeton: Princeton University Press, 1976), pp. 58–113.

109 Christensen, op. cit., 'China, the U.S.-Japan Alliance, and the Security Dilemma in East Asia', p. 73.

110 Of this 85 per cent some 60 per cent came from Hong Kong with Taiwan the next largest source. Of the ASEAN members, Singapore provided the greatest amount of FDI. For figures see Gerald Segal, 'Enlightening China', in David S.G. Goodman and Gerald Segal (eds.), *China Rising: Nationalism and Interdependence* (London: Routledge, 1997), pp. 177–178. Also see Juwono Sudarsono, 'China as an Economic Power: A Regional View', in Chan Heng Chee (ed.), *The New Asia-Pacific Order* (Singapore: Institute of Southeast Asian Studies, 1997), p. 95.

111 In order to attract FDI the Chinese government established special economic zones (SEZs) along the southeastern coast of China. In these SEZs the authorities operated largely outside the state plan and were given licence to attract foreign investors using preferential policies. By 1984, fourteen coastal towns and Hainan island were permitted to offer tax incentives as the geographical base for FDI was expanded. However, it was not until the 1990s that, with improving infrastructure, an expansion of the types of industries allowed to invest, and a populace with growing purchasing power, FDI increased to such a level that China became the second largest recipient. A consequence of the SEZs, however, is that inland areas have not benefited as greatly, leading to disparities within China. For FDI figures in China see Tan Kong Yam, 'ASEAN in a New Asia: Challenges and Opportunities', in Chia Siow Yue and Marcello Pacini (eds.), *ASEAN in the New Asia: Issues and Trends* (Singapore: Institute of Southeast Asian Studies, 1997), pp. 8–13.

112 The American machinery multinational, Caterpillar, is in the process of ending its three year joint venture with Shanghai Diesel because the expected demand for its engines did not materialise; in 1996 its losses exceeded $3.6 million. Germany's Siemens group, one of the largest foreign investors, has failed to 'earn a profit by German accounting standards', while the American appliance maker, Whirlpool, is backing out of two of its four ventures. For details see Pamela Yatsko, 'Rethinking China', *FEER*, 18 December 1997, pp. 52–57.

113 For details of the changing pattern of Chinese exports and imports see Christopher Findlay and Andrew Watson, 'Economic growth and trade dependency in China', in David S.G. Goodman and Gerald Segal (eds.), *China Rising: Nationalism and interdependence* (London: Routledge, 1997), p. 111 and p. 112.

114 Quoted from Segal, op. cit., 'Enlightening China', p. 178.

115 Leifer, op. cit., 'China in Southeast Asia: Interdependence and Accommodation', p. 161 and p. 158.

116 Quoted from Whiting, op. cit., 'ASEAN Eyes China', p. 319.

117 See Allen S. Whiting, 'ASEAN Pressures China', *FEER*, 24 April 1997, p. 28.

118 Quote from *FEER*, 25 December 1997 and 1 January 1998, p. 13.

119 Ramses Amer, 'Towards a Declaration on "Navigational Rights" in the Sea-lanes of the Asia-Pacific', *Contemporary Southeast Asia*, 20/1 (April 1998), pp. 98–99.

120 See Rigoberto Tiglao, Andrew Sherry, Nate Thayer and Michael Vatikiotis, 'Tis the Season', *FEER*, 24 December 1998, p. 19.

121 Erica Strecker Downs and Phillip C. Saunders, 'Legitimacy and the Limits of Nationalism: China and the Diaoyu Islands', *International Security*, 23/3 (Winter 1998/99), p. 117.

122 Mel Gurtov and Byong-Moo Hwang, *China's Security: The New Roles of the Military* (Boulder: Lynne Rienner, 1998), p. 278.

123 David S.G. Goodman, 'How Open is Chinese Society?', in David S.G. Goodman and Gerald Segal (eds.), *China Rising: Nationalism and Interdependence* (London: Routledge, 1997), p. 32.

124 Shambaugh, op. cit., 'Containment or Engagement of China?', p. 195.

125 Ellis Joffe, 'How Much Does the PLA Make Foreign Policy?', in David S.G. Goodman and Gerald Segal (eds.), *China Rising: Nationalism and Interdependence* (London: Routledge, 1997), pp. 54–55.

126 For a comparsion of China's actions over Taiwan and the South China Sea see Gurtov and Byong-Moo Hwang, op. cit., *China's Security*, Ch. 8.

127 You Ji, 'Missile Diplomacy and PRC Domestic Politics', in Greg Austin (ed.), *Missile Diplomacy and Taiwan's Future: Innovations in Politics and Military Power* (Canberra: Canberra Papers on Strategy and Defence No. 122, 1997), p. 32.

128 Ibid., p. 33.

129 The use of the word equal was highly significant since prior to this China had insisted upon discussions between central and provincial government.

130 For Taiwanese concern at how this encourages moves towards unification see Julian Baum, 'Dangerous Liaisons', *FEER*, 25 March 1999, pp. 10–15.

131 Shambaugh, op. cit., 'Containment or Engagement of China?', p. 190.

132 For details on how, by applying pressure on Taiwan, China could achieve unification without resorting to a military invasion see Bruce Gilley, 'Operation Mind Games', *FEER*, 28 May 1998, pp. 31–32.

133 Joffe, op. cit., 'How Much Does the PLA Make Foreign Policy?', p. 58.

134 For a detailed account of China's foreign policy apparatus and the PLA's influence see Michael D. Swaine, 'The PLA and Chinese National Security Policy: Leaderships, Structures, Processes', in David Shambaugh and Richard H. Yang (eds.), *China's Military in Transition* (Oxford: Clarendon Press, 1997), pp. 96–129.

135 Joffe, op. cit., 'How Much Does the PLA Make Foreign Policy?', p. 63.

136 Gurtov and Byong-Moo Hwang, op. cit., *China's Security*, p. 295.

137 See Matt Forney, 'New Order', *FEER*, 2 October 1997, pp. 22–25. Zhang Wannian was subsequently forced to retire over scandals involving the PLA at Jiang Zemin's request. See *FEER*, 8 October 1998, p. 17.

138 Bruce Gilley, 'Stand-Down Order', *FEER*, 10 September 1998, p. 21.

139 It was Fu Quanyou who pledged the military's General Staff Department would 'resolutely support, resolutely comply with and resolutely implement' Jiang Zemin's order for the military to withdraw from managing companies in non-defence related industries. See Susan V. Lawrence, 'Out of Business', *FEER*, 6 August 1998, pp. 68–69.
140 Swaine, op. cit., 'The PLA and Chinese National Security Policy: Leaderships, Structures, Processes', p. 128.
141 Strecker Downs and Saunders, op. cit., 'Legitimacy and the Limits of Nationalism', p. 141n120.
142 For details of new structures in the Spratlys see Cynthia D. Balana, 'Construction Boom: China putting up new structures in Spratlys', *Philippine Daily Inquirer*, 10 March 1999. The involvement of the PLA is difficult to determine. See Rigoberto Tiglao, Andrew Sherry, Nate Thayer and Michael Vatikiotis, ''Tis the Season', *FEER*, 24 December 1998, p. 19; 'Mischief structures will stay – Beijing', *The Philippine Star*, 23 March 1999.
143 Rigoberto Tiglo *et al.*, ibid., p. 18. Also see 'Peaceful resolutions to disputes with S-E Asia', *The Straits Times*, 17 December 1998, and 'Thailand warns PROC on Spratlys', *The Philippine Star*, 29 November 1998.
144 For the offer see 'RP-China Talks on Spratlys Set Here in March', *The Philippine Star*, 29 January 1999; 'China: RP may use Mischief Shelters', *The Philippine Star*, 27 January 1999. For the renunciation of the offer see Nirmal Ghosh, 'China's Spratlys structures will Stay', *The Straits Times*, 23 March 1999; 'China denies offering joint use of its structures in Mischief Reef', *The Philippine Star*, 24 March 1999.
145 The Chinese had threatened to walk out of the meeting if the South China Sea dispute was raised, and thus intially the issue was not on the agenda. See Johnna Villaviray, 'ASEM Chair Cool to Spratly Issue', *The Manila Times*, 23 February 1999; 'Concern over Spratlys Statement', *The Straits Times*, 27 April 1999.
146 Snyder, op. cit., 'Perceptions of the Security Dilemma', p. 155.
147 'China Bans Fishing in Spratly Waters', *The Philippine Star*, 25 March 1999; 'China Fishing Ban in Spratlys Will Violate Agreement', *The Philippine Star*, 27 March 1999.
148 Liberty Dones, 'RP Mulling Spratly Case against China', *The Philippine Star*, 30 March 1999.

6 Conclusion: Application and Mitigation

1 Arnfinn Jørgensen-Dahl, *Regional Organization and Order in South-East Asia* (London: Macmillan, 1982), pp. 114–115.
2 Herbert Butterfield, *History and Human Relations* (London: Collins, 1951), p. 20.
3 John Herz, *Political Realism and Political Idealism: A Study in Theories and Realities* (Chicago: Chicago University Press, 1951), p. 3.
4 Nicholas J. Wheeler and Ken Booth, 'The Security Dilemma', in John Baylis and N.J. Rengger (eds.), *Dilemmas of World Politics: International Issues in a Changing World* (Oxford: Clarendon Press, 1992), p. 30.

5   Alexander Wendt, 'Anarchy is What States Make of It: The Social Construction of Power Politics', *International Organization*, 46/2 (Spring 1992), pp. 391–425.

6   Charles L. Glaser and Chaim Kaufmann, 'What is the Offense-Defense Balance and Can We Measure It?', *International Security*, 22/4 (Spring 1998), p. 44.

7   Chaim Kaufmann, 'Possible and Impossible Solutions to Ethnic Civil Wars', *International Security*, 20/4 (Spring 1996), p. 148.

8   Robert Jervis, 'War and Misperception', in Robert I. Rotberg and Theodore K. Rabb (eds.), *The Origin and Prevention of Major Wars* (Cambridge: Cambridge University Press, 1989), p. 113.

9   Paul Roe refers to this when he writes, 'while many writers have recognized [the security dilemma's] potential utility at the interstate level, for the most part there has been a marked failure to operationalize the security dilemma in terms of its original Butterfieldian conception'. Paul Roe, 'The Intrastate Security Dilemma: Ethnic Conflict as a "Tragedy?"', *Journal of Peace Research*, 36/2 (March 1999), p. 200.

10 For details of autonomy plans and calls for independence see John McBeth and Margot Cohen, 'Loosening the Bonds', *Far Eastern Economic Review*, 21 January 1999, pp. 10–13. Hereafter known as *FEER*. John Aglionby, 'Ethnic groups flex muscle at Jakarta', *The Guardian*, 18 March 1999; 'Indigenous Indonesians rally in Jakarta', *The Straits Times*, 23 March 1999.

11 This is not intended to imply that democracy and human rights equate to power-sharing and ethnic reconstruction, rather, that these can be seen as elements within democracy and respect for human rights. The process of creating a new identity with others requires those engaged in such an activity to respect each other's differences, otherwise the process could easily degenerate into one of assimilation rather than a joint process of acculturation. Likewise providing an inclusive means of governance is an element of democracy, although only one. While Malaysia is a good example of power-sharing, the revelation from Special Branch Chief, Mohamad Said Awang, in the Anwar Ibrahim trial that he might lie to the court if told to do so by government ministers, confirmed that Malaysia cannot yet be considered democratic when the judicial process might not be free from government interference. See John Gittings, 'Anwar Victim of Smear Campaign, Says Police Report', *The Guardian*, 7 November 1998.

12 For example Khoo Boo Teik claims, '[f]or the first time, Malaysians are ready to discuss politics and no longer assume the other side is hostile'. See Murray Hiebert and S. Jayasankaran, 'Wake-up Call', *FEER*, 18 March 1999, pp. 8–11.

13 A degree of caution is required because prior to the riots against the ethnic Chinese in Indonesia, there were promising signs during the 1990s that Indonesia was becoming more tolerant of its Chinese community. See Ariel Heryanto, 'Ethnic Identities and Erasure: Chinese Indonesians in Public Culture', in Joel S. Kahn (ed.), *Southeast Asian Identities: Culture and the Politics of Representation in Indonesia, Malaysia, Singapore, and Thailand* (Singapore: Institute of Southeast Asian Studies, 1998), pp. 95–114.

14 The 1990s has witnessed a new approach by the Rangoon regime to the management of its relations with the ethnic minorities. This holds out the promise

of a changing nation-building strategy and has included allowing indigenous elites an input into the decision-making process concerning the development of their region. Critics claim, however, that this is a ploy to extend state hegemony over the ethnic minorities, and issues concerning autonomy and ethnic relations remain to be tackled. For details see Tin Maung Maung Than, 'Myanmar: Preoccupation with Regime Survival, National Unity, and Stability', in Muthiah Alagappa, *Asian Security Practice: Material and Ideational Influences* (Stanford: Stanford University Press, 1998), pp. 410–411.

15   Robert Jervis, 'Cooperation under the Security Dilemma', *World Politics*, 30/1 (January 1978), pp. 167–214.

16   A. Butfoy, 'Offence-Defence Theory and the Security Dilemma: The Problem with Marginalizing the Context', *Contemporary Security Policy*, 18/3 (December 1997), p. 49. Since it is impractical to eschew any offensive capability, even defensive force postures require some element of offence. Whether this offensive capability is sufficient to generate concern in neighbouring states, depends upon how much offensive capability exists. Charles Glaser distinguishes between the amount needed to support a defensive posture and those needed to support an offensive posture as *necessary* offence and *optional* offence. See Charles L. Glaser, 'Political Consequences of Military Strategy', *World Politics*, 44/4 (July 1992), p. 509. For details on why an offensive ability is necessary in a defensive force posture see Alan Collins, *The Security Dilemma and the End of the Cold War* (Edinburgh: Keele University Press, 1997), pp. 47–49.

17   Nayan Chanda and Shada Islam, 'In the Bunker', *FEER*, 6 August 1998, p. 25.

18   For an optimistic view that personal ties and a strong network of institutional links can still keep ASEAN united in the face of the challenges facing the organisation in the late 1990s, see the comments of Singapore's Foreign Minister, Professor S. Jayakumar, in *The Straits Times*, 16 March 1999.

19   Nayan Chanda and Shada Islam, 'In the Bunker', *FEER*, 6 August 1998, p. 25.

20   Michael Yahuda, *The International Politics of the Asia-Pacific, 1945–1995* (London: Routledge, 1996), p. 186.

21   Wheeler and Booth, 'The Security Dilemma', op. cit., pp. 29–60. Jack Snyder, 'Perceptions of the Security Dilemma in 1914', in Robert Jervis, Richard Ned Lebow and Janice Gross Stein (eds.), *Psychology and Deterrence* (Baltimore: The Johns Hopkins University Press, 1985), pp. 153–179.

22   Rosemary Foot, 'China in the ASEAN Regional Forum: Organizational Processes and Domestic Modes of Thought', *Asian Survey*, 38/5 (May 1998), p. 436.

23   Greg Austin, *China's Ocean Frontier: International Law, Military Force and National Development* (St Leonards: Allen & Unwin, 1998), p. 358.

24   Rigoberto Tiglao, Andrew Sherry, Nate Thayer and Michael Vatikiotis, 'Tis the Season', *FEER*, 24 December 1998, pp. 18–20; Johnna Villaviray, 'RP Eyes Expansion of Spratlys Facilities', *The Manila Times*, 25 February 1999; 'RP Queries Vietnam on Spratly Structures', *Philippine Daily Inquirer*, 13 March 1999; 'Seaside Boom', *FEER*, 8 July 1999, p. 14.

25   Quoted from Marichu Villanueva, 'China Staying Put in Mischief Reef', *The Philippine Star*, 18 November 1998.

26   Denny Roy, 'The Foreign Policy of Great-Power China', *Contemporary Southeast Asia*, 19/2 (September 1997), p. 132.

27 The Philippine drive to increase their defence budget in late 1998 was partly spurred on by China's action in the Spratly Islands. *The Philippine Star* writing, 'The Philippines' poor defense capabilities were highlighted during the recent dispute with China over its renewed construction at Mischief Reef in the South China Sea. Defense officials said the intrusions threatened the country's sovereignty and natural resources'. See 'Estrada Vows to Produce Modern, Professional AFP', *The Philippine Star*, 27 November 1998.

28 See Liberty Dones, 'RP Agrees to Joint Use of Chinese Structures in Mischief', *The Philippine Star*, 21 November 1998.

29 Lee Lai To, 'The South China Sea: China and Multilateral Dialogues', *Security Dialogue*, 30/2 (June 1999), pp. 165–178.

30 Details in 'China denies offering joint use of its structures in Mischief Reef', *The Philippine Star*, 24 March 1999; 'China Bans Fishing in Spratly Waters', *The Philippine Star*, 25 March 1999.

Index

Note: ASEAN has not been indexed as an entry on its own as it appears in the text throughout.

Lightning Source UK Ltd.
Milton Keynes UK
UKOW04n0046241215

265321UK00001B/3/P